How Do You Get There From Here?

Learning and Playing the Long-Term Investment Game

> Bruce,
> Tasting with you has been a tremendous experience, and helped get me through the final stages of producing this book.
> Thanks! Tim

Timothy Appelt

A Structured Capital Publication

Copyright © 2013 by Timothy Appelt

All Rights Reserved. The use of any part of this publication reproduced, transmitted in any form or by any means, electronic, mechanical, photocopying, recording, or otherwise, or stored in a retrieval system, without the prior written permission of the publisher – or, in the case of photocopying or other reprographic copying, a licence from the Canadian Copyright Licensing Agency – is an infringement of the copyright law.

For permission requests, write to the publisher, addressed "Attention: Permissions Coordinator," at the address below.

Library and Archives Canada Cataloguing in Publication

Appelt, Timothy, 1952-, author
    How do you get there from here? : learning and playing the long-term investment game / Timothy Appelt.

Includes bibliographical references and index.
Issued in print and electronic formats.
ISBN 978-0-9918741-0-1 (bound).-- ISBN 978-0-9918741-1-8 (pdf)

    1. Investments. 2. Investments--Forecasting. 3. Asset allocation. 4. Portfolio management. 5. Investment analysis. I. Title.

HG4521.A66 2013   332.6   C2013-901600-7
                                                                  C2013-901601-5

Published in 2013 by Structured Capital Inc.
Mississauga, Ontario
contact info@structuredcapital.com
website www.structuredcapital.com

Editor: Jeanne Duperreault
Cover Design: Alex McCusker Design

ISBN 978-0-9918741-0-1

Printed in the United States of America by Lightning Source, an Ingram Content company.

Contents

	Preface	v
	Introduction	1
Part 1:	**An Overview of Equity Markets History**	**13**
Chapter 1:	The US Equity Market over the Long Term	15
Chapter 2:	Inflation and the US Equity Market	21
Chapter 3:	Shorter-Term Variability in the US Equity Market	29
	Appendix: an introduction to some statistical terms	35
Chapter 4:	Variability over the Longer Term	45
Chapter 5:	International Equity Market Returns over the Long Term	51
Chapter 6:	Variability in International Equity Markets	59
Chapter 7:	The Importance of Dividends Revisited	65
	Appendix 1: understanding the dividend-based model of returns	75
	Appendix 2: the algebra of dividends and total return	79
Chapter 8:	The Impact of Currencies on Foreign Investment Holdings	87
Chapter 9:	Nominal and Real Currency Returns and Purchasing Power Parity	95
Part 2:	**Looking Towards the Future: an Approach to Building Equity Forecasts**	**111**
Chapter 10:	Economic Growth and Equity Market Returns — Round One	113
	Appendix: past real equity returns and future GDPPC growth	125
Chapter 11:	Economic Growth and Equity Market Returns — Round Two	131
Chapter 12:	Does the Future Simply Repeat the Past?	139
Chapter 13:	Future Returns and the Components of Return	147

Chapter 14:	Expected Dividend Yield.	153
Chapter 15:	Expected Real Dividend Growth	163
Chapter 16:	Expected Return due to the Change in Dividend Yield	175
Chapter 17:	Expected Returns to Foreign Exchange	189
Chapter 18:	Equity Forecasts: How do you get There from Here?	203

Part 3:	**Diversification, Fixed Income and Other Assets...**	**213**
Chapter 19:	Investment Opportunities and Diversification	215
Chapter 20:	Historical Returns to Fixed Income.	225
Chapter 21:	Yields, Changes in Yield, and Returns.	235
Chapter 22:	Forecasting Returns to Nominal Bonds	249
Chapter 23:	Inflation and Real Return Bonds	257
Chapter 24:	Correlations and Other Asset Classes	267

Part 4:	**The Realities of Investing: Costs, Investment Vehicles and Portfolio Construction.**	**275**
Chapter 25:	The Challenges of Active Management within Asset Classes	277
Chapter 26:	Certain Cost Reduction versus Uncertain Value-Added	285
	Appendix: more on the trading costs of ETFs	293
Chapter 27:	The Key Component of a Comprehensive Investment Strategy: Asset Mix.	297
Chapter 28:	Returns, Risks and Correlations in Portfolio Construction.	305
	Appendix: more on risk aversion, utility, and optimal portfolios, part 1	317
Chapter 29:	Applying Dynamic Forecasts to Portfolio Construction.	321
	Appendix: more on risk aversion, utility, and optimal portfolios, part 2	333
Chapter 30:	A Summary of Key Concepts	335
	Bibliography	341
	Index	343

Preface

Over a period of 16 months, essentially half of the wealth invested in North American equity markets was wiped out.

- From the end of October 2007 to the end of February 2009 the S&P500 Total Return index fell 50.95% in US dollars.
- The Canadian market held up until May 2008, but from then until the end of February 2009 the Canadian S&P/TSX Total Return Index fell 43.35% in Canadian dollars.

The devastation wasn't limited to North America, as developed markets in the rest of the world fell by 56.4%,[1] and emerging markets fell by 61.4%.[2]

It wasn't the market downturn itself that motivated me to write this book. It wasn't even the anger and, in some cases, fear for the future that I saw in friends and acquaintances, although that certainly fueled my passion. Three other, related points struck me.

First, for many individuals there was a real sense of bewilderment, and a lack of understanding of how such a thing could happen — not just to the world in general, but more importantly to themselves, their savings and potentially their lives. How could so many people, in many cases with a long history of working, sometimes in management and often with financial matters, find themselves so at sea? Second, given that most of these people had gone to the

---

1 As measured by the MSCI EAFE (Europe, Asia and Far East) developed markets index, in US dollars, from October 2007 to February 2009.

2 As measured by the MSCI EM (Emerging Markets) index, in US dollars, from October 2007 to February 2009.

financial system for advice, why were people in pre-retirement or well into their retirement, positioned to lose as much as 25%, 35%, or even more of their retirement savings? That is, how could financial advisors be so at sea? And third, the consequences of the crisis clearly hit professional investors as well. For example, the OECD reported 2008 real returns (that is, return after inflation) to private pension funds of -26.2% in the United States, -21.4% in Canada, and -23% across 23 countries.[3] If professionally managed funds did so badly, how could anyone else expect to do better?

There is another point that has become important as I have worked on this book over the past two years. The "crash" was already far in the past as I began to write, and since then newspapers and analysts have been focused on soaring equity market returns. Clearly both the financial services industry and the markets themselves were well on their way to recovery. But what about investors: have they recovered, have they learned from this experience, and are they better prepared for the future?

Sadly, I think the answer is "largely not", at least for individual investors. Anecdotal evidence suggests that many investors were over-committed to equities prior to the crash, and lowered equity weights far too late in the game. Then fear kept many out of equities as markets rebounded. Four years later in early 2013, the Toronto Globe & Mail featured a two-page spread entitled "The End of Fear", with the sub-heading:

> Since the crash of 2008, scared investors have been stashing their cash. But now, they're getting over their painful memories and betting that the rebounding market still has room to grow.[4]

This is appalling. By the end of 2012 US equities had regained their pre-crash highs, while Canadian equities were just a few points below them.[5] Yet the Globe reports that many smaller investors are now

---

3 Whitehouse, Edward, "Pensions and the Crisis", OECD media briefing, OECD 2009, pp.1-2
4 Report on Business Weekend, Feb 2, 2013, p.8.
5 Specifically, as of the end of December 2012, the S&P Total Return index had gained 110.66% from its February 2009 low, ending 3.33% above its October

thinking about getting "back in" at new market highs, at a time when some rational investors might be contemplating a reduction of equity exposures. It's enough to make one think that Mark Twain's cynical view of mankind might be right:

> It is not worthwhile to try to keep history from repeating itself, for man's character will always make the preventing of the repetitions impossible.[6]

Now I'm not saying that I skated through all of the turmoil unscathed. Looking at my own situation, while I could say that my personal investments and retirement savings fell less than the average, this good fortune wasn't necessarily due to a well-thought-out and systematic approach to investing. As a professional investor I have focused on specific strategies, often with shorter-term investment horizons, that were used as just one part of large multiple-strategy portfolios. I seldom thought about "the big picture". But as I will discuss, and as many others have pointed out, the big picture — in this case the allocation of investments between asset classes — is where almost all of the return of most portfolios comes from. And yet I know I spent little or no time on that issue.

So when I began to consider what any investor needs to know and understand in order to manage investments for the long term, I started by thinking about asset allocation, and how such decisions should be made. Deciding on an asset allocation implies that you have formed expectations of return and risk for the assets in which you are potentially investing, and from my point of view these are expectations that should evolve as market conditions evolve. To give two extreme examples, one's long-term market expectations should have been very different in December of 1999 versus March of 2009, and I will develop tools to help you understand why this is so. In 1999 the prospects for equities should have been viewed as poor while those of bonds were strong. By contrast, in early 2009,

---

2007 monthly high. Over the same period the Canadian S&P/TSX Total Return index had gained 70.95% from its February 2009 low, remaining just 3.15% below its May 2008 high.

6 *Mark Twain in Eruption: Hitherto Unpublished Pages About Men and Events*, ed. Bernard DeVoto, Harper, New York, 1940.

after equities fell dramatically, the prospects for equities should have been viewed as good, close to historical average levels of return, while the prospects for bonds were below average. The implication is that even with a long-term view of markets, your allocation should have changed over this time frame.

However, when I started to talk to non-professionals, and even to many professionals, I began to realize how little awareness there was about past levels of return and risk from stock and bond markets, let alone what you should expect at any particular time as you look ahead.

From these observations the outline of my project took shape. First, I wanted to explore and analyze the history of global equity and fixed income markets. Knowing what has happened in the past is not in itself a guide to what will take place in the future, but in many cases what does occur will lie within the bounds of past experience, at least if that experience is broad and extensive. Second, I wanted to take the analysis further and develop a fairly systematic and straightforward approach to generating plausible expectations about broad investment opportunities. Finally, I wanted to show how these return expectations, along with an understanding of their risks, could be turned into a workable investment portfolio strategy.

This analysis and investment program is aimed at anyone who has to oversee long-term investments, whether for themselves or for others. It can provide both a background primer and a first-level decision-making framework for those who have fiduciary responsibilities as members of investment committees for pension funds and foundations. I also think that many professionals, who, like me, have seldom focused on the long term and the big picture, can benefit as well. I hope that individual "do it yourself" investors will also find value, though this approach is far from the main stream of thought that they will encounter. But in talking with the "friends and neighbours" who were part of my original motivation to write this, I've come to believe that in almost all cases they find the prospect of seriously managing their investment future too daunting to take on, and they want to hire advice and management. Perhaps this book will give them a little information, background and structure that will help them to better understand, monitor and evaluate such advisory services.

While I like to think that the basic principles I propose are quite straightforward, the process of showing that this is so can be rather complex. I don't want to pull any punches and condescend to a serious reader, so I don't want to downplay the complexities. Yet I also don't want the exposition to bog down in so much detail that any reasonable reader would get discouraged. Many of the technical details can be skipped or skimmed, at a first reading at least.[7]

I would like to acknowledge some of the intellectual sources for this book. The roots of my thinking about the equity version of the simple analytical framework I outline here really stem from the Gordon Growth Model, first discussed in finance classes many years ago. At various times I've returned to think about that model and its implications. In 1992 or 1993, Gerry Rocchi showed me a paper he'd written in which, as I recall, he laid out the algebra of dividend yields, dividend growth and returns that form the basis of the analytical framework for equities that I use. While the paper was mislaid years ago in one of many office moves, it was the first time I had seen a systematic treatment of this material, so I knew that it could be worked out again if I set my mind to it.

Keith Ambachtsheer also used elements of this framework to generate an analysis of expected returns in his newsletter for pension clients in the late 1990s,[8] trying to wean them from continued use

---

7 One simplification that I have made has caused me some discomfort at several points in the book: this is my decision to couch all discussions of returns and risks in terms of percentage returns and their distributions. Using percentage returns is the standard practice of investment industry reporting, and is used for most "investment research". But any serious quantitative research, analysis and forecasting must in the end use logarithmic returns, since the distribution of the natural logarithm of investment returns is approximately normal, while the distribution of percentage returns is clearly not. At several points (Chapters 4 and 28) I hint that analysis using logarithmic returns would lead to clearer or sounder analysis, and I hope that quantitative investors will understand the need to remain within the chosen (but sometimes awkward) framework.

8 *The Ambachtsheer Letter*, a private newsletter for his pension and investment management clients.

of historical average returns as expected returns in asset allocation decisions. I'm not sure what success he had then, but the power of that simple approach resonated with me, as I remained embroiled in the short-term concerns of active management. These themes were revisited in a very important article to which I make numerous references in the text, and which I've reread many times over the years: "What Risk Premium is 'Normal'?" by Rob Arnott and Peter Bernstein.[9] They present a version of the analytical framework and use it in a similar fashion to Ambachtsheer, but they also raise and discuss many of the important questions that are often glossed over by others, and extend the framework to fixed income assets.

And of course Dimson, Marsh and Staunton, whose international database is an important resource for this book, have written numerous articles in this area. After writing out the algebra of the equity relations in the Appendix to Chapter 7, I found that they had published the algebra in DMS 2006, not surprising given their important use of these concepts.

I want to thank a number of people who have read and helped me improve this book: Robert Bertram, Gordon Divitt, Michael Doran, Ken Gordon, Ramaswamy Krishnan, Morgan McCague, and Gerry Rocchi. I am astounded and gratified at their willingness to read, think about and comment (sometimes in great detail) on drafts at various stages of writing. And of course my in-house editor, my wife Jeanne Duperreault, read and edited at least three drafts of the book, and supported the project with unflagging encouragement and good cheer.

---

9 A&B 2002. For full citation information please refer to the Bibliography.

Introduction

Suppose you want to teach someone about baseball. It's pretty hard to describe the point of baseball to someone who's never seen a game, although there are better and worse ways of going about it. Those of us of a certain age might remember Bob Newhart's classic skit of an executive at game manufacturer Olympic Games.[1] Newhart picks up the phone and we hear his comments as he tries to make sense of Abner Doubleday's description of his new game. Newhart has puzzled through the fact that the game is played outside and that there are two teams of nine players. The conversation continues:

> **Newhart speaking to Mr. Doubleday:** You got a pitcher and a catcher. They throw this ball back and forth. That's all there is to it?
>
> ...... [Mr. Doubleday responds out of our hearing on the phone]
>
> **Newhart:** All right. A guy from the other side stands between them. With a bat. I see. And he just watches them?
>
> ......
>
> **Newhart:** Oh, I see. He swings at it?
>
> ......
>
> **Newhart:** He may or he may not swing at it. Depending on what?
>
> ......
>
> **Newhart:** If it looked like it were a ball.... Uh, what's a ball, Mr. Doubleday?
>
> ......
>
> **Newhart:** You've got this plate. Uh-huh.....

---

[1] The skit "Nobody Will Ever Play Baseball", is from the record album *The Button Down Mind of Bob Newhart*, Warner Brothers, May 6, 1960. I transcribed these excerpts.

Things spiral out of control as Newhart tries to understand what happens if the batter swings and hits a ball, and what happens if the ball stays fair: " ... *and what's fair, Mr. Doubleday?*" In the end he rejects the game: how could anyone expect people to learn and play such a complicated game? Surely no one will ever play baseball!

Of course when most of us learned about baseball, we watched from the stands or saw games on TV, and with a little explanation here and there we got the basic idea of the game. Probably no one learns about the infield fly rule on his first visit to the ballpark, but most will understand how runs are scored, and what it is to win or lose. Over a period of time you can learn some of the intricacies — how fielders shift depending on the hitter and what pitch is being thrown; or what type of pitch is thrown depending on the hitter and whether or not there are runners on base. What's interesting is that you can learn a huge amount about the game, you can hold your own in discussions about strategy and second-guess the manager, and yet not have a clue about how to actually *play* the game. That is, you can't hit, catch, throw or run.

And when it comes to actually playing, there are again layers within layers. You might be able to hit a fastball, but not a curve. You might be great at a Sunday afternoon pickup game, but wouldn't know how to actually turn a double play, or throw to the right base in the heat of action of a more competitive game.

I suspect that most people who have money to invest have heard an incoherent sales pitch like poor old Abner Doubleday's. Perhaps they've done a bit of watching from the stands. They read newspapers, and maybe follow some of the investment programming on TV. But I'm fairly sure that most people who have started to learn about the investment game in this way do not have a clear idea of what the game is really about, and don't understand some of its very basic rules and parameters. A poor understanding of baseball doesn't really matter, and certainly doesn't have a significant impact on your life. But a poor understanding of investing can have a serious impact on your future, and it shouldn't be surprising to find that investing is quite a bit more complicated than baseball.

So my goal with this book is to elucidate some key aspects of the most important part of investing, what you might call *the long-term investing game*. I will cover some of the background information that you need to know, and some of the rules or parameters you need to understand, in order to monitor and evaluate a long-term investment plan. While things get pretty detailed at times, I am not really trying to teach you all of the "on field" skills you need to play the game seriously. However, there are a lot of hints if you are motivated to build and monitor your own investment strategy.

To begin this process, I want to go back to basics and start by asking what investing really is. Defining it in a very general way might help identify the kinds of things you have to know or believe in order to understand the process. Here is a definition from one of my favourite finance textbooks. In its broadest sense,

"Investment is the sacrifice of certain present value for (possibly uncertain) future value."[2]

That goes by really quickly, doesn't it, so let's slow it down a little. The *certain present value* is an asset you have today, such as money you have earned, but it could be other things as well. You sacrifice it — give it up, trade or exchange it — for some future benefit. That future benefit or value is the return on your sacrifice or investment. And here's one of the really crucial points: in most cases that future benefit is uncertain. You may or may not actually receive that return or future value.

All sorts of quite ordinary activities can be described as "investing". For example:

- A farmer plants part of his stored wheat, the sacrifice being that he can't sell it now or eat it. Assuming that the crop grows, he will receive many times the amount he planted at harvest. But the crop could fail entirely, produce a small amount due to pests, disease or drought, or at the other end of the scale, produce a bumper crop. What he actually gets is uncertain.

---

[2] *Investments*, 3rd Edition, William F. Sharpe, Prentice-Hall, Inc. Englewood Cliffs, New Jersey 1978, p. 3.

- We often say that someone is *investing in his education*. You might take a night course such as a part-time MBA, investing both money (for tuition and books), as well as time (that you might otherwise have spent at leisure or at a part-time job). The future benefits might be a higher-paying job and a more lucrative and satisfying career over the long run. Of course there is uncertainty, not only as to whether you graduate, but as to the extent that the more lucrative career materializes.
- You can view putting "sweat equity" into a new business venture as an investment, perhaps giving up the income from your current job, in the hope of building a viable business with a larger income. The range of possible outcomes covers the spectrum of abject failure to wild success.

Notice that in all three cases the investment outcome is something attractive and desired, a gain of some kind, but that isn't actually built into the original definition. For example, many forms of institutionalized gambling can be viewed as investments: you place your bet in exchange for an uncertain future return. The fact that the average return is negative due to the known house take might make gambling irrational in some obvious sense, but that doesn't prevent casinos from being full, and lottery tickets being sold like hotcakes.

While those are all valid examples of investing in the broadest sense, this book will focus on a subset of investing that can be called *financial investment*. In a financial investment the investor purchases a security — a GIC, stock, bond or other asset — or deposits money in a bank, in exchange for a more or less uncertain future financial outcome. It is worth noting that I will only be discussing financial investments that are marketable or traded in active regulated markets, although most of the principles discussed here apply to financial investments that are difficult to trade.

All of these examples of investing, including financial investment, share three elements: (1) the sacrifice or outlay of some asset that you now have, that is, the cost or investment; (2) a future benefit or return; and (3) a greater or lesser uncertainty surrounding that future benefit. The basic idea is pretty clear, and in a very general way it describes what happens with an investment. But up to this point I have avoided using a very important term when outlining parts (2) and (3): the term is *expectation*. This is a term that you need to understand if you want to treat investing as a sensible, rational endeavour.

Let me return to the wheat farmer. Were I, a non-farmer, to plant wheat, I might believe that it would grow and that I would end up with more wheat than I had originally planted. I might *say* that I expect 20 bushels an acre, but with my lack of knowledge and experience that's just a vague hope, perhaps based on what a neighbour has told me.

The experienced farmer is in a very different situation. Perhaps he believes that *on average*, his best field yields 35 bushels an acre. In an exceptionally fine year it might yield as much as 42 bushels per acre, and in a drought year it might yield less than 20 bushels. Of course hail could wipe out the crop completely. He understands the range of possible outcomes of planting (investing), and has an *expectation* or *expected outcome* that is essentially the average of those possible outcomes, with each outcome (intuitively) weighted by the likelihood of its occurrence.

In fact, he might be very poor at developing his expectations or estimating the average outcome. For example, his expectation might be biased to the positive side. By that I mean that other experienced farmers might take the same information and formulate an expectation of 30 rather than 35 bushels per acre from that same field. Or we might find that if we looked back at the 35 years of records kept by him and his father, the historical average yield was just 25 bushels per acre, and that would make us wonder why he expected 35 bushels.

On the other hand, the farmer might have excellent reasons for thinking that future returns will be more like 35 bushels per acre rather than the 25 bushels from his past. He might have instituted new farming practices, such as irrigation, new fertilizers, better equipment, and so on, that justify such expectations.

So you can see that the sense of "expectation" in *expected return on investment* is very different from my *vague hope*. You can also see what I believe is a key point, one that I think many sophisticated investors do not understand, that a true *expectation* of return is implicitly the weighted average of a range of possible outcomes. This formulation might be very formal and (perhaps misleadingly) precise, or it may be informal and based on intuition and experience.

With this in mind I will refine the concept of investing. There is not much point in discussing investments that are merely based on vague hopes, and there is certainly no point in writing a book about them. The context here will be to think about investment as a considered or rational process:

> <u>Reasoned or rational investing</u> involves (1) the sacrifice or outlay of some asset that you now have, that is, the cost or investment; (2) an expectation of a future benefit or positive return; and (3) an expectation of the level of uncertainty with respect to receiving that future benefit.

Those expectations in (2) and (3) might be biased, naive, based on misinformation, and so on, but they are the result of some kind of considered process — rational in an everyday sense of the word. I have added that the expected return must be positive, for surely no rational person would invest, sacrificing their current resources, without a positive expectation or forecast of return.

Yet many investors seem to be reluctant to make forecasts, or at least to acknowledge that they are forecasters. You might come across one of the amusing shtick lines of certain "value" investors: "We don't forecast — we buy what is cheap today". I've often heard value investors making fun of forecasters and forecasting, and this may be partly because forecasting is hard to do. But if you think about it for two seconds, you will see that the comment that "we don't forecast" is downright silly.

Assuming that such an investor actually has a meaningful definition of what it is to be "cheap today", why should his clients buy or continue to hold those currently cheap assets? Is it because he believes that those assets will be even cheaper (that is, sell at a lower price) in a few years? No, presumably he thinks they will rise in price and provide a good, healthy return, ideally a better return than average. And if you probe and pry a little deeper, you might find that those investors act as though the cheaper an asset is today by their standard, the higher its future returns will be. They "prefer" cheaper stocks, the cheaper the better. That's a forecast of future returns, although it may not be a very clear and explicit one.

Moreover, the shtick obscures the fact that a good value investor takes into account a view of the distribution of possible future outcomes. Not only does he believe that greater value (as he defines it) implies higher return and conversely, he often suggests that the downside outcomes of cheap (high value) stocks are limited. He is doing exactly what the revised concept of rational financial investing suggests, forming expectations of return and risk. If a value investor is a good and successful investor, it is because he is a good forecaster.

Not only do we have to make forecasts, we have to make quite explicit forecasts. First, we need to make forecasts of return in order to estimate how much our investment will grow, which in turn is necessary for determining how large an investment we must make in order to achieve our goals. This is important, because at any point we have limited resources that we can either consume now, or save and invest for future consumption. Explicit forecasts of expected gains are a crucial part of making that allocation decision.

A second related point is that forecasts of both return and risk are required in order to choose some subset of investments from a range of possible alternatives. On the one hand almost no investors literally try to hold every possible asset, and their beliefs about expected return and risk are the basis for this. On the other hand most investors intuitively understand that holding just one asset can be very risky. I won't discuss the idea of investment choice until Part 4, but I'm confident that all investors who choose assets understand at some level that their return expectations (no matter what they are based on) are a key part of this decision. The part that needs explanation, though I think it is quite intuitive once it is pointed out, is that expected risk is, or should be, an important part of making more effective choices as well. In sum, making explicit forecasts is part of a disciplined approach to investing.

In the following chapters I will be working towards the goal of formulating expectations of long-term return and risk, first for equities, and then bonds. This will be followed by a discussion of how forecasts can be turned into an investment portfolio that best meets the needs of a particular investor. But I will begin by examining what has happened to markets historically.

You should not think that my study of history implies that I believe that the future will mimic the past in any simple or straightforward way. For example, as I write these thoughts in the early months of 2011, which part of the past would you think will repeat? The last ten years ending in December 2010, in which the S&P 500 equity index returned 1.41% annually including dividends? What about the ten years ending in December 1999 in which the S&P 500 returned 18.21% annualized including dividends? Probably neither. Or perhaps the future will average the whole of whatever arbitrary portion of history that I happen to have in my databases. Surely not, but that is often how people come up with estimates for the future.

Yet there is a lot to learn from history. You have likely heard the well-worn aphorism that "History doesn't repeat itself, but it sometimes rhymes".[3] I take this as a succinct expression of a very complicated, but in the end very obvious, idea. Conditions are always changing and evolving, but the underlying principles that govern change or generate outcomes, remain more or less the same. We couldn't function in any part of our lives if we didn't implicitly believe that future conditions are the result of current conditions, transformed through the laws or principles of nature and human behaviour.

From this very general point of view, I see the description and analysis of past market behaviour as having many educational benefits. Bearing in mind that investors are interested in forecasting the returns of their potential investments, I will mention two of them. First, if enough financial history has been gathered, it is very likely that future performance will fall somewhere within the

---

[3] Often incorrectly attributed, it seems, to Mark Twain, whom I have correctly quoted in the Preface.

range of that past performance — the past begins to show *the range of what is possible*. For example, the recent downturn in equity markets was by no means unprecedented: there are several similar examples over the history of the US market, and if you look beyond the US to international markets there are many more. Knowing such facts is one step towards understanding the potential risks you face by holding equities. Moreover, if you had reason to forecast returns that stepped outside the bounds of the past that we know of, isn't that an important thing to acknowledge?

Second, studying history can sometimes help investors *understand the mechanisms that can lead to desirable or undesirable consequences*. I may be able to discover relationships that have held across markets and over time, which in turn may help me forecast some part of what might happen in the future. So keep in mind that in examining market history I am both looking at the range of possible outcomes, as well as searching for possible relationships that might hold over time.

My emphasis on both history and on forecasting is focused on returns to asset classes or broad market indexes, such as returns to Canadian, US or international equities, or Canadian fixed income. One useful way of thinking about this is whether or not it is likely that an asset such as Canadian equities is likely to outperform or underperform its historical average return over some specific period.

I am also going to make the case that most investors have little hope of reliably outperforming those broad market averages through active management or stock selection within those asset classes. So my view is that a strategy that employs a mix of broad asset classes at the lowest possible cost will be the ideal approach for most investors. You will not be surprised to find that the majority of industry practitioners, especially those selling high-cost investment products to retail investors, will reject this approach. My views are more closely aligned to those who oversee large institutional portfolios, although even in that area there will be disagreement. I hope that at least some investors will have the patience to think through the main lines of the argument, so that even if they do not accept my conclusions they are challenged by the reasoning.

In Part 1, I present a comprehensive history and analysis of equity markets. Chapter 1 summarizes 140 years of history of the US equity market, while introducing the concepts of price returns (capital gains) and total returns, along with real or inflation-adjusted returns. In the subsequent three chapters I examine US inflation and introduce the concept of volatility, using the US market as a case study. In Chapters 5 and 6, I extend the perspective to cover 19 international equity markets, applying the concepts that have been introduced, and fine-tuning conclusions based on that broader experience. I add another interesting level of detail to the historical analysis in Chapter 7 by developing a return attribution analysis that will eventually provide the necessary framework for forecasting equity returns. In Chapters 8 and 9, I analyze the effect of currencies on investments. All of this is retrospective.

In Part 2, I develop a framework from which I can begin to make forecasts of future equity returns. By way of a preliminary analysis, I examine the relationship between economic growth and equity returns in Chapters 10 and 11, to see whether forecasting economic growth can help us in any way with our equity forecasts. The results are largely negative, but they provide some insights into how equity markets respond to information. In Chapter 12, I discuss some of the problems with assuming that average past returns provide a good forecast of future returns. I show how the attribution framework developed in Part 1 can be used as a framework for forecasting equity returns in Chapter 13, while details of this framework are examined in Chapters 14 through 17, as each component of return is handled separately. These ideas are summarized in Chapter 18, and a full set of forecasts is developed to illustrate the methodology. I also show how the framework can be used as a sounding board against which forecasts made by others can be evaluated.

In Part 3, fixed income assets are examined in some detail, along with a small set of other investment opportunities. I begin by discussing the concept of diversification in Chapter 19: why investors should want to diversify, what the benefits might be, and how those benefits are gained, if indeed they are. Chapter 20 examines the historical returns and risks to nominal fixed income assets, along with the impact of inflation. In Chapter 21, I develop an attribution framework for fixed income that is analogous to the framework developed for equities, and use this to clearly show why the returns and risks of bonds are different from those of equities. In Chapter 22, this is turned into a forecasting framework for nominal bonds. Chapter 23 adds the concept of inflation-linked or real return bonds, modifying the fixed income framework both for historical attribution and forecasting. Chapter 24 concludes Part 3 by presenting correlations between equities and nominal fixed income assets. But I also develop a conceptual framework for weighing the benefits of adding additional asset classes to an investor's opportunity set, and give several examples of this.

Finally, in Part 4, I discuss how all of this work can be put together into a comprehensive investment strategy. My belief is that for most investors, a sensible asset mix, implemented by investments in the lowest-cost investment vehicles that are available, is the ideal approach. Up to this point, active management within asset classes has not been examined, and Chapter 25 discusses both the difficulties of adding value through active management within asset classes, as well as the difficulty faced by investors who try to choose specific active funds managed by others. Chapter 26 extends the analysis by showing why, again for most investors, a guarantee of lower costs is more beneficial than holding out the hope for added value from active management. Chapter 27 highlights the importance of asset mix in determining investment returns: *on average* asset mix determines 90% of the variability of investment returns and 100% of the investment returns themselves. In Chapter 28, I develop a framework for portfolio construction based on the historical returns and risks to asset classes, and show how you might think about choosing from the myriad of opportunities available. The natural result is an ongoing *static mix* of assets, that maximizes your expected benefit or utility given your aversion to risk. Chapter 29 extends this analysis by applying my dynamic forecasts, and some of the consequences of using those forecasts are explored. The natural result of this more refined approach is an asset mix that slowly *evolves* as your forecasts adapt to changing market conditions and other information. I summarize some key issues in Chapter 30.

Historical or retrospective analysis can help investors understand the past and answer the question: *how did we get here?* But investors need to make forecasts, and my systematic approach to forecasting both allows me to make objective forecasts and to justify them. Just as useful is the fact that my framework allows me to analyze the forecasts of others, and show what has to happen for those forecasts to come true. That is, in both these cases it helps answer the question: *how do you get there from here?*

Part 1:

An Overview of Equity Markets History

Chapter 1:

The US Equity Market over the Long Term

> **OVERVIEW**
>
> The long-term performance of the US Equity market is measured.
>
> Key concepts:
> - total returns versus price returns or capital gains;
> - nominal returns versus real returns (which is return adjusted for inflation).

Investors who hold stocks or equities receive returns from two sources. First they receive returns due to changing asset prices: *price returns* or capital gains and losses. Second they receive *returns from dividends* and their reinvestment. Many investors, analysts and financial reporters who follow markets over what I would call the short term, that is days, weeks and even months, focus almost exclusively on asset price movements. For example, when you hear or read that on December 31, 2010 the S&P500 index closed at 1257.64, this number reflects only the changing price levels of its component members because it is a *price index*. By contrast, a *total return index*, which you almost never see in newspapers, adds the impact of dividends as they are paid day by day, and which are then reinvested in the index. On this same date the S&P 500 Total Return Index closed at 2114.29. In a moment you will see why investors should be concerned with total returns and not just price returns.

The longest equity market history in my database is drawn from the publicly available data provided by Robert Shiller on his website,[1]

---
[1] The data are available for download at http://www.econ.yale.edu/~shiller/data.htm along with remarks on the sources.

which covers the US Equity market from January 1871 to the current day, along with a record of monthly dividends, earnings, bond yields and CPI inflation. Over this 140-year period ending December 31, 2010, the price index returned 4.12% annually. When I use these data to calculate total returns,[2] including reinvested dividends, the return was 8.88% annually, or 4.57% in excess of the annualized price return.

Most people are surprised that more than half of the historical annualized total return of the US market has come from dividends and their reinvestment. From day to day, short-term price changes grab headlines, and the impact of dividends is quite minor. But as you measure equity performance over multi-year spans, the volatility of price movements becomes less significant relative to the stability and accumulation of dividends.

You might also be surprised at the magnitude of these numbers, although here the reaction is somewhat mixed. For example, given the way some of the financial press and sellers of financial products talk, you might think that returns of 8.88% on average are rather small and disappointing. On the other hand, the US economy and market has been one of the most successful in the world in the 20th century, with no major disruptions and on the winning side of two world wars. So perhaps these returns are much higher than average.

Figure 1-1[3] presents one way of dramatizing the significance of this total return: the red line shows that $100 invested at the beginning of 1871, with all dividends reinvested, would have grown to $14,763,903.[4] Had dividends been spent and not reinvested as shown by the blue line, that $100 would only have grown to $28,325;

---

[2] From 1970 onward I use the S&P 500 Total Return Index as provided by Standard and Poors, but prior to that I calculate total returns from monthly prices and dividends, in line with Appendix 2 of Chapter 7.

[3] All Figures and Tables are numbered in this style: the first number refers to the chapter number, and the second to the sequence of Figures or Tables within that chapter. Since this labeling is unambiguous, I will refer to Figures and Tables in other chapters directly using these labels, without additional descriptors.

[4] As with several of the graphs in this book that show investment returns accumulating over long periods of time, the vertical axis of Figure 1-1 is on a

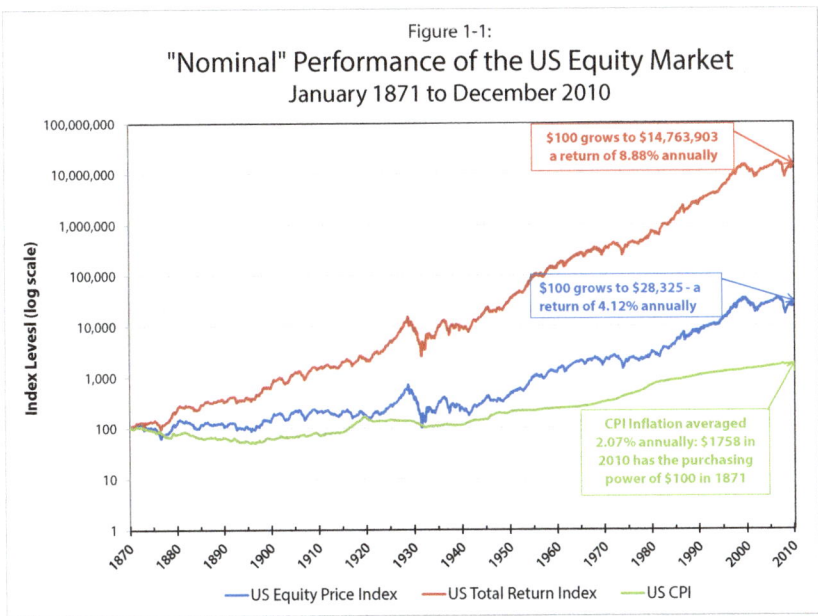

still strong, but fully 538 times smaller than the total return. So whether or not you think that 8.88% is a strong long-term return, it is large enough to accumulate a great deal of wealth over the long run.

A second important distinction is between *nominal returns*, the returns just calculated from the values of the prices and dividends that we see day by day over time, and *real returns*, returns adjusted by a measure of inflation such as a CPI index or other price deflator. At a minimum, long-term investors hope to maintain the purchasing power of their capital, and ideally would like to earn returns in excess of inflation. Over the 140-year period the US Consumer Price Index (CPI) rose by 2.07% annually, and is shown as the green line in Figure 1-1. This means that the purchasing power of $100 at the beginning of 1871 is equivalent to the purchasing power of $1758 in 2010, a significant erosion of value. When inflation has been removed from nominal returns to create real returns, for the full 140-year period:

---

logarithmic scale. You can see that the value for each horizontal grid line is 10 times larger than the previous one below.

- the price index generated real returns (net of inflation) of 2.01% annually, and
- the total return index generated real returns of 6.67% annually, which is 4.57% in excess of the annualized price return.

A return of 6.67% over inflation is still a very strong return: $100 invested in 1871 would have become $867,211 by the end of 2010, while the total would have been just $1,611 if dividends had been spent and not reinvested (as before, smaller by a factor of 538). This is all summarized in Table 1-1 below.

Table 1-1:
US Equity Market Returns
1871/02 to 2010/12

	% Return	Proportion of Return
Total Nominal Equity Return	8.88%	100%
Consisting of:		
CPI	2.07%	24%
Real Total Returns	6.67%	76%
Real Total Returns consisting of:		
Real Price Returns	2.01%	23%
Impact of Dividends	4.57%	52%

While the long-run US CPI number of 2.07% per year might not seem like a very large number, I cannot overemphasize the importance and impact of inflation on potential investment returns on the one hand, or on the potential rising costs of living on the other. We are all aware that gasoline prices in particular and energy prices in general, along with those of food and shelter, continue to rise. To some extent this trend may be countered by technological change, which causes the prices of some items to actually fall over time. But one of our highest priorities as investors must be to protect our investments against the damaging costs of inflation.

From this very high-level 140-year perspective, the US equity market has been a profitable investment. Remember that the United States was on the winning side of two world wars and several other major conflicts, and emerged from the global depression of the 1930s and the Second World War as a dominant economic force. This long-term perspective also masks many of the serious bumps and bruises investors would have picked up along the way.

Chapter 2:

Inflation and the US Equity Market

I discussed the importance of having investments outpace inflation over the long term, and showed that the US equity market did a marvelous job of this over the 140-year history in the database. But a careful look at Figure 1-1 in the previous chapter can add a little context and colour to the annual CPI inflation number of 2.07%.

To set the stage for this, I will divide the data into two parts. Roughly in the centre of Figure 1-1, and almost coinciding with the depths of the 1929–1932 market crash,[1] you can see that the green CPI inflation line begins a long stretch of rising inflation that has lasted to the present day. Prior to this point inflation was not always positive.

After the first year in 1871, the CPI index, which I based at 100, fell below its starting point, reaching a low of 50.4 in 1896 and 1897.

> **OVERVIEW**
>
> The impact of inflation is examined in more detail. Six inflation environments are isolated.
>
> Key findings:
>
> - inflation has a negative correlation with real returns;
> - equities may not protect investors from the impact of high levels of inflation.

---

1 You can locate the great market crash of 1929, roughly in the centre of Figure 1-1. The month-end peak of the equity market prior to the crash was August of 1929. The subsequent market downturn finally bottomed in June of 1932, with the price index (blue line) falling just below its starting point at the beginning of 1871, sixty-two years earlier. The return over the two years and ten months from August 1929 was -83.8% (-80.3% including dividends). You can see from the graph that this was the largest continuous downturn in the history of the US market as recorded here.

This was a stretch of serious deflation that lasted for 26 years. From this trough it began rising, returning to 100 in 1917, before peaking at 167.7 in 1920. It then began to stabilize and decline, hitting a low of 101.9 in May of 1933 at the depth of the Great Depression, just after the equity market bottomed in mid-1932. From that point inflation began its upward trend to the present day.

This means that over the 62-year period from February 1871 to May 1933, CPI inflation averaged just 0.02% per year — essentially zero. In the subsequent 77-year period from June 1933 to December 2010, CPI inflation averaged 3.75%. In other words the long-run inflation number of just 2.07% can be viewed as the combination of a long period of virtually no net inflation, followed by a long period of 3.75% inflation — a rather different story. So May 1933 is a good place to divide the history and to take a first look at the impact of inflation on equity returns. Table 2-1 summarizes the results.

Table 2-1:
US Equity Market Returns

	% Return 1871/02 to 1933/05	% Return 1933/06 to 2010/12	Difference (Compounded)
Total Nominal Equity Return	6.78%	10.59%	3.56%
Consisting of:			
CPI	0.02%	3.75%	3.73%
Real Total Returns	6.77%	6.59%	-0.16%
Real Total Returns consisting of:			
Real Price Returns	1.23%	2.63%	1.38%
Impact of Dividends	5.46%	3.86%	-1.52%

First, note that there is a significant performance difference between the two periods. The total nominal return of the first period, 6.78% annualized, is 3.56% less than the total nominal return over the second period, which is 10.59%. Second, it is intriguing that this difference in total nominal return is reflected in the difference in inflation, which was just 0.02% annualized in the first period, but 3.75% in the second, for a difference of 3.73%. The flip side of this is that the total real returns for the two periods are almost the same: 6.77% for the first period and 6.59 % for the second period. These bracket the total real return of 6.67% for the whole history (Table 1-1).

The lesson here is that inflation can have a significant impact on total nominal returns, but don't jump too quickly to the conclusion that real returns were stable at around 6.5%, as suggestive as that may be.

Let me look again at the first half of the data. Earlier I sketched three major trends from 1871 to 1933, which suggested that inflation was quite volatile. Using this broad brush, I can describe inflation performance in these three sub-periods:[2]

- 1871/02 to 1897/07: a span of 26 years in which CPI inflation averaged -2.55% per year. Of the 26 years, 17 (65.4%) were negative.
- 1897/08 to 1920/06: a span of 23 years in which CPI inflation averaged 5.39% per year. Of the 23 years, only 5 (21.7%) were negative.
- 1920/07 to 1933/05: a span of 13 years in which CPI inflation averaged -3.82%. Of the 13 years, 8 (61.5%) were negative.

In the second half of the sample, from 1933/06 to the end of 2010, CPI inflation averaged 3.75%. The green CPI line in Figure 1-1 rises fairly consistently, and inflation was negative in only three of the 77 calendar years: 1938, 1949, and 1954. Inflation has been positive since 1955, although the recent financial turmoil has raised questions and concerns about the possibility of negative CPI (deflation) if economic growth were to falter.

This period of positive inflation has faced a different issue: extended periods of high inflation. Counting those years with inflation greater than the average level of 3.75% as "high", 27 of the 77 years would qualify. Of those high-inflation years, 20 were concentrated in a 23-year span from 1968 to 1990, and I use this fact to break down the second half of the data as follows:

---

2 I first came across this idea of looking at equity returns relative to long-lasting investment "eras", though not necessarily defined by inflation trends, in Keith Ambachtsheer's private newsletters to pension funds and investment managers in the mid to late 1990s.

- 1933/06 to 1967/12: a span of 34 years in which CPI inflation averaged 2.91%. In just 6 of those calendar years (17.1% of the time), inflation was greater than 3.75%.
- 1968/01 to 1990/12: a span of 23 years in which CPI inflation averaged 6.15%. In 20 of those years (87% of the time) inflation was greater than 3.75%.
- 1991/01 to 2010/12: a span of 20 years, in which CPI inflation averaged 2.5%. In just 1 of those years inflation was greater than 3.75%.

So now US equity history is divided into six sub-periods: two with negative inflation, two with moderate inflation averaging between 2.5% and 3%, and two with high inflation averaging over 5%. For each of these sub-periods, total nominal returns are calculated and are then divided into inflation and real total returns. Real total returns are further subdivided into real price returns and the impact of dividends. These calculations are summarized in Table 2-2.

Table 2-2:
US Equity Market Returns Segmented by Inflation Regimes

	Period 1 1871/01 to 1897/07 (26 yrs)	Period 2 1897/08 to 1920/06 (23 yrs)	Period 3 1920/07 to 1933/05 (13 yrs)	Period 4 1933/06 to 1967/12 (34 yrs)	Period 5 1968/01 to 1990/12 (23 yrs)	Period 6 1991/01 to 2010/12 (20 yrs)
Total Nominal Return	5.50%	7.79%	7.61%	12.04%	9.78%	9.11%
Consisting of:						
CPI	-2.55%	5.39%	-3.82%	2.91%	6.15%	2.50%
Real Total Returns	8.26%	2.28%	11.88%	8.87%	3.42%	6.45%
Consisting of:						
Real Price Returns	2.64%	-2.70%	5.55%	3.88%	-0.62%	4.31%
Impact of Dividends	5.48%	5.13%	5.99%	4.80%	4.06%	2.05%

There is a lot of information here, so let me take it step by step. First, take the time to compare average inflation (second row of numbers) and average real returns (third row of numbers) period by period, and think about how different the investing world must have been in each inflationary "era" relative to the one just prior to it. Then follow across on the fourth row, and you will see that not only are real price returns very different from period to period, but that in two periods they are negative. The final row, showing the impact of dividends, is relatively stable compared to the others, and only in the last two periods have average dividends fallen significantly below 5% annually.

Table 2-3 helps tell a little more of the story, by re-orienting all of the data in Table 2-2 and then ignoring dates and sorting the results by the level of CPI inflation, from the lowest to the highest. Look down each of the columns and you can begin to see some patterns.

Table 2-3:
CPI versus Nominal and Real Total Returns
Ranked by CPI Inflation (low to high)

Period	US CPI	(1) Nominal Total Returns	(2) Real Total Returns	(3) Real Price Returns	(4) Impact of Dividends
3	-3.82%	7.61%	11.88%	5.55%	5.99%
1	-2.55%	5.50%	8.26%	2.64%	5.48%
6	2.50%	9.11%	6.45%	4.31%	2.05%
4	2.91%	12.04%	8.87%	3.88%	4.80%
2	5.39%	7.79%	2.28%	-2.70%	5.13%
5	6.15%	9.78%	3.42%	-0.62%	4.06%
Correlation with CPI		0.56	-0.87	-0.72	-0.48

Column (1) shows that nominal total returns are positively correlated[3] with CPI at 0.56. This means that generally in periods

---

3 When higher values of one series seem to coincide with higher values of a second series, and lower values of the first seem to coincide with lower values of the second, then the two series appear to be positively correlated. When higher values of the first series seem to coincide with lower values of the second, the two series appear to be negatively correlated. Statistical correlation is a concept that quantifies the positive or negative relation that appears to hold between two data series.

I will broach the subject of statistical significance in the Appendix to Chapter 3. The correlations between CPI and each of columns 1 and 4 are suggestive, but are not in fact statistically significant. The correlation between CPI and column 2 is significant and negative, while the correlation between CPI and column 3 is negative but only marginally significant. For those who have an interest, there is when CPI was high, so were nominal returns. Over time, equities seem to respond to higher levels of inflation with higher nominal returns. Does this imply that equities are a full hedge against high levels of inflation?

Column (2) confirms that in all six periods real total returns were positive. But the results raise an important concern. The fact that the correlation between CPI and total real returns is strongly negative at -0.87 means that real total returns were highest when inflation was negative, and lowest during the two periods of high inflation. The strength of the relationship certainly raises the question as to whether equities have been, and will continue to be, a hedge against inflation in times of very high inflation.

Column (3) shows that real price returns also have a strong negative relationship with CPI, and in fact price returns have not kept up with inflation in the two periods of higher inflation.

Column (4) shows a slightly weaker negative relation between CPI and the real returns due to dividends. Note that at least in these examples, real returns from dividends did not significantly decline in the two periods of relatively high inflation.

I will revisit the question of how equity returns relate to inflation when I extend the analysis to international stocks. But I want to highlight one point here, the concern suggested by column (2) that periods of high inflation might in fact be times when real equity returns trail inflation, and that when an inflation hedge is needed the most, equities might not provide one.

In the 140-year history of the US market there is only one extended period of significantly high inflation, the nine-year span from January 1973 to December 1981, which is a subset of the fifth inflation era defined above. Over this nine-year period inflation averaged 9.22%, a seriously high level but certainly not the excruciatingly high inflation that devastated Germany in the years

---

a 5% probability that the correlation between CPI and Column 2 is 0 (so a 95% probability that the relation is indeed negative), and a 10% probability that the correlation between CPI and Column 3 is 0 (and so a 90% probability that the relation is indeed negative). These are strong results with so few data points.

Table 2-4:
Nominal and Real Returns when CPI is "High"

	Nominal Price Returns	Nominal Total Returns	CPI	Real Total Returns	Real Price Returns	Impact of Dividends
9-year span from 1973/01 to 1981/12	0.42%	5.01%	9.22%	-3.86%	-8.06%	4.57%
Average of 26 years with CPI Inflation greater than 6%	1.89%	7.19%	10.85%	-3.25%	-8.02%	5.18%

following the first World War and culminated in the hyperinflation of 1922–1923. Table 2-4 summarizes the nominal and real price returns, total returns and the impact of dividends for this period. Table 2-4 also shows the same data for the average of 26 individual (not contiguous) years in which inflation was greater than 6%. For this sample the (arithmetic) average CPI was 10.85%.

In both cases nominal price and total returns were significantly lower than CPI, so real total returns were negative: -3.86% annualized for the contiguous nine-year span, and -3.25% for the sample group of 26 individual high-inflation years. Price returns trailed inflation by about -8% in both cases, and dividends contributed 4.57% and 5.18% respectively.

This confirms the idea strongly suggested by the data in Table 2-3, that equities may not provide a full inflation hedge in periods of high inflation. But it is interesting that the impact of dividends hovered around 5% in both examples, slightly above the 4.6% provided by dividends over the whole 140-year span of data.

Chapter 3:

Shorter-Term Variability in the US Equity Market

While the main purpose of Table 2-2 was to highlight the fact that inflation has a significant impact on equity returns, the analysis also gave a first look at how very different total nominal and total real returns could be from one extended period to another. But I can also examine the *variability of returns* or *volatility* directly, not with respect to inflation experience but just as a function of period-by-period returns. Our ultimate goal is to estimate potential long-term returns from any point in time, and an important stepping stone is to be aware of the range of returns that have occurred in the past and that might occur in the future.

> **OVERVIEW**
>
> The fact that equity returns are highly variable is illustrated, and this variability is identified as an important measure of the riskiness of equities.
>
> Key concept:
>
> - *standard deviation* is introduced as a measure of risk or variability.

To recap some fairly recent events and to highlight what I mean by variability or volatility over the shorter term, remember that 2008 was one of the worst calendar years on record for US equities, with the S&P 500 falling 37%. Moreover, the 16-month period from November 2007 through February 2009 encompassed a gut-wrenching decline of 50.95%. This period was followed by 21 months from March 2009 to December 2010, in which the S&P

500 generated a positive total nominal return of 77.85%.[1] These are huge and disturbing numbers and it is important to find a way of measuring and comparing the variability of assets you invest in.

Let me begin with a picture of the US equity market in Figure 3-1 that shows year-by-year returns as the blue bars. The horizontal red line shows the average nominal total return of 10.59%. The highest return was 52.35% in 1954, and the lowest was -43.21% in 1931. It is interesting that the yearly return was within plus or minus 1% of the average in only five of the 140 years — the average return rarely occurred, and "variability" is the operative word.

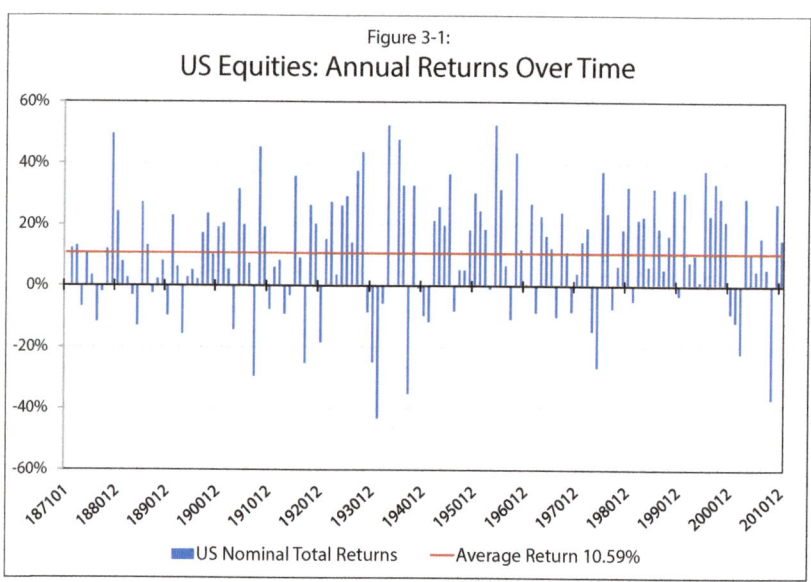

While Figure 3-1 shows that equity returns were quite variable from year to year, it is very hard to draw any specific conclusions from it, or to compare the variability inherent in these returns with, for example, the variability of some other asset you may want to consider. So in order to get a handle on the concept of variability I have to introduce a simple but important statistical concept that measures variability. While I don't want to focus on statistics in this book, it is

---

[1] After a 50% downturn you need a 100% return to get back to where you were — so as of December 2010 the S&P 500 was still well short of its high. I will briefly return to this point in the Appendix to this chapter.

important to introduce several statistical terms to help describe asset returns and measure some of the relations between them.

One way to illustrate the variability of US equities is to take all of the yearly returns from Figure 3-1 and order them from lowest to highest as displayed in Figure 3-2. As in Figure 3-1, the red line is the average nominal total return of 10.59%, and it is clear that half of the returns are above the line (actually 71 of 140 for 50.7%), while half the returns are below the line (69 of 140, for 49.3%). Ignore the mauve and green lines just for a moment.

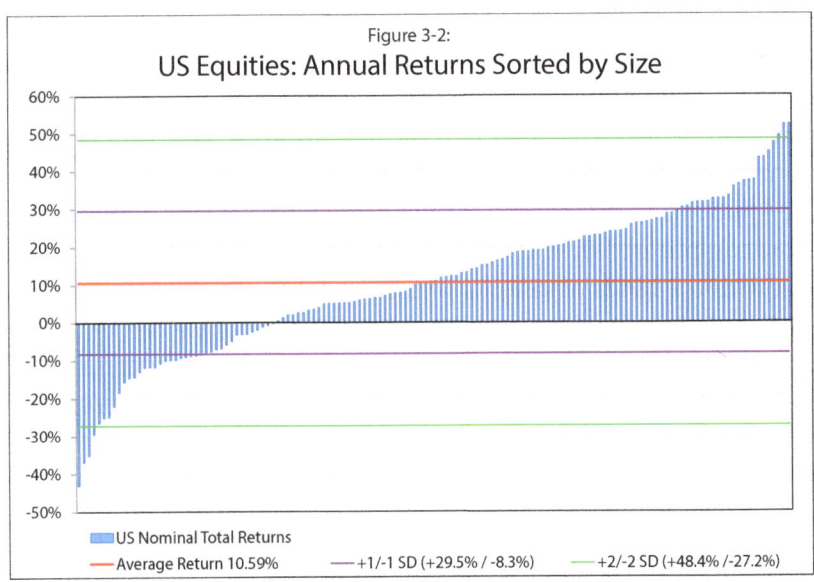

The visual impression that these one-year returns are variable is based on the observation that lots of them are very high or very low — they are very far away from the mean or average. For example, if I circled those returns that were within plus or minus 5% of the mean, you would find only 26 of the 140 observations (18.6%) in that range, 14 below the mean and 12 above. In other words 81.4% of the yearly returns are more than 5% away from the average return of 10.59%. Similarly, just 56 of the 140 observations (40%) are within plus or minus 10% of the mean, 29 below and 27 above, so that fully 60% of the returns are more than 10% below or above the mean.

Another interesting question is: how many returns are negative? Of the 140 returns, 39 (or 27.8%) are negative, which means that they are more than 10.59% below the mean or average.

You can make any number of similar observations to describe the variability of the data we are observing. But the problem is that when you turn to another set of data, say returns from another country's equity market, or returns from the US or Canadian bond market, you will find it very difficult to compare the variability of one data set to another just using these kinds of observations.

The simple answer to this is to introduce the concept of *standard deviation*. Most people know what an *average* or *mean* is, and I've used the term without explaining or defining it. But I'm guessing that most people have forgotten the definition of standard deviation from Grade 9 or 10 math. You can look it up on Wikipedia, or check the Appendix to this chapter, and you will find that it's only a little bit more complicated than the definition of an average. What is useful is that with the kinds of samples of financial data that investors usually observe and work with, *approximately two-thirds of the sample will lie between plus or minus one standard deviation around the mean, and approximately 95% of the sample will fall within plus or minus two standard deviations of the mean.*[2]

This works for the sample of 140 years of US total nominal equity returns. The standard deviation is calculated to be 18.91%, and in Figure 3-2 the mauve lines show the mean plus or minus one standard deviation, while the green lines show the mean plus or

---

[2] Think of these characterizations as useful approximations or rules of thumb. Strictly speaking, these are properties of the standard deviation of samples for which the data are normally distributed, and none of our samples of percentage returns to equities or other assets are literally normally distributed. You can see this because while there is no theoretical limit to the magnitude of positive returns, negative returns are limited to -100%, the case where an asset price falls to $0. In other words, the negative "tail" of the distribution is abruptly truncated. This is one of the important reasons why serious quantitative research uses the natural logarithms of returns rather than percentage returns, as mentioned in the Preface. The distribution of logarithmic returns is empirically normal.

minus two standard deviations. You can actually count the returns within each category.

- 44 returns fall between minus one standard deviation at -8.3% and the mean, for 31.4% of the total observations; 49 returns fall between the mean and plus one standard deviation at 29.5%, for 35% of the total observations. Thus 93 returns in total, or 66.4% of the observations, fall between plus or minus one standard deviation of the mean. This is very close to two-thirds of the sample.
- 133 observations fall within plus or minus two standard deviations, for exactly 95% of the sample.
- you can see in Figure 3-2 that three returns fall above plus two standard deviations, for 2.14%, while four returns fall below minus two standard deviations, for 2.86%. This totals 5% of the observations falling outside the plus or minus two standard deviation band.

Let me tie this back to recent history. If you turn to Figure 3-1 again, you will see that the return for 2008, the third-last return on the right-hand side of the chart, is the second-lowest return for any calendar year. It is one of the four returns in the "bottom tail" of the return distribution, below minus two standard deviations from the mean. So while 2008 was a very bad year in the US equity market, it was not unprecedented, and it is consistent with the normal distribution of annual returns.

With the tool of the standard deviation, I can compare the *variability* or *risk* of returns for different samples or assets: one set of returns is more *variable* than another if its standard deviation is higher. Here are two examples of ways you can use this approach. First, if you look carefully at Figure 3-1, you can see that the first third of the data, to about 1915, appears to be slightly less variable than the remaining data. When I measure variability in each part, this observation is confirmed: the standard deviation is 16.0% up to 1915, and 20.1% thereafter. It actually turns out that the mean of the first part is lower, at 8.1% annualized, versus 11.8% for the second part.

In the second kind of example that is used throughout the book, I will use the standard deviation to compare the variability of different data sets. These could be nominal versus real returns, stock markets around the world, or equities versus other assets such as bonds and "cash" or short-term investments. For example, I reported that the mean and standard deviation of total nominal returns for the US market were 10.59% and 18.91% respectively. By comparison the mean and standard deviation of total real annual returns over the same period were 8.38% and 18.70%. Thus the variability of real and nominal one-year returns has been almost identical.

Researchers, theorists and (less frequently) investors study risk in some detail. They might try to parse or analyze equity risk, for example, into component factors that explain both its magnitude and its relationship to returns. But here I will simply characterize the overall risk of an asset in terms of the standard deviation or variability of its returns; sometimes I will use the term *volatility* as a synonym of the phrase *variability of return*.

Appendix: an introduction to some statistical terms

It is possible to comprehend the basic information and investment ideas developed in this book without being well-versed in statistics. But a rough understanding of some key concepts is important, not only for this book but, in my opinion, for understanding any approach to investing. So here is an informal primer that describes a few basic concepts. I will use a little algebra where necessary, but my main goal is to describe the concepts in words.

I will also relate the concepts to some of the specific data, graphs and calculations that have been discussed so far. While the actual data used to this point have been based on monthly data, for the purposes of this exposition I am going to assume that yearly total nominal returns were used, starting with 1871 and ending with 2010. I symbolize the first year's return as r_1, the second as r_2, and so on, with the last one as r_{140}. Each of the annual returns r_n (where "n" is a variable ranging over years 1 to 140) is potentially different from every other return. In Figures 3-1 and 3-2 these were the vertical blue bars.

Cumulative Return

In Figure 1-1 the red line showed the cumulative total return of US equities: $100 would have grown to $14,763,903. If I start with $100, and r_1 (the first year's total nominal return) is 12.28%, then you can see that at the end of year one my $100 becomes $112.28. That is, multiply $100 by r_1, which means that my gain in dollars is $12.28, and then add it to $100. You can write this as $100*(1+ r_1). Then take that result, $112.28, and multiply it by r_2, the percentage gain for year 2, and add it to our growing investment, continuing this all the way to the end. The chain of calculations looks like this:

(a) $100*(1+ r_1) * (1+ r_2) * (1+ r_3) * ... *(1+ r_{140}) = $14,763,903

Annualized Return

Now, early in Chapter 1, I said that the total nominal return for the 140-year period was 8.88%. Remember that each of the individual annual returns r_n was potentially different from 8.88%, although it is quite possible that the returns for two or more individual years are identical. But when I talk about investment returns over multiple years, I want to know what the return is which, if received every year, would give the ending value that was actually achieved. In one sense of "average" this is the average return. I am going to denote this type of return as "r_g". Were I to replace each of the different annual returns r_n in formula (a) with the single value r_g I would have

(b) $\$100 * (1+r_g) * (1+r_g) * (1+r_g) * \ldots * (1+r_g) = \$14{,}763{,}903$

where $100 is multiplied by $(1+r_g)$ 140 times. A much clearer way of writing this that identifies that I am multiplying by $(1+r_g)$ exactly 140 times (the power of 140) is

(c) $\$100 * (1+r_g)^{140} = \$14{,}763{,}903$

Solving for r_g you obtain 8.88%. This is the annualized return. It is also called the <u>geometric average</u>, hence the "g" in r_g.

Arithmetic Average Return

In Figure 3-1 the horizontal red line is the average of the actual annual returns r_n. As opposed to the geometric average r_g that was just calculated, this is the more familiar arithmetic average or mean which I will call r_a. That's the one we all learned first in school: you add up all 140 of the yearly numbers r_n and divide by 140.

But if you were paying attention, you will have noticed that the arithmetic average r_a was said to be 10.59%, substantially higher than the geometric average (annualized average return) of 8.88%.

The Effect of Variability on Annualized Returns

The reason that the arithmetic average return is higher than the geometric or annualized return is because the individual yearly returns are very volatile, that is, they vary from year to year. Note that if they were identical every year, say 8.88%, then the geometric return would equal the arithmetic return. So it is the fact that the various yearly returns are not identical that causes the difference between the geometric and arithmetic averages.

You saw how dramatic this effect can be when I mentioned in footnote 1 of chapter 3 that after a 50% downturn you would need a 100% rally to recover. That is, if you start with $100 and lose 50%, you have $50. To earn your way back to $100 you need to gain $50, which is a gain of 100% ($50 on your starting point of $50). The average return over these two periods would be 25% (-50% + 100% all divided by 2), which sounds huge. But the geometric return is 0% — you started with $100 and ended with $100 two periods later.

<u>Defining Variability of Returns or Volatility</u>

The idea behind variability is very simple: when I say that annual returns vary from year to year, I mean that they differ from each other. But of course that also means that they differ from the (arithmetic) average return.

In order to describe and measure this variability, you might start by adding up all these differences from the mean and then divide by the number of observations to get an average difference. But when you think about the distribution of return in Figure 3-1, and realize that roughly half of the differences will be positive and half negative, that's probably not going to work very well. The trick used is to square the differences, and then take their average. That gives what is known as the *variance* of the data, which can be written in symbols as:

$$Var(r) = \frac{\sum_{n=1}^{140}(r_n - r_a)^2}{n}$$

where r_a is the previously defined arithmetic average of the 140 yearly returns to the US market and each of the r_n is one of the 140 annual returns to the US market.[1]

The concept that I have introduced in this chapter, the standard deviation, is the *square root* of the variance as just defined.

---

1 This is the definition for the Variance of a population as opposed to a sample.

The properties that two-thirds of the observations fall within +/- 1 standard deviation, and that 95% of observations fall within +/- 2 standard deviations are properties of a particular distribution called the *normal* distribution. While most of the financial data I will be examining are not strictly normal in this sense, monthly, quarterly and annual data are "close enough" to normal that these properties are likely to hold.

<u>Relating Average and Annualized Returns through Variability</u>

To put the concepts of average and annualized returns in perspective, I always try to use the term "average return" to mean *arithmetic average return*, and the terms "annualized return" and "cumulative annualized return" to mean the *geometric average return*. I am concerned about annualized returns when looking at how wealth would accumulate over a long time span. I am interested in average returns when describing returns on a period-by-period basis (for example, monthly or yearly). It was no accident that the arithmetic average was shown in Figures 3-1 and 3-2, when I wanted to show the distribution of the individual annual returns. Both arithmetic averages and standard deviations help to describe the distribution of returns, while strictly speaking, geometric average returns do not.

So given any sample of period-by-period returns, you can calculate the actual average return and standard deviation that describe the data, as well as the annualized cumulative return. But it can also be useful to know that under certain circumstances, if you know the standard deviation, and one of either the arithmetic or annualized return, you can estimate the number you don't know using a statistical formula. I won't elaborate further here, but the idea is that if data are normally distributed and independent, the annualized geometric average return is a function of the variance and arithmetic average of the data. A simple rule of thumb that roughly estimates the relationship, is that the geometric return is approximately the arithmetic return less half of the variance, or in symbols:

$R_g \approx R_a - Var/2$

This tends to overstate the difference between the two averages, but provides a good first approximation. There are more accurate formulations of the relationship based on certain assumptions about the nature of asset returns, but the details are not necessary in our context. To illustrate with the US numbers we have seen, since R_a was 10.59% and the standard deviation (square root of the variance) was 18.91%, the formula suggests that R_g should be approximately 8.86%, very close to the actual number of 8.88%

The Correlation Between Two Series of Data

In Chapter 2, I appealed to the concept of correlation, when I stated that inflation appeared to be *positively correlated* to nominal total returns, and *negatively correlated* to real total returns (see Table 2-3). While we use the term "correlation" in ordinary English, and people generally understand its meaning, it is also a statistical concept with a precise definition. Statistical correlation is a measure that ranges from 1.0 to -1.0, with a correlation of 1.0 meaning that two series change identically: if series A increases, then series B increases by exactly the same proportion, and if series A decreases, then series B decreases in exactly the same proportion. A correlation of -1.0 means that if series A increases, then series B decreases by exactly the same proportion, and conversely. A correlation of 0 means that there is no relation between the two series.

To see some real examples of correlations, look back to Table 2-3. There I reported a positive correlation of 0.57 between CPI Inflation and Total Nominal Returns over six time periods, and a negative correlation of -0.87 between CPI Inflation and Total Real Returns over the same periods.

A positive correlation between two factors A and B does not mean that one series "causes" or "drives" the other. They can be merely coincident, or perhaps both are driven by some third factor C. On the other hand, if we happen to believe that factor A causes factor B, then we expect to find a positive correlation between them, and lack of such a correlation would undermine any notion of causation. The existence of a correlation between two factors is a necessary but not sufficient condition for causation.

Line of Best Fit

The correlation between two series is closely related to the concept of the *line of best fit*, which is found by a *linear regression*, and the best way to show this succinctly is with a graph. Using the data from Table 2-3, the following graph plots the Real Total Return (vertical axis) against the CPI Inflation (horizontal axis) from each period. The dark blue line is the line of best fit, which is a function of the negative correlation (-0.87 in this case) between the two series.[2]

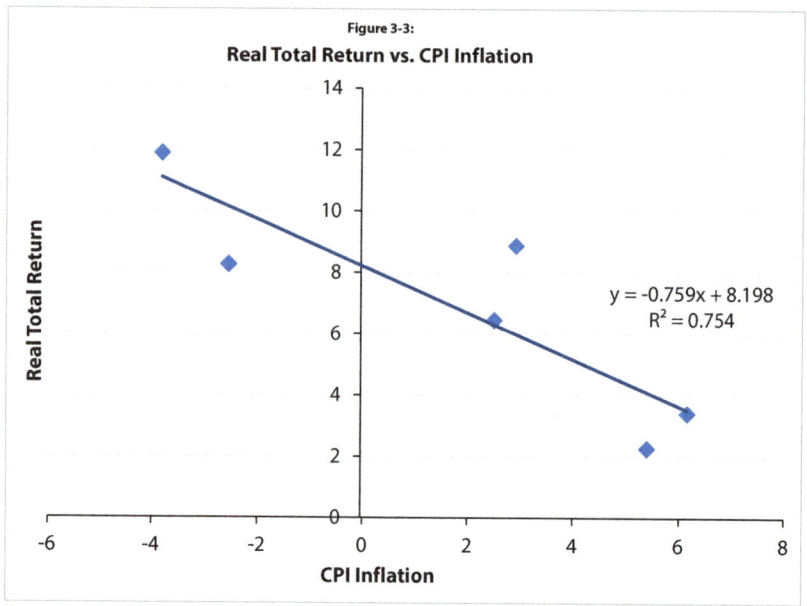

The linear regression uses the given data to calculate the line of best fit, which is an equation for a line that says: y (in this case Real Total Return) is a function of x (CPI Inflation). You might remember that a line is defined by a simple equation: in Grade 9 algebra we used the symbols y = mx + b, where m is the slope of the line and b is a constant, the value at which the line crosses the vertical y axis.[3]

---

[2] Specifically, one definition of the slope of the line shows it to be a function of the correlation between the two variables and the ratio of their standard deviations.

[3] In finance we often use trivially different symbols: y=a+bx, where "b" is pronounced "beta" and "a" is pronounced "alpha". In different contexts there are

The fact that the linear regression defines a line gives some important added information relative to the correlation. While a correlation statistic may indicate that a relationship holds between two variables, it does not give a scale or ratio between them. The slope of the line estimates such a relation.

You can see the equation on the graph: y = -0.7988x + 8.198. So when x (inflation) is 0 then y (real return) is 8.198. When inflation is 3%, the equation says that real return will average 0.7988*3 + 8.198 = 5.922 (which is 5.922%). You can figure out that for real return to equal 0, x (inflation) would average 10.8%.

It would be risky to use just six data points to make predictions here, but the graph is suggestive. While all of the real return data are positive (vertical axis), the downward slope of the line suggests that real returns may become negative as inflation rises past 10.8%, the point where y is 0. Indeed the implications of this equation are quite compatible with what was shown in Table 2-4, where real returns were negative with inflation in the 9%–10% range. So this regression is, broadly speaking, in line with those findings.

Statistical Significance

When I measure relationships such as correlations or regression coefficients from the line of best fit, the results have to be interpreted relative to their *statistical significance*. It is just as important to know that a measured relationship is not significant as that it is, and for all such measured relationships I will say whether or not it is "significant", and will footnote a number that measures this significance. When a relationship is not statistically significant, I may say that it is not significantly different from 0. If the relationship is statistically significant, I will give the small probability that it is 0, and usually this probability will be less than 5%. I will only use relationships that are deemed to be significant as part of a further analysis. For those not familiar with statistics, you probably don't need to go beyond these observations: if the relationship is significant, then the statistics

---

financially interesting interpretations of b and a, but in this book I will simply use the equation to determine the constant and slope of a potential relationship.

suggest that the relationship holds and is meaningful; if it is not significant then assume that there is no meaningful relationship.

The following table shows how this works. It gives a small subset of the statistical information available about the linear regression portrayed in Appendix Figure 3-3 above. Associated with each of the coefficients in the equation is a number called the *t-statistic* and the associated probability that it is not significant (that it is really just 0). For the constant, the probability that the coefficient is really 0 is just .001 or 0.1%, and for the slope of the line the probability that it is really 0 is 0.025 or 2.5%. That probability is a function of the calculated t-statistic and the number of observations — the more observations the less chance of insignificance for a given t-statistic. In most contexts, if the probability that the coefficient is 0 is greater than 5%, I will not count the result as significant.

Appendix Chapter 3 Table 1:

Linear Regression: Inflation vs. Real Return

Dependent Variable: **REAL_RETURN**

6 Observations

Variable	Coefficient	t-Statistic	Prob.
Constant	8.198	9.142	0.001
INFLATION	-0.759	-3.501	0.025
R-squared	0.754		
Adj. R-squared	0.692		
F-statistic	12.25		
Prob(F-statistic)	0.02		

The final concept I want to mention is the adjusted r-squared. The value of 0.692 says that 69.2% of the variability of the relationship is explained by this regression, which means that the data fit very well indeed.

There is a delicate balance here. On the one hand, for those who are not familiar with statistics, I don't want to present a flurry of confusing numbers that might hinder understanding of the main ideas in this book. On the other hand, talking about relationships that might be used in making investment decisions, without measuring them and understanding their significance, is futile. And for those

Appendix: an introduction to some statistical terms 43

who understand this, it's very frustrating not to have a measure of significance associated with a number that is said to be important.

In general, I will try to give enough information to show that statistical relationships are measured and understood, without overwhelming the readers who find the statistics difficult. I think it's wrong to pretend that statistics aren't necessary and important, and yet I believe that all the concepts in this book can be understood without a deeper understanding of statistics than is contained in this Appendix.

Chapter 4:

Variability over the Longer Term

How does the very high one-year variability of equities translate into volatility over the longer term, such as a 10-, 20- or 30-year investment horizon? If you have an expectation of a certain level of return over a very long period, you should understand the extent by which you might be wrong, and the impact that might have on your future wealth.

> **OVERVIEW**
>
> The impact of variability of longer time periods is examined.
>
> Key findings:
> - the dispersion of annualized equity returns narrows as the time frame increases;
> - yet equities are just about as risky over the long term as they are over the short term.

The simplest way to proceed is to present the data pictorially as in Figure 4-1. Nominal US equity returns are calculated for 1-, 5-, 10-, 20- and 30-year periods and the multi-year returns are then annualized. In this example the multi-year periods are overlapping. That is, if I calculate 30-year returns from the beginning of every calendar year, the 30-year return from year one is very similar to that from year two, since they overlap for 29 of 30 years. We can't really count them as completely different or *independent* observations, yet they represent what investors experienced over those time spans. Consequently, when I provide certain kinds of analysis using these data, I will be careful to use non-overlapping independent data points to ensure that the results are not distorted by the overlapping data.

The most important and interesting phenomenon is that as the time spans increase, the dispersion of returns falls quite dramatically.

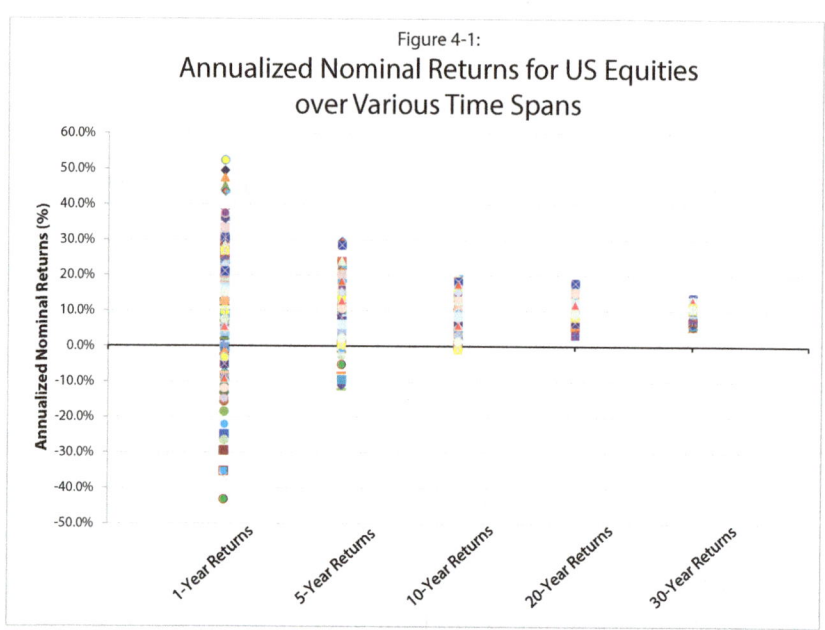

While one-year real returns have ranged from 52.35% to -43.21%, the range for five-year spans is 29.6% annualized to -12.1% annualized, and for 30-year spans the range is just 13.6% annualized to 5.2% annualized. Table 4-1 presents averages and standard deviations for each of these samples. To show the distribution more clearly, it also presents the average plus or minus one standard deviation, along with the actual maximum and minimum values.

The second row of Table 4-1 shows the standard deviation falling from 18.9% for one-year spans to 2.3% for 30-year spans. In

Table 4-1:
Nominal Annualized Total Returns
for Sub-period Samples of US Equities 1871 to 2010

	Annual	5-year	10-year	20-year	30-year
Average of Samples	10.6%	9.2%	9.3%	9.4%	9.4%
Std. Dev. of Samples	18.9%	8.0%	5.1%	3.3%	2.3%
Average +1 Std. Dev.	29.5%	17.2%	14.4%	12.7%	11.6%
Average -1 Std. Dev.	-8.3%	1.3%	4.2%	6.0%	7.1%
Actual Maximum	52.4%	29.6%	19.9%	17.8%	13.6%
Actual Minimum	-43.2%	-12.1%	-1.4%	3.2%	5.2%

line with the declining variability number is the fact that the average returns are also falling, from 10.5% for one-year spans to 9.4% for the 30-year spans, close to the long-run geometric mean of 8.88%.[1]

There is some evidence that equities, and many other asset classes, exhibit less risk over the long term than is implied by their short-term volatility, and I will speak to this point briefly. But it is important that you understand that the narrowing dispersion of *annualized* returns as your time frame increases does not in itself imply that equities are less risky in the long run than they are in the short run. Indeed the standard deviation numbers suggest that equities are just about as risky as we would expect them to be, given the risk of equities in the short term.

What I mean by this is that if I assume that equity returns are truly random and independent across time, the variance of unannualized returns (standard deviation squared) should increase with time, so that standard deviation increases with the square of time. This is in fact happening here, but since it is usual to express multi-year returns as annualized numbers, the magnitude of the numbers shrinks. For example, the ten-year standard deviation of the sample in Table 4-1 is 5.1%, which is equivalent to an unannualized return of 64.4% over ten years, much higher than the one-year standard deviation of 18.9%.

To make this point clear, in the second row of Table 4-2 I have extrapolated the standard deviation of the one-year sample of 18.9% to the longer time spans assuming that variance increases with time. The numbers are then annualized. The standard deviations of the

Table 4-2:
Actual Standard Deviations of Multi-Year Samples Versus Multi-Year Standard Deviations Extrapolated from Annual Data

	Annual	5-year	10-year	20-year	30-year
Std. Dev. From Samples	18.9%	8.0%	5.1%	3.3%	2.3%
Std. Dev. Extrapolated	18.9%	7.3%	4.8%	3.1%	2.4%

---

1 See chapter 1 for the long-run geometric return, and the Appendix to Chapter 3 for a brief discussion of the difference between geometric and arithmetic average returns.

samples in the first row are slightly higher than the extrapolated numbers until 30 years, at which point the sample standard deviation is marginally lower.

While you should understand that the narrowing dispersion of annualized multi-period returns does not indicate lower risk over longer-term periods, there is in fact some evidence in Table 4-1 that equities are indeed less risky over the longer term than we might otherwise expect. If you carefully examine the numbers, you will find that the minimum returns for the 20-year and 30-year samples are higher (that is, less risky) than -2 standard deviations. So while the standard deviations as calculated are similar to those you would expect for a normal distribution over time, the extreme "tails" of the distribution have narrowed, particularly on the downside.

There is actually much stronger evidence that longer-term returns exhibit lower-than-expected risk, at least when the analysis is done within a more appropriate framework.[2] But there are several reasons why I think most investors do not need to be concerned about this issue. First, the long time frames over which this becomes very important are too long to impact most real-life investment decisions. Second, there is evidence that this risk reduction occurs in most asset classes,[3] and the question of how the moderation of risk for longer-term holding periods should impact long-term investment decision-making is difficult to untangle. In sum, while we can

---

[2] In the preface I mentioned that to keep things simpler for most readers, I have chosen to couch all analysis and reporting in terms of percentage returns to assets, indexes and portfolios. This is the perspective taken by all investors when reporting returns, and by most traditional investors when they do their research. But here we have a case where working with percentage returns rather than the natural logarithm of returns obscures the picture. The fact that variances increase at a rate significantly less than one-to-one with time over longer time spans is easily discernible within the framework of logarithmic returns. This means that log returns to assets tend to exhibit negative serial correlation over the longer term, and that distributions are narrower than what is expected if returns are completely independent over time.

[3] For example, in CPS 1991, Cutler, Poterba and Summers show that all of equities, bonds, currencies, real estate and precious metals exhibit negative serial correlation over longer-term holding periods.

acknowledge that long-term returns to equities and other assets likely exhibit less risk than might otherwise be expected, that fact will not affect our ongoing discussions.

Longer-term real equity returns show much the same pattern in Figure 4-2. Even in the robust and very successful US equity environment, there are a number of five- and ten-year time spans with negative real returns. The minimum real return over a five-year span is -11.8%, while the minimum real return over a ten-year span is -4.2%. Indeed the lowest real return over a 20-year span is a sobering 0.5%. The actual maximum and minimum returns, along with averages and standard deviations, are given in Table 4-3.

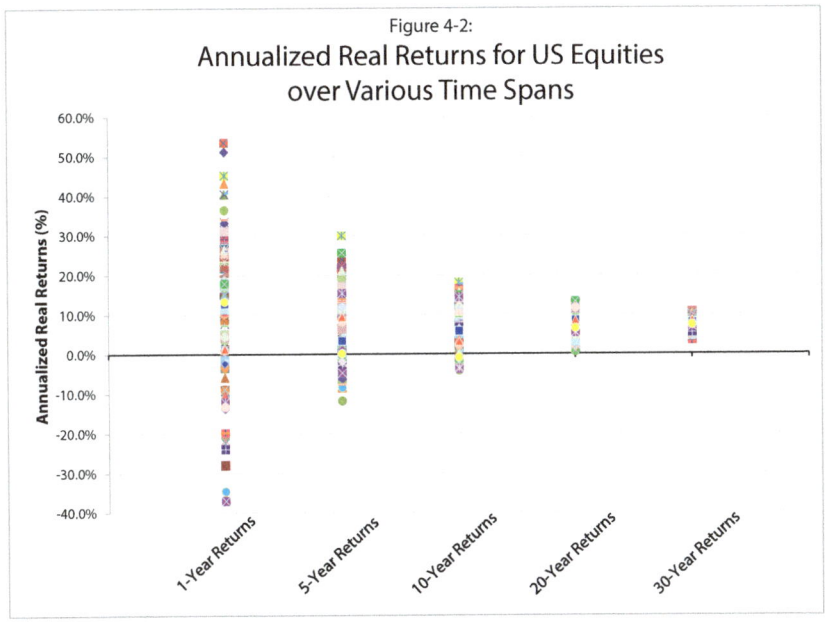

Figure 4-2:
Annualized Real Returns for US Equities over Various Time Spans

Table 4-3:
Comparing Nominal and Real Total Returns for Multi-Year Samples

	Annual	5-year	10-year	20-year	30-year
Average Real Return	8.4%	7.0%	6.9%	6.8%	6.6%
Std. Dev. Of Real Return	18.7%	7.9%	5.2%	3.1%	1.7%
Actual Maximum Real Rtn	53.5%	29.9%	18.0%	13.2%	10.6%
Actual Minimum Real Rtn	-37.4%	-11.8%	-4.2%	0.5%	3.3%

You might see these numbers and think that if the worst case for a 30-year time span is a nominal return of 5.2% annualized (Table 4-1) or a real return of 3.3% annualized (Table 4-3), what's the problem? Just invest in equities and forget about it. While that's an initially convincing position to take, and one that has justified many not-very-good investment decisions in the past, I will just mention three kinds of problems.

The first is that our sample of US data comes from what has been one of the most successful economies in the world, which has survived one significant economic disruption, the Great Depression, and has been on the winning side of two major world wars, while (apart from Hawaii) suffering almost no home country infrastructure damage. Not all other countries, economies and equity markets have been so fortunate. You will see some evidence of this when we look at equities from a global perspective.

Second, if you embark on a 30-year investment plan and expect returns closer to the average, then only obtaining the historical minimum might have a devastating impact. With a real return matching the historical average of 6.6% annualized over 30 years, $100 grows to $675. But at a return matching the historical minimum of 3.3%, $100 would grow to $264, just 39% of what you might have been expecting.

Third, remember that if you have a 30-year investment horizon in which to accumulate wealth, it is only the first year for which your investment has 30 years to grow. As you accumulate wealth and contribute assets to your investment program, your investment horizon necessarily shortens, with minimum returns for those investments being much lower. And of course those minimums are not unbreachable.

Chapter 5:

International Equity Market Returns over the Long Term

Now with this perspective on the US market and a toolkit of concepts to work with, I can convey some key information about global equity markets in a fairly efficient manner. While individual markets could be examined in just as much detail as the US market, I will keep this as a very brief overview, primarily presenting summary information across markets. In several cases I will "pool" the market information, and draw some tentative conclusions about equity markets as a whole.

Remember the point of this exercise: I want to explore what has happened in the past, in order to provide some insights into a range of possible investment outcomes. When you invest, and place your bets on what you think are likely future outcomes, understanding the range of past outcomes can act as a touchstone for forecasts, although not as a direct template for the future. Think of it as an accident that you are living and investing in the particular country, economic environment and time in which you happen to

> **OVERVIEW**
>
> Real and nominal returns to 19 equity markets over 111 years are compared.
>
> Key findings:
>
> - the distribution of returns to equity markets is quite wide;
> - US equity nominal returns have been close to the average;
> - but real returns to US equities have been very strong relative to those of other markets — so it may be misleading to use the US historical experience as your main guide to future equity returns;
> - the study confirms that inflation is negatively correlated with real returns.

find yourself. Observing other countries, markets, environments and time frames is a sobering indicator of what could happen to you.

The obvious starting point is to compare US market experience with other markets. The information presented in this chapter is derived from the DMS database.[1] Table 5-1 summarizes local

Table 5-1:
Local Total Equity Returns: 1900 to 2010

	Nominal Total Returns			Inflation	Real Total Returns		
	Geom. Mean	Arith. Mean	Std. Dev.	Geom. Mean	Geom. Mean	Arith. Mean	Std. Dev.
Australia	11.58	13.15	18.48	3.86	7.43	9.07	18.18
Belgium	8.00	10.74	25.44	5.33	2.54	5.14	23.62
Canada	9.07	10.46	17.16	3.05	5.85	7.26	17.22
Denmark	9.18	11.13	22.14	3.89	5.09	6.94	20.85
Finland	13.09	16.80	31.45	7.32	5.38	9.24	30.33
France	10.49	13.20	25.36	7.21	3.06	5.66	23.51
Germany	8.18	13.61	34.01	4.97	3.06	8.14	32.26
Ireland	8.17	10.65	23.39	4.26	3.75	6.40	23.16
Italy	10.62	14.76	33.67	8.45	2.01	6.06	28.99
Japan	11.10	14.50	29.33	7.01	3.82	8.49	29.82
Netherlands	8.04	10.31	23.22	2.92	4.97	7.11	21.79
New Zealand	9.78	11.52	20.67	3.75	5.82	7.57	19.73
Norway	8.11	11.11	28.39	3.74	4.21	7.23	27.41
South Africa	12.59	14.77	23.29	4.92	7.31	9.54	22.56
Spain	9.60	11.83	23.03	5.83	3.56	5.82	22.26
Sweden	10.12	12.52	23.46	3.57	6.32	8.73	22.86
Switzerland	6.64	8.31	19.10	2.30	4.24	6.07	19.78
United Kingdom	9.48	11.38	21.73	3.95	5.33	7.21	19.97
United States	9.40	11.36	20.05	2.96	6.25	8.27	20.28
Average	9.64	12.22	24.39	4.70	4.74	7.37	23.40
World (USD)	8.60	10.04	17.29	2.96	5.48	7.00	17.69
World ex US (USD)	8.16	10.02	20.22	2.96	5.04	6.99	20.36

---

[1] This database was compiled by Elroy Dimson, Paul Marsh and Mike Staunton (DMS) of the London Business School, and is distributed by Morningstar Canada. Data for 2010 were updated manually from the Credit Suisse Global Investment Returns Sourcebook 2011, and a number of error corrections were made to bring the electronic historical data in line with this publication.

The database consists of annual local market-level returns to stocks, bonds and bills for each of 19 countries, along with annual CPI inflation and US dollar exchange rates. The "World" series are calculated using either GDP or capitalization for weighting. From these basic data all other series are calculated.

nominal and real total returns for the equity markets of 19 countries, based on annual returns for the 111 years from the start of 1900 to the end of 2010.

All of the individual country returns are "local": that is, they represent the return to an investor of each individual country, without exposure to foreign exchange effects.[2] The row labelled "Average", the third row from the bottom of the table, is the simple arithmetic average of the items in the column above. No investor could have achieved that average, which mixes results from different currencies, since any particular investor must have a home country and a home currency, and his investments outside his home market will be subject to currency effects. View this as a summary statistic only.

By contrast, the last two rows entitled "World (USD)" and "World ex US (USD)" are returns from the perspective of a US dollar (USD) perspective, which means that returns include the effects of each country's currency movement relative to the US dollar. Each country return contributes to the US dollar-based return series in proportion to its size (measured by each country's GDP prior to the use of market capitalization data from MSCI starting in 1969.) The World series includes the US along with all the other countries, while the World Ex US series includes all countries except the US.

At this point I want to focus on the blue columns, Geometric Average Total Nominal Returns and Geometric Average Total Real Returns. First let's look at the geometric mean nominal total returns.

Earlier I suggested the possibility that US market experience might be a slightly misleading representation of past equity investment experience, given the political and economic success of the country in the 20th century. While the US total geometric average return of 9.4% is higher than the returns both to the World index (8.6%) and the World ex US index (8.16%), it is just below the arithmetic

---

2 In creating these time series, German local nominal equity returns and inflation are excluded for 1922 and 1923, because DMS report that hyperinflation over that period totalled 209 billion percent. (DMSW 2010, p. 34.) Real local equity returns were -38.76% and 25.28% for 1922 and 1923 respectively, and are included in the real total return series reported in Table 5-1.

average of 9.64% with more than half of the countries having higher nominal returns. So this initial observation might suggest that the US results are quite normal, being right in the middle of the pack, roughly 3% below the highest nominal return of 12.59% for South Africa, and 3% above the lowest return of 6.64% for Switzerland.

However, the second blue column brings a little more perspective, as inflation has been removed to generate geometric average real total returns. Here only Australia, South Africa and Sweden posted higher real returns than the US return of 6.25%, which is substantially above the average real return of 4.74%.

Figure 5-1 shows both nominal (red bars) and real (blue bars) geometric average total returns, with the countries ordered by real returns. The large blue highlighting arrows indicate the average return of all individual country markets, along with returns to the two size-weighted USD World indexes. The green arrow is just there to highlight the US return.

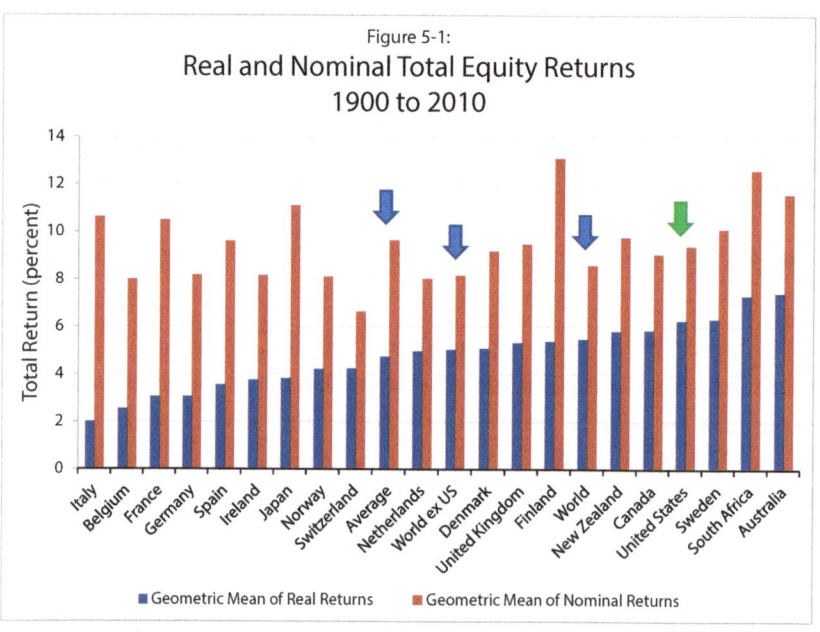

The ranking of the blue bars shows that the US real return was indeed a significant achievement, especially when you realize that on average the US had 50% of the capitalization of the 19 countries.³ In addition, Figure 5-1 suggests that there is a modest tendency for higher real returns to be associated with higher nominal returns, since the red bars to the right are slightly higher on average than those towards the left. The correlation is 0.40.⁴

You can also use Figure 5-1 to see the relationship between long-run inflation and real returns, because inflation is the difference between the height of the real return bars and the height of each associated nominal return bar. But to make this crystal clear I replace the red bars representing total nominal returns with the green bars that show CPI Inflation directly, in Figure 5-2 below. It is apparent that on the left, where real returns are lower, the green inflation bars tend to be much higher than those on the right, where the real returns

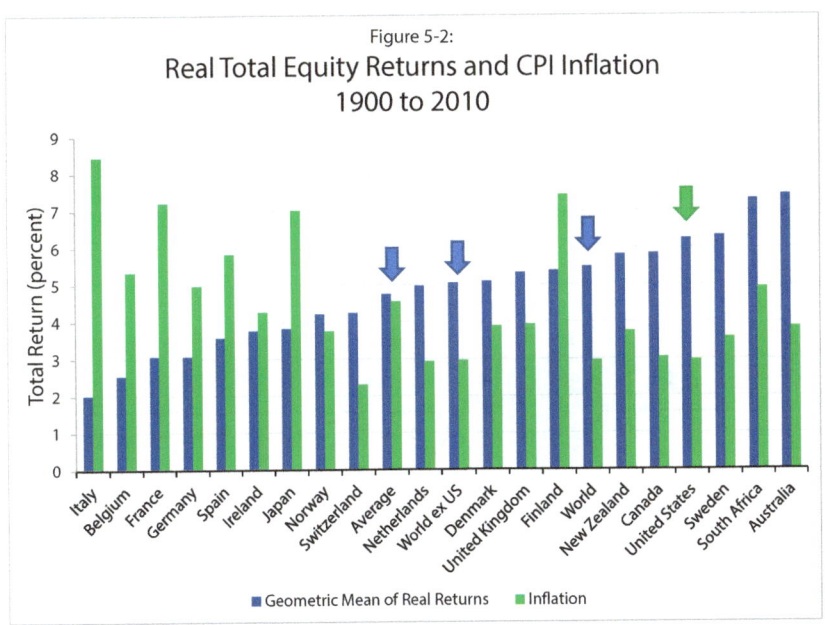

---

3 Extrapolating from the DMS data for the US and the two World indexes, the average weight of the US was 50.7%, with a low of 30.0% and a high of 72.7%.

4 Significant at the 5% level with a t-statistic of 1.97. I mention the concept of statistical significance in the Appendix to Chapter 3. If you are not familiar with the concept, just remember that this means that statistics show that the relationship is strong.

are higher. So the US market, with the fourth-highest real return, had the third-lowest inflation rate. Finland is a noticeable exception, with the seventh-highest country real return, and the second-highest inflation rate. But despite Finland, the correlation is negative and very significant at -0.53.[5] This negative relationship between real returns and inflation supports the relationship found within the US market.

To take this a step further, we can pool all the year-by-year data (111 individual years) for all 19 markets, rather than just the 19 spans of 111 years as in Figures 5-1 and 5-2. So Figure 5-3 shows the relationship between annual real returns and annual CPI inflation for all countries. The correlation is -0.23 and again is highly significant.[6] The line of best fit is plotted in red.[7] You can see that as inflation

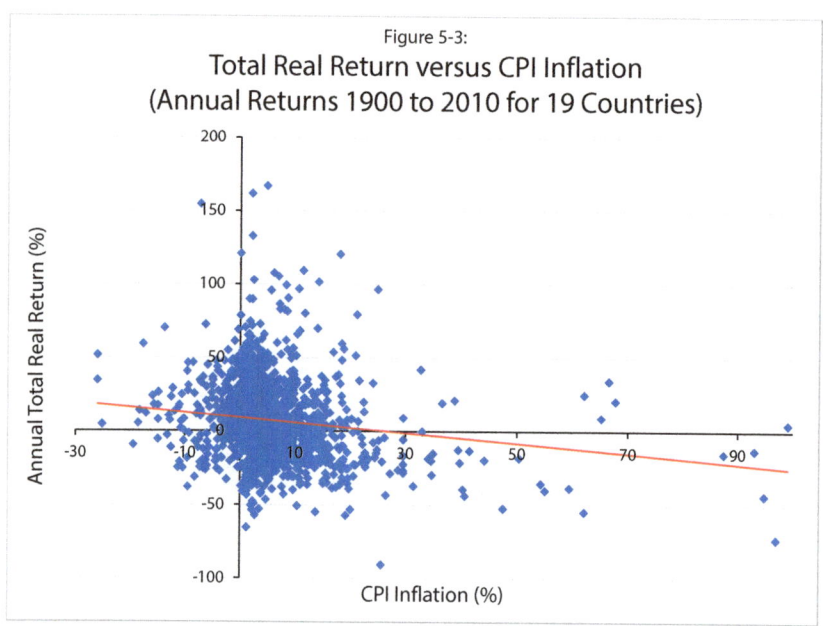

---

5 Significant at the 1% level with a t-statistic of -3.04.

6 The t-statistic is -10.88, and the correlation is significant at far greater than the 0.001% level.

7 Five very high inflation data points ranging from 171% to 360% have been dropped from the graph in order to keep the scale more useful. However the calculation of the line of best fit uses those points.

rises, the red line slopes downward to the right, meaning that total real returns are falling. The line crosses into negative territory at 26.5% inflation. This means that within the more usual range of inflation that we have faced in North America, and for most of the time elsewhere, real returns have been positive on average, although of course in many individual years this is clearly not the case.

Inflation will be addressed again when I look at developing forecasts for equities in Part 2, and study fixed income assets in Part 3. Suffice it to say that almost no one in the modern mainstream investment world has had to deal with extended periods of high inflation in the last 30 years, although some people fear that this could change in the future.

Chapter 6:

Variability in International Equity Markets

In the previous chapter, Table 5-1 showed nominal and real returns and risks for the whole history of the 19 DMS countries, along with averages and composite indexes. In order to put the risk numbers in perspective, Figure 6-1 plots the local real arithmetic average return for each country and composite index on the vertical axis, against the annualized historical real standard deviation or risk which is plotted along the horizontal axis.

> **OVERVIEW**
>
> The risk or variability of international equity markets is examined.
>
> Key findings:
> - many markets have displayed much higher risk than the US market;
> - many markets have delivered negative real returns for ten years and longer.

Canada is positioned farthest to the left (red diamond), which means it has shown the lowest risk (standard deviation) at 17.22%, and slightly higher-than-average real return. Australia stands out as having substantially higher real return along with modestly higher risk at 18.18%. South Africa has the highest real return but substantially higher risk at 22.56%. The United States (green diamond) is nestled towards the top left-hand corner, with both higher historical risk and higher historical real return than Canada. Notice that there is also a group of five countries to the right, with varying returns, but with much higher risk in the 27% to 33% range.

So for those of us with a North American point of view, you can see that while many countries have generated higher average annual

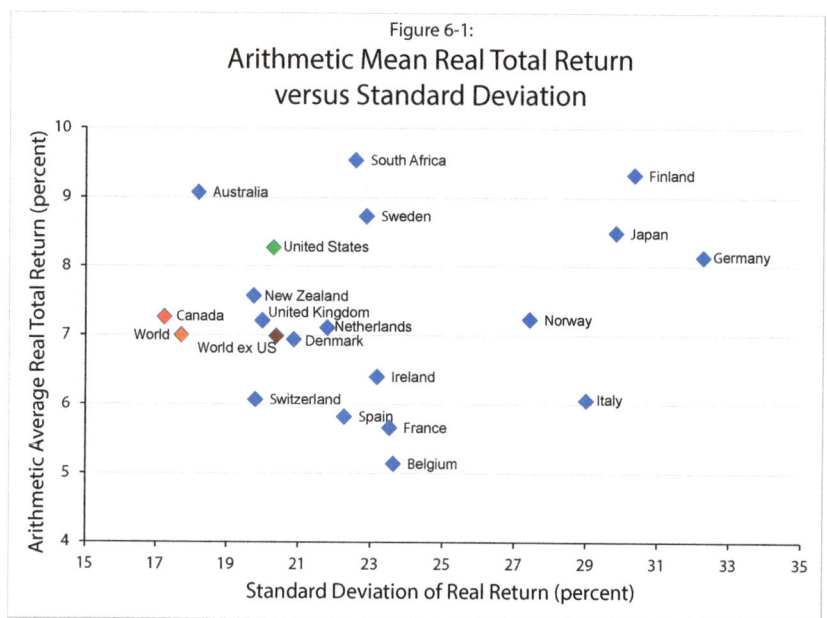

real returns, many also generated lower real returns. But in almost all cases they were subject to higher risk or volatility.

Rather than using complex tables, I will take a visual approach to show you the effects of long-term volatility. With 19 countries, as well as the US-dollar-based World and World ex US indexes, there are 21 data series spanning 111 years, which gives eleven non-overlapping ten-year spans for each series. For each country and composite index Figure 6-2 shows the ten-year annualized average real total returns for each of the non-overlapping decades ending 1910, 1920, 1930, and so on. The market with the lowest dispersion of returns is New Zealand on the left, and the dispersion widens as you move to the right.

I have highlighted Canada (fourth from the left) and the US (fifth from the left). You can see that apart from New Zealand, Australia and Denmark, ten-year real returns to North American markets were less variable than those of most other countries.

The average annualized ten-year geometric mean real return of the data pooled across all countries was 5.03%, with a standard deviation of 8.08%, so you might expect that roughly two-thirds of

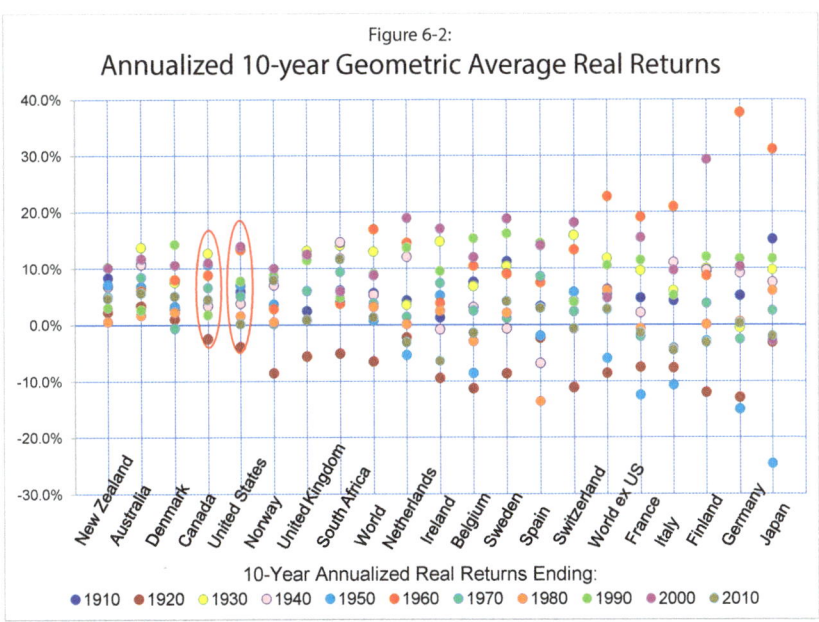

the returns are within +13.11% and -3.05%. In fact slightly more than two-thirds of the observations (153 of 209 for 73.2%) are within that range, with 13.9% (29 observations) above and 12.9% (27 observations) below. Interestingly, all of the Canadian returns are within the plus/minus one standard deviation band, while the US has just one observation above and one below it.

Ten years is a very long time to be under water relative to inflation, and it is noteworthy that almost one-quarter of the real returns shown here (47 of 209 for 22.5%) were negative. For example, in the ten years ending December 2010, eight countries experienced negative real returns (taupe dots on Figure 6-2), and the US just barely eked out a positive real return of 0.16% annualized (2.5% nominal).[1] Just think how difficult this level of equity return has been for individual investors and institutions who have depended on equity returns to fund future liabilities.

---

[1] Our DMS database uses a broad index of 5,000 stocks from 1971 on. By contrast, the S&P 500 index, used in the first four chapters over the same time period, had a nominal return of 1.4% and a real return of -0.91% over this period.

Many of the other negative ten-year spans have been in two other decades: the ten-year span ending in 1920 (brown dots) has 16 negative real returns, while the ten-year span ending in 1950 (blue dots) has 8 cases. Both periods spanned world wars and the economic disruptions caused by them. By contrast the poor real returns for the decade ending in 2010 were caused by a series of financial disruptions and bubbles, but as in the two other decades the problems were global in nature. Three other decades with noticeable negative returns are the ten years ending in 1980 (5 countries), the ten years ending in 1970 (4 countries) and the ten years ending in 1940 (4 countries). Whatever the cause, it's fair to say that ten years of negative real returns can be devastating and we are not immune from them today.

To look beyond ten years, I have prepared a similar graph of annualized 30-year geometric average real total returns in Figure 6-3. Each 30-year span ends in 1930, 1940, and so on, which means that each span partly overlaps two previous spans. This yields a sample of 171 returns with 9 from each country. As you might expect, given the analysis of the US market, the annualized returns have "tightened" into a narrower band: the average across the pool is almost identical

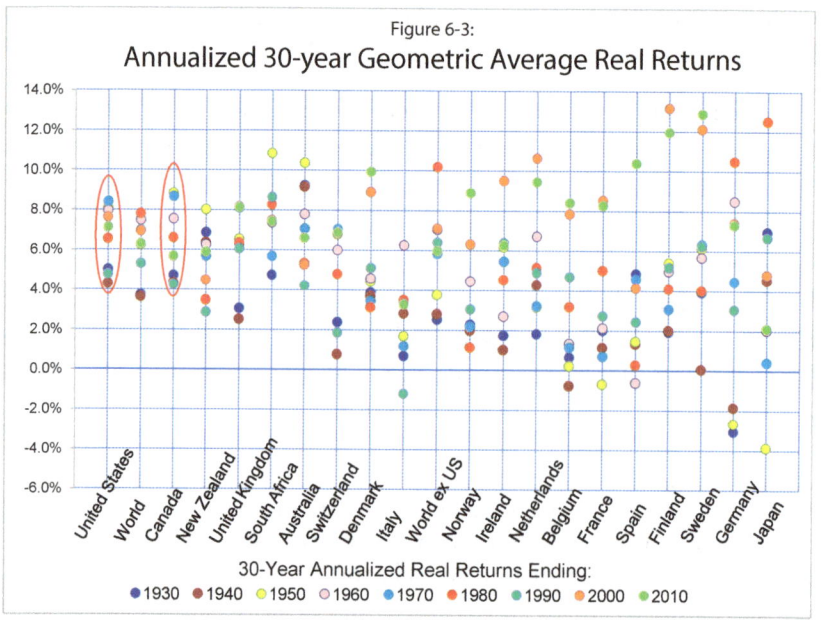

to that of the ten-year returns at 5.04%, but the standard deviation is much smaller at 3.21%.

When you examine Figure 6-3, please be aware that the scale is very different from that in Figure 6-2: the highest return is 13.18% for Finland (versus the maximum ten-year return of 37.68% for Germany in Figure 6-2), while the minimum return is -3.86% for Japan (versus the minimum ten-year return of -24.66% also for Japan in Figure 6-2). Once again I have highlighted the Canadian and US data, and over this longer time frame they have the smallest dispersions of return for individual country markets.

With a mean of 5.04% and a standard deviation of 3.21, the range of plus/minus one standard deviation around the mean is from 1.83% to 8.25%, and 118 of the 171 observations (69%) fall within that range; 26 (15.2%) are above and 27 (15.8%) are below.

You can also count that eight 30-year real returns were less than 0%. If ten-year spans trailing inflation are disruptive, then 30-year spans are disastrous. The only slightly reassuring thing is that six of the eight cases are directly related to the two world wars and hyperinflation in Germany, the 30-year spans ending 1930, 1940 and 1950, with three being attributed to Germany, and one each to Belgium, France and Japan.

By contrast, the 30-year span ending in 2010, with its final difficult decade, still showed robust returns over the full period, which you can verify by observing the bright green dots across the board. The lowest real total return over this period was 2.12% for Japan, and the average return of 7.74% was actually the highest average of the nine sample periods.

Chapter 7:

The Importance of Dividends Revisited

The importance of dividends as a major component of total return has already been noted several times. For example, the study of the US equity market in Chapter 1 reported that dividends contributed 4.57%, which is more than half (52%) of the 8.88% annualized total nominal return over 140 years. This is also 69% of the annualized total real return of 6.67% over the whole period.

In chapter 2, I discussed the impact of inflation and looked at equity performance over various sub-periods. I mentioned, but did not dwell on the fact that the contribution of dividends and their reinvestment was very stable and positive in all of the inflation regimes that were isolated, including the high inflation and outright deflation regimes (summarized in Tables 2-2 and 2-4). By contrast real price returns were much more varied, and were quite negative in high inflation regimes.

> **OVERVIEW**
>
> The importance of dividends as the main source of long-term real equity returns is highlighted and summarized.
>
> Key concepts:
>
> - total return can be defined in terms of three aspects of dividend yield:
>   - dividend yield itself;
>   - dividend growth;
>   - the return due to the change in dividend yield (a change in valuation).
> - this is a complete attribution of total local market return.

With the addition of standard deviation to our tool kit, I can make this point more directly. Chapter 4 examined the arithmetic averages and standard deviations of nominal and real total returns to

US equities over varying time spans. Now I will calculate the averages and standard deviations of the impact of dividends as well. Table 7-1 presents this material, based on the same samples used in Chapter 4.

Table 7-1:
Arithmetic Averages and Standard Deviations
of Returns for US Equities over Various Time Spans

Period	(1) Nominal Total Returns	(2) US CPI	(3) Real Total Returns	(4) Real Price Returns	(5) Real Impact of Dividends
Annual Returns					
Average	10.59%	2.24%	8.38%	3.67%	4.58%
Std.Dev.	18.91%	5.86%	18.70%	18.02%	1.68%
5-Year Returns					
Average	9.07%	2.14%	6.92%	2.25%	4.58%
Std.Dev.	6.65%	3.94%	7.49%	7.19%	1.49%
10-Year Returns					
Average	9.00%	2.12%	6.83%	2.17%	4.58%
Std.Dev.	5.36%	3.51%	6.12%	6.00%	1.39%
20-Year Returns					
Average	9.20%	2.28%	6.80%	2.11%	4.61%
Std.Dev.	3.26%	2.67%	3.17%	3.36%	1.17%
30-Year Returns					
Average	9.26%	2.44%	6.67%	1.91%	4.68%
Std.Dev.	2.40%	2.04%	1.78%	1.96%	0.97%

The relative stability of dividends is most obviously apparent with annual returns. While annual nominal total returns, annual real total returns and annual real price returns have a variability of more than 18%, the variability of the impact of annual dividends is just 1.68%. As the time span is extended, the standard deviation of annualized return compresses for all components of return, and with the 30-year sample the variability of the impact of dividends has fallen to just 0.97%, still much less than the variability of the other return series.

To summarize, here are three important points about dividends in the US equity market:

- historically, dividends have provided more than half (52%) of total nominal returns, and two-thirds (69%) of total real returns.
- dividends have provided a very stable element of return under all inflationary environments, ranging from deflation to the highest inflation regimes experienced during this time span.
- dividends have been the most stable component of return from the perspective of the direct measurement of volatility.

But I can add several additional points that will lead to a more comprehensive analysis. Figure 7-1 shows the dividend yield on a year-by-year basis across our history, and it is easy to see why in most periods the impact of dividends on return was in the 4% to 6% range, as shown in Table 2-2.

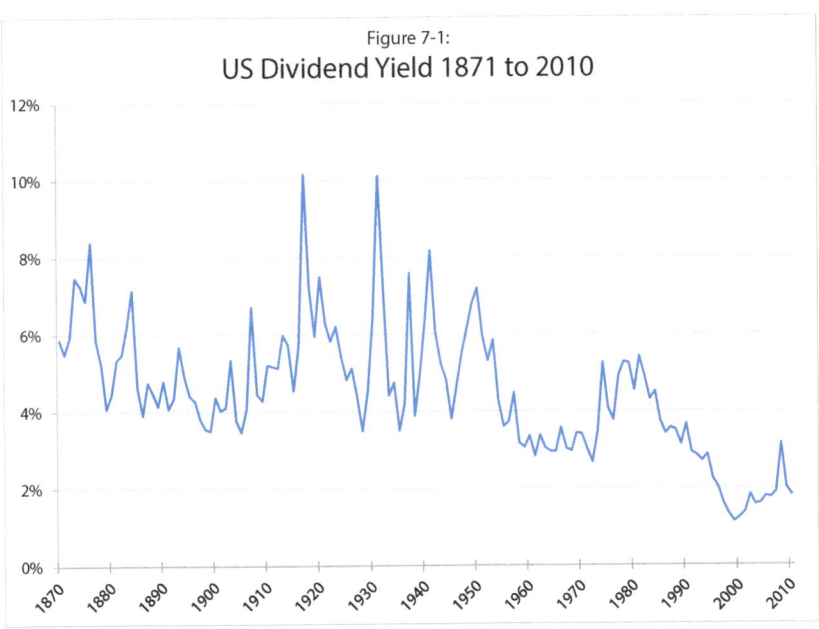

The arithmetic average dividend yield is 4.48%[1] over the whole 140-year sample. Notice that the yield stayed well above 4% during most of history prior to 1958, averaging 5.3%, but since then there has been a steady decline. Indeed from the beginning of 1997 the

---

1 The arithmetic average using annual data.

yield has stayed at or below 2%, apart from the spike upwards caused by the 2008-9 market decline.

The very low dividend yields over the last 20 years relate directly to the very low impact of dividends in the final low inflation regime distinguished in Table 2-2. During the twenty years from 1991/01 to 2010/12, the impact of dividends was only 2.05%, far lower than in any other time period, while the average dividend yield was 1.98%.

A second important fact about dividends is that while the yield averaged 4.48% over history, the dividends themselves grew significantly in both nominal and real terms. Figure 7-2 shows nominal dividend growth: starting at $100,[2] dividends grew to $8,742, for an annualized nominal return or growth rate of 3.25%.

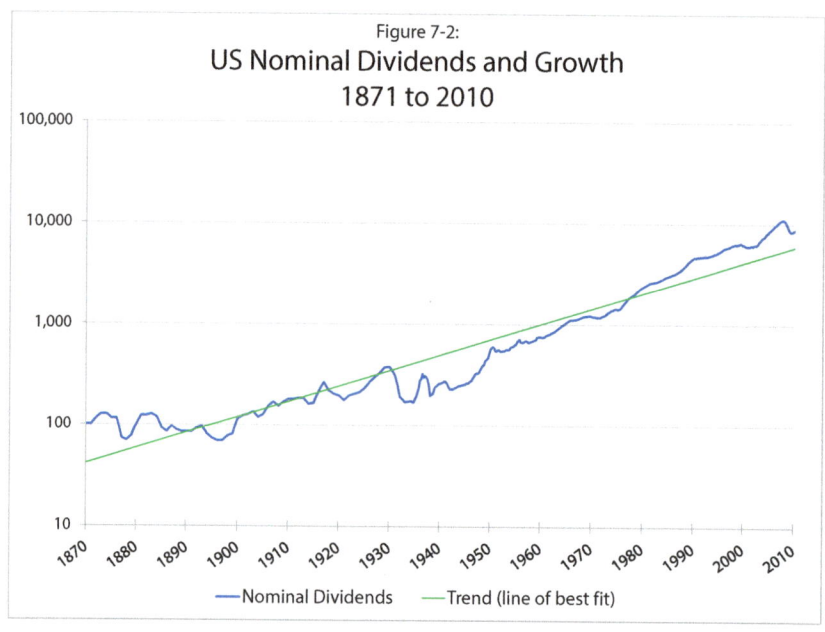

The green line on the graph is the trend line or line of best fit. It is interesting because comparing it to the dividends themselves makes it easier to see that the nominal growth of dividends has not

---

[2] As with Figure 1-1, the left hand scale is logarithmic: each horizontal line is 10 times larger than the one below it

been very constant over time. For example, over the 30 years prior to 1900 there was no net growth in nominal dividends, as they more or less moved sideways and fluctuated around the starting level of $100. Remember that during this time there was a serious deflation. From about 1900 dividends grew roughly along the trend line until 1930, followed by more sideways movement or decline during the Great Depression and until the end of World War II. From that point dividends grew at a higher rate than the trend line, corresponding to the era of higher inflation that has carried on through the second half of the twentieth century.

Figure 7-3 compares the growth of real dividends to that of nominal dividends, and shows the trend growth of real dividends as well. Real dividends grew by 1.15% annualized, and you can see that the trend growth line fits well. Despite volatility from the Great Depression to the end of World War II, the general upward trend continues. It is interesting that until 1917, real dividends actually outpaced nominal dividends, but since then nominal dividends have grown faster.

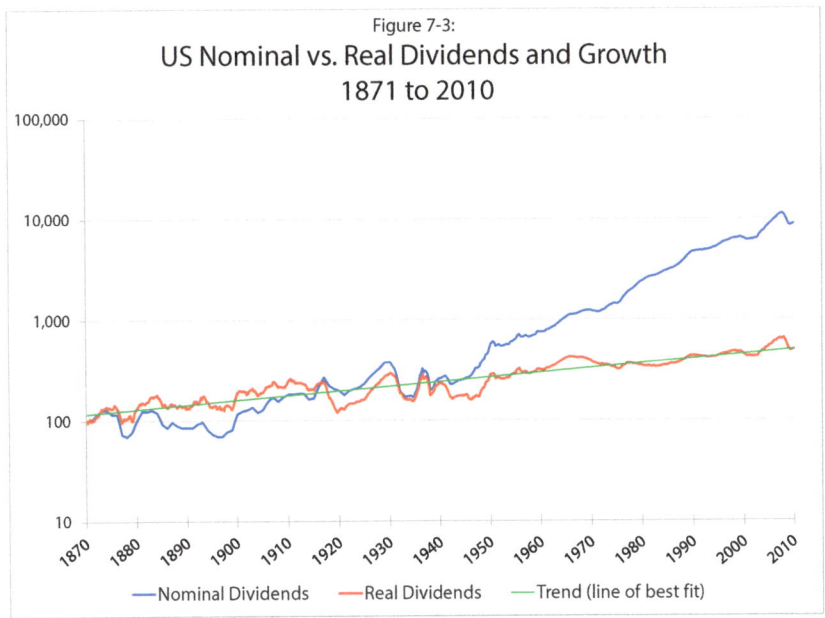

I want to introduce a final important concept relating to dividends. Returning to the history of dividend yield in Figure 7-1, I pointed out the overall decline in yield. The actual starting yield was 5.86% at the beginning of 1871 and the ending yield was 1.81% at the end of 2010, 140 years later. In 1871, the 5.86% yield meant that an investor was paying $17.08 for each dollar of dividends ($1.00/5.86%). By the end of 2010 an investor was paying $55.33 for each dollar of dividend ($1.00/1.81%).

So not only did dividends grow over the 140 years (nominal dividends by 3.25% and real dividends by 1.15%) but each dollar of dividend *was worth more, as valued by the market*. This as part of the return received by an investor who held equities over this period: the growth in the value of a dollar of dividends was 224% over 140 years or 0.84% annualized. I am going to call this concept *the percent return due to the change in dividend yield*.[3]

Here is something interesting. For the full US history, the arithmetic average dividend yield was 4.48%, the nominal dividend growth was 3.25%, and the return due to change in dividend yield was 0.84%. Adding these three numbers gives a total of 8.57%, pretty close to the total return of 8.88% given in Table 1-1. This can be written as the following approximation:

$$TR_g \approx DY_g + DG_g + r\Delta DY_g$$

where TR_g is the total geometric return over a period
DY_g is the geometric average dividend yield
DG_g is the geometric average dividend growth rate, and
$r\Delta DY_g$ is the geometric average return due to the change in dividend yield.

If I substitute the real dividend growth rate of 1.15% for the nominal growth rate, adding the numbers gives a total of 6.47%, again very close to the total real return of 6.67% stated in Table 1-1. This can be written as a second approximation:[4]

---

3 I believe that Keith Ambachtsheer used this or a similar concept in his 1990s newsletters (*The Ambachtsheer Letter*), and it is made explicit by Arnott and Bernstein (A&B 2002, p. 71).

4 A&B 2002 p. 71.

$$RTR_g \approx DY_g + RDG_g + r\Delta DY_g$$

where RTR_g is the total geometric real return over a period, and RDG_g is the geometric average real dividend growth rate

It is no coincidence that these approximations come very close to the actual return numbers. In fact if you ensure that you have the true geometric averages for each of the components, and compound (add geometrically) the three components of return, this is not a mere approximation but an exact calculation of total return.[5] Table 7-2 shows this exact identity, where I have substituted the geometric average dividend yield of 4.57% for the arithmetic average of 4.48%.[6]

Table 7-2:
Three Aspects of the Impact of Dividends
Monthly Data, 1871 to 2010

	Nominal Return	Real Return
Total Return (Chapter 1)	8.88%	6.67%
Compared with		
Geometric Average Dividend Yield DY_g	4.57%	4.57%
Geometric Average Dividend Growth DG_g	3.25%	1.15%
Return due to Change in Dividend Yield $r\Delta DY$	0.84%	0.84%
Total: $(1+DY_g) * (1+DG_g) * (1+r\Delta DY) - 1$	8.88%	6.67%

The exact equations are:

$$1+TR_g = (1+DY_g)*(1+DG_g)*(1+r\Delta DY_g)$$

and

$$1+RTR_g = (1+DY_g)*(1+RDG_g)*(1+r\Delta DY_g)$$

I will derive these true relationships in Appendix 2 to this chapter, and as I proceed I will use these results many times. But for now, I think it is worth noting that the third component, return due to change in dividend yield, $r\Delta DY$, was by far the smallest

---

[5] With the additional pedantic point that dividends have to be assumed to occur at the end of each period, and that the compounding has the same periodicity as the most basic unit of return.

[6] The geometric average is calculated from monthly data, to make it compatible with the US return data in Table 1-1.

component at 0.84%. This component, which should be understood as the change in the way investors value dividend flows, has only contributed about 9.7% of the total nominal return and 12.8% of the real return over the whole history. All the rest of the returns are a function of dividend yield and dividend growth.

Unfortunately, the global DMS database does not provide us with either dividends or price-only returns, but the authors have released summary information for geometric mean dividend yields, growth of real dividends and the return due to the change in dividend yields for the 19 countries over the total time span.[7] Using these three data items, along with the geometric mean inflation numbers compiled from the data, I derived Table 7-3, which shows the components for both total real and total nominal geometric returns, following the approach in Table 7-2. You can verify that the real and nominal return numbers match those of Table 5-1.[8]

As with Table 5-1, the individual country returns are local returns not subject to foreign exchange. Simple inspection suggests that dividend yield is by far the largest component of long-term real returns, and this is supported by the summary average row. The average dividend yield of 4.49% is 94.7% of the average local real return of 4.74%. Average real dividend growth was negative at -0.11%, meaning that dividends did not quite keep up with inflation, while the return due to the change in dividend yield averaged 0.35%. Note that for 7 of the 19 countries, average dividend yield is actually higher than total real return. This is because in those cases the combination of dividend growth and the return due to the change in dividend yield has been negative.

For total nominal returns, the average impact of inflation was 4.7%, much higher than its impact in North America, and this raises average nominal returns to 9.65%. So you can see that outside of North America, inflation tended to be a much larger component of nominal returns, slightly higher than dividend yield.

---

7 DMS 2011) page 31.

8 With a small rounding error to the second decimal place.

Table 7-3:
Dividend-Based Components of Total Return
DMS Data: 1900 to 2010

	Geom. Mean Dividend Yield	Growth of Real Divs.	Return due to Change in Div. Yield	Total Real Return	CPI Inflation	Total Nominal Return
Australia	5.76	1.10	0.48	7.44	3.86	11.58
Belgium	3.72	-1.48	0.36	2.55	5.33	8.02
Canada	4.39	0.84	0.56	5.86	3.05	9.08
Denmark	4.58	-1.13	1.64	5.09	3.89	9.18
Finland	4.76	0.49	0.09	5.37	7.32	13.08
France	3.81	-0.90	0.18	3.06	7.21	10.49
Germany	3.66	-1.16	0.58	3.05	4.97	8.17
Ireland	4.57	-0.94	0.16	3.75	4.26	8.17
Italy	4.06	-1.52	-0.47	2.00	8.45	10.62
Japan	5.22	-2.39	1.08	3.81	7.01	11.09
Netherlands	4.94	-0.51	0.55	4.98	2.92	8.04
New Zealand	5.38	1.26	-0.84	5.81	3.75	9.78
Norway	4.00	-0.13	0.33	4.21	3.74	8.10
South Africa	5.82	0.95	0.46	7.32	4.92	12.60
Spain	4.18	-0.60	0.01	3.57	5.83	9.60
Sweden	4.02	1.77	0.43	6.32	3.57	10.11
Switzerland	3.48	0.46	0.28	4.25	2.30	6.64
United Kingdom	4.63	0.46	0.20	5.32	3.95	9.48
United States	4.24	1.37	0.56	6.26	2.96	9.41
Average	4.49	-0.11	0.35	4.74	4.70	9.65
Std. Deviation	0.69	1.18	0.52	1.56	1.74	1.66

This idea of analyzing returns into components is often called an *attribution analysis*. It is important to understand exactly how this analysis works, and in Appendix 1 of this chapter I present a number of examples that spell out how returns can be calculated and attributed. Working through the examples will convince most people that the analysis really does work. I have also provided a semi-formal derivation of the analysis from first principles in Appendix 2, just by way of proof that this analysis really is complete: it fully explains total returns to equities.[9]

---

[9] Since individual stocks do not always pay dividends, the analysis is more appropriately applied to portfolios or broad indexes.

Since dividends are real and tangible cash flows that reach the hands of investors, and since growth in those dividends or cash flows is also real and measurable, these two components are important *sources of return* that can be isolated, and possibly forecast. The attribution analysis is retrospective, and might be said to give a partial answer to the question: *how did you get here?* In Part 2 I am going to suggest that a form of this analysis can be used to forecast future returns, which will help us start to answer the question: *how do you get there from here?*[10]

---

10 An interesting side-note for this attribution analysis is the question of how share buybacks are accommodated. Briefly, the issue is that companies sometimes use earnings to purchase and then retire a portion of existing shares, rather than distributing earnings to shareholders by paying dividends.

While this is an inconsequential issue for most markets, it is significant for the US market. For example, over the 27 years spanning 1985 to 2011, annual share repurchases averaged 1.61% of market capitalization in the US equity market. (See Mauboussin 2012, p 3 — 1.61% was calculated from the data presented there.) If you add this to S&P500 dividend yield of 2.32% over the same period, total corporate payouts rise to 3.9%, much closer to the higher historical levels of dividend yield in the US market, and closer to the levels of dividend yields in other major equity markets.

Some analysts call the sum of dividends and share buybacks the total yield, and seem to suggest that the total yield better represents shareholder benefits. But this way of looking at the impact of share buybacks can be a little misleading from a return attribution perspective. A closer analysis shows that share buybacks contribute to shareholder returns by generating higher earnings and dividend growth rates than would be achieved without the buybacks. In other words, share buybacks lower current dividends in exchange for higher future dividend growth, and you can show that under certain ideal conditions (but by no means all conditions), returns for buy-and-hold shareholders are roughly equivalent with or without buybacks.

The implication for our attribution analysis is that the historical impact of US share buybacks is already contained in the historical dividend growth data. That is, while running dividend yields would have been higher over the past 27 years without buybacks, dividend growth would have been commensurately lower. So share buybacks are fully accounted for in this analysis. Treating them as additive to dividend yield would "double count" their impact.

To see a more detailed treatment of this analysis, please refer to my article Share Repurchases and their Impact on Forecasting Returns, in the supplementary articles for this book at http://www.structuredcapital.com/.

Appendix 1: understanding the dividend-based model of returns

In this Appendix, I want to walk through some examples of how the dividend-based components of return interact. I do this because while most investors would say they understand the mathematics of these simple relationships, they don't fully appreciate the explanatory power of the model.

Assume that at the beginning of an investment period your portfolio is worth $100.00 and over the last period it received a dividend of $4.00. Thus at the beginning of the current investment period the dividend yield is 4% ($4/$100). In the simplest case, assume also that the dividend doesn't change or grow, and that the dividend yield at the end of the period remains at 4%.

What is your investment return? Since the dividend didn't grow or change, you received $4.00 in dividends over this period. Since the dividend yield remained at 4%, then the price must have remained at $100.00 (divide $4.00 dividend received by the 4% dividend yield). So the investment return is 4%: an ending price of $100.00 plus $4.00 in dividends from a starting price of $100.00. In this case all of the return is due to the dividend received.

Here's how I summarize Case 1:

<u>Case 1 parameters</u>
starting price:	$100.00
starting dividend:	$4.00
starting dividend yield:	4%
dividend growth:	0%
ending dividend yield:	4%

from these calculate
- ending dividend: $4.00
- ending price ($4/4% yield): $100.00
- ending price plus dividend: $104.00
- period return: 4%

In Case 2, I assume that dividends grow by 5%, but that the other assumptions are unchanged. Since the dividend started at $4.00 and it grows by 5% or $0.20, it becomes $4.20. And since the ending dividend yield remains unchanged at 4%, the ending price must have risen to $105.00 ($4.20/4%). Here is Case 2:

Case 2 parameters
- starting price: $100.00
- starting dividend: $4.00
- starting dividend yield: 4%
- dividend growth: 5%
- ending dividend yield: 4%

from these we can calculate
- ending dividend: $4.20
- ending price ($4.20/4% yield): $105.00
- ending price plus dividend: $109.20
- period return: 9.2%

As always, total return is a function of change in price plus dividends received, for a total of 9.2%. But you can *attribute* the change in price in Case 2 to the dividend growth of 5%, along with 4% dividend yield: $(1+0.04)*(1+0.05)-1 = 0.092$ or 9.2%.

Case 3 will go one step further, and allow for the dividend yield to change as well. Here I assume that it takes a significant fall from 4% to 3.5%. Here is what happens:

Case 3 parameters
- starting price: $100.00
- starting dividend: $4.00
- starting dividend yield: 4%
- dividend growth: 5%
- ending dividend yield: 3.5%

from these we can calculate
- ending dividend: $4.20
- ending price ($4.20/3.5% yield): $120.00
- ending price plus dividend: $124.20
- period return: 24.2%

Appendix 1: understanding the dividend-based model of returns

I can divide the $24.20 gain or 24.2% rate of return into three components. First, $4.20 or 3.5% (ending dividend yield) is due to the dividend received, second, 5% is due to dividend growth, and third, I can attribute 14.2857% of return due to the change in dividend yield. You can figure out this last number in two ways. On the one hand you can calculate 14.2857% directly as the growth of $1.00 of dividends, as I did in the text of the chapter, from the starting value of $1.00/4% = $25 to an ending value of $1.00/3.5% = $28.57, for a return of 14.2857%. On the other hand you can solve for x in:

(1+.035)*(1+.05)*(1+x)-1 = 0.242

Case 4 is similar to Case 3, but shows the impact of a rising dividend yield instead of a falling one: the ending dividend yield is assumed to rise to 4.5%.

Case 4 parameters
- starting price: $100.00
- starting dividend: $4.00
- starting dividend yield: 4%
- dividend growth: 5%
- ending dividend yield: 4.5%

from these we can calculate
- ending dividend: $4.20
- ending price ($4.20/4.5% yield): $93.33
- ending price plus dividend: $97.53
- period return: -2.467%

Now, I still received $4.20 in dividends, and so gained 4.5% (ending dividend yield) due to the dividend. Since the dividend grew by 5%, I also would have received 5% in price change had the dividend yield stayed the same. The loss due to the rise in dividend yield can be calculated directly as the change in the value of a dollar of dividends, which is from $1.00/4% = $25 to $1.00/4.5% = $22.22, for a return of -11.11%. Again you can verify this by solving for x, which will turn out to be -11.11%:

(1+.045)*(1+.05)*(1+x)-1 = -0.02467

What I am illustrating here is a model of *return attribution*. Instead of looking at total returns in each period as a combination of two things, dividends received and price change, I am dividing the price change or capital gains component into two further parts. The first is price change due to the growth of dividends (assuming that dividend yield is unchanged), and the second is price change due to the change in valuation or dividend yield. Since the price change due to growth in dividends is just the dividend growth rate for the period, I refer to it as dividend growth.

Appendix 2: the algebra of dividends and total return

I observed that total nominal return over an investment period is approximately the sum of average dividend yield, dividend growth, and the return due to the change in dividend yield. In order to approximate total real return you can substitute real for nominal dividend growth. In Tables 7-2 and 7-3 I showed what I said was the true relationship, which gives the exact result. Finally, I illustrated how this works by example in Appendix 1.

Here I want to prove the true relationship, and show why the approximations work. I don't think that most readers should worry about following this derivation. The only reason for presenting it here is to prove that this attribution is complete. I'm always amazed at how investors, particularly professionals, continually dismiss these simple ideas, as though they were irrelevant. While many pay lip service to the importance of dividends, few act on that reality. Some argue that dividends are somehow arbitrary because they can be manipulated by corporations, as though their reported earnings were not. But dividends are real cash flows received by investors, and equity returns are fully explained in terms of dividends, yields, dividend growth and changes in yields. The algebra is very straightforward, and proves that there is no gap in the analysis.

For a given period of time, perhaps one day, but for the data in this book either one month or one year, I can calculate the total rate of return for an individual stock or an equity market index as:

the change in price plus any dividends received, all divided by the beginning price.[1] That is,

$$TR_t = (P_t - P_{t-1} + D_t)/P_{t-1}$$

where TR_t = total return (the impact of prices plus dividends)
P_t = price at the end of the period
P_{t-1} = price at the beginning of the period (that is, the end of the previous period)
D_t = the dividend received during period t

The equation can be rewritten as:

$$TR_t = (P_t + D_t)/P_{t-1} - P_{t-1}/P_{t-1}$$

or

$$TR_t = (P_t + D_t)/P_{t-1} - 1$$

which means that

$$1 + TR_t = (P_t + D_t)/P_{t-1}$$

or in English, that the sum of ending price plus dividends received over a period, all divided by the beginning price, equals one plus the total return for the period.

Similarly define

D_{t-1} = the dividend at the beginning of the period (that is, the dividend from the previous period).

Now let's explicitly define dividend yield or DY:

$$DY_t = D_t/P_t = \text{end of period dividend yield,}$$

and

$$DY_{t-1} = D_{t-1}/P_{t-1} = \text{end of previous period dividend yield.}$$

Another way to define the price at a point in time is to divide the current dividend by the current dividend yield. That is, if the dividend is $4 and the dividend yield is 5%, then the price must be $80. So:

---

[1] This formulation makes the assumption that the dividends are accounted for at the end of the period, whether one day, one month, or longer. For periods of longer than one day this can distort returns, but for our purposes this issue will be ignored.

Appendix 2: the algebra of dividends and total return

$$P_t = D_t/DY_t$$

and of course

$$P_{t-1} = D_{t-1}/DY_{t-1}$$

Now I define the last two concepts used in the body of the chapter, dividend growth and the return due to the change in dividend yield. The dividend growth rate, DG, for a period is just a percentage return or change of the dividend:

$$DG_t = (D_t/D_{t-1}) - 1$$

so that

$$1 + DG_t = (D_t/D_{t-1}).$$

The return due to a change in dividend yield is a little trickier, but think of it this way: if the dividend is the same at the beginning and end of the period, say $1.00,[2] by the definition given above the price at the beginning would be $1/DY_{t-1}$, while the price at the end of the period would be $1/DY_t$. So the return due to the change in dividend yield, which I will symbolize as $r\Delta DY$, is just the percentage return from those two prices:

$$r\Delta DY_t = (1/DY_t)/(1/DY_{t-1}) - 1$$

so that

$$1 + r\Delta DY_t = (1/DY_t)/(1/DY_{t-1})$$

or more simply

$$1 + r\Delta DY_t = (DY_{t-1}/DY_t)$$

With these definitions I need to do a little bit of simple reordering and substitution. Let's begin with the initial definition of total return:

$$1 + TR_t = (P_t + D_t)/P_{t-1}$$

which means that

$$1 + TR_t = (P_t/P_{t-1}) + (D_t/P_{t-1})$$

---

[2] Any change in the dividend amount is accounted for in the dividend growth calculation.

That is, $1+TR_t$ is the price change or capital gain (P_t/P_{t-1}) for the period plus the dividend for the period divided by the beginning price.

It is less confusing to treat the two components separately for now. First look at the capital gain or price change, and substitute for P.

$$P_t/P_{t-1} = (D_t/DY_t) / (D_{t-1}/DY_{t-1}) \text{ [definition of } P_t \text{ and } P_{t-1}]$$
$$= (D_t/DY_t) * (DY_{t-1}/D_{t-1}) \text{ [rewriting]}$$
$$= (D_t/D_{t-1}) * (DY_{t-1}/DY_t) \text{ [regrouping]}$$
$$= (1+DG_t) * (1+r\Delta DY_t) \text{ [definition of terms]}$$

Second let's deal with the dividend/price component.

$$D_t/P_{t-1} = (D_t/P_{t-1}) * (P_t/P_t) \text{ [1=x/x, for any x]}$$
$$= (D_t/P_t) * (P_t/P_{t-1}) \text{ [reordering]}$$
$$= DY_t * (1+DG_t) * (1+r\Delta DY_t) \text{ [definition of terms]}$$

Now, returning to the starting point $1+TR_t = (P_t/P_B) + (D_t/P_B)$ and substituting in for each part

$$1+TR_t = [(1+DG_t) * (1+r\Delta DY_t)] + [DY_t * (1+DG_t) * (1+r\Delta DY_t)]$$
$$= (1+DY_t) * (1+DG_t) * (1+r\Delta DY_t) \text{ [regrouping]}$$

I will call this equation (7.1):

(7.1) $1+TR_t = (1+DY_t) * (1+DG_t) * (1+r\Delta DY_t)$

In order to move from the world of nominal returns to real returns, I remind you that nominal dividend growth is a function of real dividend growth and inflation:

$$1+DG_t = (1+RDG_t) * (1+I_t)$$

or,

$$(1+RDG_t) = (1+DG_t)/(1+I_t)$$

where I_t is the percent inflation for the period

and so

(7.2) $1+TR_t = (1+DY_t) * (1+RDG_t) * (1+I_t) * (1+r\Delta DY_t)$

But remember that real total return is a function of total return and inflation, specifically:

Appendix 2: the algebra of dividends and total return

$$1+RTR_t = (1+TR_t) / (1+I_t)$$

So dividing both sides of equation (7.2) by $(1+I_t)$, you derive the equation for real return:

(7.3) $1+RTR_t = (1+DY_t) * (1+RDG_t) * (1+r\Delta DY_t)$

In using the definitions of real return and real dividend growth to generate equations (7.2) and (7.3) I took a bit of a shortcut. While I have implicitly appealed to these definitions at various points in the text, I haven't properly defined what "real" means.[3] Suffice it to say for now that dividend yield must be the same whether you use real prices and yields or nominal prices and yields, and since nominal and real dividend yields are the same, so are real and nominal $r\Delta DY$.

Moreover, while I have simplified things and shown the equations for a single period, you can see how equations (7.1), (7.2) and (7.3) can be extended over multiple periods, since all the terms are multiplicative. Here's how it works. In the Appendix to Chapter 3, I reviewed the concept of a geometric mean. For example, the geometric mean of nominal total return over periods 1 to t, in symbols TR_g, would be derived from the equation

$$(1+TR_g)^t = (1+TR_1)*(1+TR_2)* ...* (1+TR_t)$$

so

$$1+TR_g = ((1+TR_1)*(1+TR_2)* ...* (1+TR_t))^{(1/t)}$$

I can use equation (7.1) to substitute in for each of the terms $(1+TR_1)$ in the right-hand side of the previous equation. Moreover since all of the terms in (7.1) are multiplicative, they can be regrouped

---

3 This all comes together when you realize how "real" prices and dividends are defined. For example, for your first price data point, call it P0, the real price RP0 equals the nominal price P0. For period 1, the real price RP1 equals the nominal price divided by 1+the percent inflation for the period: P1/(1+I1). For period 2 the real price RP2 equals the nominal price P2 divided by the cumulative inflation since the beginning of the series, that is P2/((1+ I1)*(1+ I2)), and so on.

Working with this concept of cumulative inflation, you can easily extend the definition of real prices, real dividends, real returns and real dividend growth as needed.

so as to create the following equation, where each of the terms is a geometric mean over the time frame from t=1 to t:

(7.4) $1+TR_g = (1+DY_g)*(1+DG_g)*(1+r\Delta DY_g)$

where TR_g is the geometric mean total return
DY_g is the geometric mean dividend yield
DG_g is the geometric mean dividend growth
and $r\Delta DY_g$ is the geometric mean return due to the change in dividend yield

In a similar fashion multi-period versions of (7.2) and (7.3) can be defined:

(7.5) $1+TR_g = (1+DY_g)*(1+RDG_g)*(1+I_g)*(1+r\Delta DY_g)$

(7.6) $1+RTR_g = (1+DY_g)*(1+RDG_g)*(1+r\Delta DY_g)$

I used equations (7.4) and (7.6) to generate nominal and real returns in Table 7-2, while (7.5) and (7.6) were used in Table 7-3.

You can think of equations (7.4), (7.5) and (7.6) as an attribution model of return for explaining history in a useful and informative way. But as we move forward, these equations, or approximations of them, can be used to conduct research, and potentially to make forecasts of future returns. I will leave the issue of forecasting for now, but here I will present some approximations of the equations that we can use as we do research in the following chapters.

For example, analogous to equation (7.4) is the approximation (7.7) for nominal total returns, and analogous to equation (7.6) is approximation (7.8) for real total returns:

(7.7) $TR_g \approx DY_g + DG_g + r\Delta DY_g$

and

(7.8) $RTR_g \approx DY_g + RDG_g + r\Delta DY_g$

The difference between the approximations and the correct equations is the lack of compounding. In some circumstances compounding can make a lot of difference, but the amount is often rather small when we are looking at long-term market returns. Taking the data from Table 7-2, the total nominal return of 8.88% is achieved by compounding the three components of return 4.57%,

Appendix 2: the algebra of dividends and total return

3.25% and 0.84%, while adding them up as in (7.7) yields 8.66%, a reasonable approximation. Substituting the real dividend growth of 1.15% gives a total real return of 6.67%, while adding them as in (7.8) gives an approximation of 6.57%, again quite close.

Whenever possible I will use the geometric versions, but it is often convenient to use the approximations and I will use them when appropriate. For example, when I use statistics to look at the impact of these three components of return over time, I am using approximations (7.7) and (7.8) rather than the exact geometric relations (7.4) and (7.6).

Chapter 8:

The Impact of Currencies on Foreign Investment Holdings

Since investment opportunities are global, you have to be prepared to deal with the impact of foreign currencies on your investments. When I presented the overview of global equity returns in Chapter 5, and the variability of those returns in Chapter 6, I glossed over the issue of currencies by examining and comparing all foreign returns in *local* terms: US dollar-based equities in US dollar terms, Canadian dollar-based investments in Canadian dollars, Euro-based investments in Euros, and so on. While this gives a picture of return and volatility across markets, it can be misleading because as presented there, the opportunities are not "investable".

> **OVERVIEW**
>
> Currencies can have a dramatic impact on investment returns.
>
> Key findings:
>
> Relative to returns received by foreign investors in their own markets, your currency exposures can
>
> - significantly add to or subtract from your total return;
> - significantly add to or subtract from the variability of your returns.

That is, no investor can measure the returns to a multi-currency portfolio without translating the returns from each currency into some common *base* or *home* currency.[1] For example, I noted but

---

1 So by way of summary, when I talk of foreign markets this normally implies a perspective from my home market and home currency. In that case it is clear that foreign market returns should be viewed as being subject to foreign currency exposures. But at the same time, I can talk about the local market returns of each of those foreign markets, as I do in Chapter 5. Both the context of discussion and this terminology should make this clear.

did not elaborate on the fact that the World Index calculations in Table 5-1 were made in the common currency of US dollars, so the index reflects the returns that a US dollar-based investor would have received.

Non-US-based investors have to be particularly careful about this, because the world's most-followed equity indexes, the S&P 500 and (sadly) the Dow Jones Industrial Average,[2] along with most commodities including oil products and gold, are denominated in US dollars and are usually reported in US dollar terms. This leads to what I call *currency illusion*, to which Canadian investors are particularly susceptible, since so much of our financial news is from or oriented to the United States. There are countless examples, but here is just one.

Using month-end levels, from its low of September 2002 to its peak in October 2007, the S&P500 total return was 108.39% or 15.54% annualized over 61 months. Canadian investors saw these numbers day after day, year after year, reported by television, radio and newspapers, with scant notice being taken that these were the returns received by local US investors. A Canadian who held and reinvested dividends from an S&P500 fund would have been gravely disappointed, receiving a gross return of just 23.86%, or 4.30% annualized. How could he end up with a shortfall of 68.25%, or 10.78% annualized? Well, the US dollar depreciated from 1.5868 CAD/USD (Canadian dollars per US dollar) to 0.9431 CAD/USD, a fall of 40.57% or 9.73% annualized. Conversely, the Canadian dollar rose by — you guessed it — a gross return of 68.25% or 10.78% annualized.

As a Canadian investor, the depreciation of the US dollar relative to the Canadian dollar significantly lowered the value of your US assets, yet I wonder how many investors really understood what was going on here. Figure 8-1 shows this graphically. In the bottom section of the chart (left-hand scale) the blue line is the S&P500 in US dollars, as the local US investor saw it, while the red line is the

---

2 Sadly for "The Dow" because it is a poor representative of the US equity market: it is narrow in coverage and is calculated in an unusual manner.

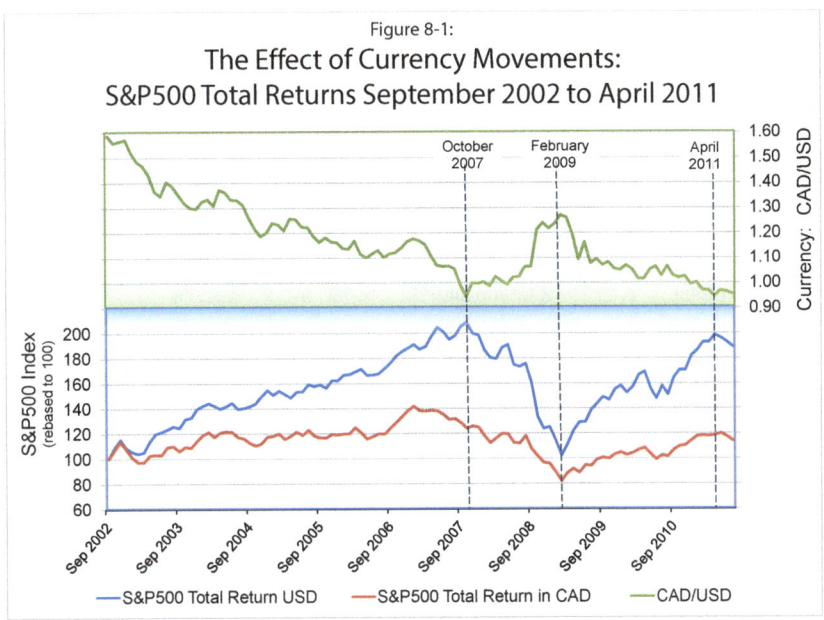

Figure 8-1:
The Effect of Currency Movements:
S&P500 Total Returns September 2002 to April 2011

S&P500 translated into Canadian dollars, as the Canadian investor would have experienced it. The dramatic rise ending in October 2007 is shown as the blue line moves from 100 to 208.39 (the unannualized gain of 108.39%), while the red line moves from 100 to just 123.85 (the unannualized gain of just 23.85%). The green line in the top section shows the US dollar (as CAD/USD) falling from 1.5868 to 0.9431 CAD/USD (right-hand scale).

The chart highlights two other periods that are also summarized in Table 8-1 below. From its high in October 2007 the S&P500 fell by 50.95% (-41.39% annualized) to its month-end low at February 2009. It subsequently rose by 93.95% to the end of April 2011, or 35.76% annualized. Combining the results from all three periods, from the September 2002 low a US investor received 98.25% or 8.30% annualized, which is a very respectable long-term return.[3]

But from a Canadian dollar perspective the "currency illusion" continued, for while the S&P500 fell less in Canadian dollars from

---

[3] Remember that if you go back a few more years to the end of 1999, an S&P500 investment would be up by just over 1% annualized to the current peak in April 2011. We always need perspective when we measure historical returns.

Table 8-1:
S&P500 Returns for Various Periods in USD and CAD

Total Return	Number of Months		S&P500 Total Return in USD	S&P500 Total Return in CAD	Gain/Loss of USD (vs. CAD)
From Sept 2002 to Oct 2007	61	Annualized	15.54%	4.30%	-9.73%
		Unannualized	108.39%	23.86%	-40.57%
From Oct 2007 to Feb 2009	16	Annualized	-41.39%	-26.70%	25.06%
		Unannualized	-50.95%	-33.91%	34.74%
From Feb 2009 to Apr 2011	26	Annualized	35.76%	18.50%	-12.72%
		Unannualized	93.95%	44.45%	-25.52%
From Sept 2002 to April 2011	103	Annualized	8.30%	1.97%	-5.84%
		Unannualized	98.25%	18.24%	-40.36%

October 2007 to February 2009, it also gained less from February 2009 to April 2011. The total S&P500 return in Canadian dollars over the whole 103-month period was just 1.97% annualized, the return being dampened by the -5.84% annualized decline in the US dollar.

Of course this phenomenon applies to any US dollar denominated asset over these periods, such as commodities in general, or gold and oil in particular. For example, the Goldman Sachs Commodity Index, which covers 24 commodities but is heavily weighted to oil and gas,[4] rose by 183.17% (20.83% annualized) over the five and one-half years from December 2002 to June 2008, while the Canadian dollar-based investor in this index gained just 84.03% (11.73% annualized). While the Canadian investor received a fine return, it was far less than the glorious returns he was reading about in the paper.

The reverse has happened as well: from trading at about par with the US dollar at the end of 1973, the Canadian dollar began a long period of decline, ending at 1.5963 CAD/USD at the end of 2001. This means that the US dollar gained approximately 60% versus CAD, or an annualized amount of 1.7%. Thus Canadian investors in US dollar-based assets benefited from this 1.7% average annual

---

4 The commodities are weighted relative to their economic value, which puts oil, gas and derivative products at roughly 70% of the index.

windfall over the 28-year period, a welcome reward to pension funds and other long-term investors who were building foreign exposures during this time.

While currencies can have either a positive or negative impact on the cumulative returns to our foreign investments, they also impact the volatility of those investments. You can guess that this must be the case when you observe that the green line in the top half of Figure 8-1, depicting the level of CAD/USD, itself has intrinsic volatility. In the bottom half of Figure 8-1 you can observe the impact of the currency movement on the S&P500 investment, which in this case appears to dampen the volatility of the foreign investment. Just compare the S&P500 in US dollars with the S&P500 translated into Canadian dollars. There the red line expressing the Canadian dollar return is clearly less volatile than the blue line. To give a numerical value, over this whole period the returns implied by the blue line have an annualized standard deviation of 15.09%, while the returns implied by the red line have a standard deviation of 12.13% annualized.

But currencies do not always interact with the underlying foreign asset to dampen volatility. Since the Canadian equity market performed similarly to the US market over this period in local terms, you might guess that the performance of the USD/CAD would have to add to the volatility of the Canadian market from a US investor's point of view.[5] Indeed that is the case: the annualized standard deviation of the Canadian market was 14.66% over this period in Canadian dollars, but jumps to 22.3% annualized when translated into US dollars. You can see why even seasoned investment professionals can be perplexed and mystified by currencies.

In sum, currencies add a layer of complexity to foreign investment returns. First, compared to the foreign or "local" returns of a market in its own currency, the currency translation into your home currency has the potential to add or subtract significantly from

---

5 With our S&P500 example, CAD rose as the S&P rose in the first period, fell as the S&P fell in the second period, and rose again as the S&P rose in the third period. Assuming that the TSX rose and fell roughly in step with the S&P500, then the converse would be happening to USD: it would be falling when the TSX rose, and rising when the TSX fell, magnifying returns and volatility.

those cumulative local returns. Second, the currency translation can either reduce or increase the volatility of the foreign investment relative to its volatility in local terms. You can think of this as leading to four cases. An investor clearly benefits from currency exposures if, over an investment period, the foreign currency translation both enhances cumulative return and reduces volatility. An investor clearly loses from currency exposures if the currency translation both reduces cumulative return and increases volatility. The other two cases, increases to both return and volatility, and decreases to both return and volatility, probably depend on your perceptions combined with the facts of the case.

To see what I mean by this, look at the last section in Table 8-1. Over the period from September 2002 to April 2011, the cumulative annualized return in USD was 8.30%, while translated into CAD this fell to 1.97%. In the text I mentioned that the volatility in USD for this whole period was 15.09%, while the volatility of the CAD return was 12.13%. I suspect that for most investors, the reduction in volatility from 15.09% to 12.13% would not have compensated for the drastic reduction in return, and they would have been disappointed with the result. But if returns had been reduced by (say) just 0.50% with the same volatility reduction, I believe that almost all investors would have been quite satisfied with the result.

There is actually a way to dramatically reduce the effects of currency exposure by *hedging* the currency exposure associated with a foreign investment. However, unless you invest in a managed investment vehicle such as an ETF that provides currency hedging for you, direct currency hedging is out of the reach of any but very large investors. But when foreign investments are made on an institutional scale, investors can arrange to sell their currency exposures forward, locking in specific future exchange rates.[6] It has sometimes been argued that this process always reduces volatility, at just the cost of

---

[6] Of course even this is only partially true: normally one sells currencies forward (i.e. sets a price and commits to buy back their local currency at some specified date in the future) over short periods such as one to four months, and then "rolls" the hedge over the next period, adjusting amounts as necessary. This means that gains or losses from the hedge are realized along the way.

the currency hedge, which gives investors a "free lunch" that should be exploited by investors as their default starting point.[7] But once you understand the mechanisms of currency hedging, you will find that this idea is simply not true.

When a well-constructed currency hedging strategy is applied to a foreign investment, the total package of foreign asset, intrinsic currency exposure, plus the currency hedge will deliver returns and volatility that more or less mirror the return and volatility of the foreign asset in its local currency, allowing for the cost of the hedge and the fact that no hedge is perfect.[8] You can think of the currency hedge as largely undoing the effects of the currency translation between the foreign currency and the home or base currency. However, since we have already seen that unhedged currency exposures on foreign assets can provide both higher or lower cumulative returns and higher or lower volatility, then reducing the currency effect through hedging will obviously have the opposite effect in each case. That is, *relative to the correct comparison base which is unhedged currency exposures*, currency hedging can either add or subtract to cumulative returns and either dampen or enhance volatility.

A recent carefully-researched study published by MSCI[9] shows this empirically, by examining the effects of hedging 40 different currencies with respect to five base currencies. The article shows that the "free lunch" from currency hedging, which would be 0% or higher excess return combined with equal or lower risk, is not a frequent occurrence. Generally lower risk is accompanied by lower returns, and higher risk is accompanied by higher returns, which should be the expected outcome. So the idea that currency-hedged

---

7 In "The Free Lunch in Currency Hedging", (P&S 1988) Perold and Schulman look at just the US side of the equation, over a very limited span of data.

8 The basic problem is that you hedge an amount at the beginning of a period, but as the asset you are hedging moves differently than the currency, your hedge may be too small or too large at any point. A perfect currency hedge requires ongoing adjustments, but it may be too costly to do this. Sometimes hedging mismatches can lead to significant unexpected gains or losses relative to the ideal hedge.

9 Chang, 2009

foreign exposures should be taken as the default, low-risk starting point, neither makes sense theoretically nor holds up empirically when tested with a comprehensive dataset and careful scrutiny.

In Part 2, Chapter 17, when I discuss forecasting returns to foreign exchange or FX, and in Part 4 as we build actual portfolios to meet our investment needs, I will briefly return to the concept of currency hedging. Depending on your investment horizon, your home market and the investment vehicles available to you, I will outline a possible role or strategy for using currency-hedged products in your portfolio.

Chapter 9:

Nominal and Real Currency Returns and Purchasing Power Parity

As presented in Chapter 7, the model of return did not include a reference to currencies. In order to complete the model and include currencies, I need to examine more closely how currencies interact with underlying assets. In particular, I need to show how returns to currencies can be broken down into real and nominal returns. Real equity returns are nominal equity returns net of inflation, and the definition for currency returns proceeds along similar lines.

In the process of defining real and nominal currency returns, I will illustrate a theory that helps explain currency movements, at least over the longer term. Let's start with the reasonable economic view that very similar items should have very similar prices. You may be familiar with the *Big Mac Index*, which has been published by The Economist Magazine for many years. In its simplest form, the index compares the local market cost of the same hamburger across the many countries and currencies in which it is sold. This is an interesting comparison because it is essentially the same product made to company specifications, but

> **OVERVIEW**
>
> The theory of Relative Purchasing Power Parity is introduced as a way to explain long-term currency movements.
>
> Key concepts:
>
> - absolute and relative purchasing power parity are introduced;
> - returns to real and nominal exchange rates are defined;
> - real and nominal exchange rates are integrated into the attribution of total return; and
> - these concepts are applied to historical data for major market indexes

is produced locally from largely local ingredients. So if a hamburger is sold for 2 Euros (EUR) in Paris, and 3 US dollars (USD) in New York, the exchange rate that would make them the same price in both currencies is 2 EUR to 3 USD: 0.6667 EUR/USD or 1.5 USD/EUR.

But suppose the actual exchange rate is 1.4 USD/EUR. In USD terms the current price of a hamburger in Paris is 2.80 USD (2 Euros times the exchange rate of 1.40 USD/EUR). This implies that the Euro is undervalued relative to the USD (at least in terms of hamburgers), since in Paris an American pays $2.80 for a $3.00 value at home. Of course from the point of view of the Parisian, dining on hamburgers in New York would be expensive, since its 3 USD cost would be 2.14 Euros at that exchange rate. This comparison can be made across any of the markets which have the same hamburger, and gives us a basis for saying which currencies are undervalued and which may be overvalued relative to your base currency.

The hamburger index provides a specific illustration of the Purchasing Power Parity (PPP) theory, which is meant to apply across goods and commodities generally. On the assumption that prices should be equivalent across markets and currencies, the theory suggests that in a world of freely traded goods and widely dispersed information, exchange rates should gravitate towards a state that would make prices equivalent.

There are many reasons why an absolute "one price" world can never be reached, including the high cost of arbitraging physical goods, lack of information about pricing, and price discrepancies purposefully generated by both governments and companies. And while the theory of absolute Purchasing Power Parity is interesting, a more useful and more general variant is called *Relative* Purchasing Power Parity (RPPP). The relative theory focuses on how changes in inflation (the general level of price changes) within each currency block affect exchange rates.

Here's an easy way to see how RPPP works. Pretend for a moment that absolute PPP holds, and that in my hamburger example the exchange rate is indeed 1.5 USD/EUR, with the burger costing 2 EUR in Paris and 3 USD in New York. To take an extreme case in which the numbers are easy to work out, suppose that the price in New York rises to 4 USD, while the price in Paris stays at 2 EUR. Absolute PPP says that the exchange rate should move to 2 USD/EUR, which equates the prices of 4 USD and 2 EUR for the hamburger.

But I can also analyze this exchange rate move by looking at inflation: how the *prices have changed*. The starting exchange rate is 1.5 USD/EUR, and American inflation has risen by 33.33%, as the 3 USD cost of the hamburger has become 4 USD (4/3-1=33.33%). In the Eurozone inflation is 0%, since the price has not changed. So the *relative* inflation rate, the difference between US inflation and Eurozone inflation, is 33.33%. This is the same as the percentage change in USD/EUR, which rises from 1.5 to 2 or 33.33%: the USD has fallen (the EUR has risen) exactly in step with the change in relative inflation.

The actual formula I used was that the percentage change in the foreign exchange rate,[1]

$$(FX_{USD/EUR(2)} / FX_{USD/EUR(1)}) - 1$$

changes in proportion to the percentage change in *relative inflation rates*, which are defined as:

$$(1+\text{Inflation}_{USD}) / (1+\text{inflation}_{EUR}) - 1$$

where $FX_{USD/EUR(1)}$ is the exchange rate at time 1
$FX_{USD/EUR(2)}$ is the exchange rate at time 2, and
Inflation in either currency is the percentage change in prices from time 1 to time 2

---

[1] Currencies are confusing for many reasons, starting with the fact that you can look at the ratio from either "direction" and that the percent changes differ depending on which way you orient the ratio. For the sake of consistency, and also for the sake of correctly orienting our return model later in the chapter, I will try to always quote currencies as Home/Foreign. This means that a percentage gain in the ratio is a gain in the foreign currency, and a percentage loss is a loss in the foreign currency.

So if you wanted to estimate the exchange rate at the end of the period, $FX_{USD/EUR(2)}$, and knew the inflation rates in each country, you would calculate:

$$(FX_{USD/EUR(2)}) = (FX_{USD/EUR(1)} * (1+\text{Inflation}_{USD}) / (1+\text{inflation}_{EUR})$$
$$= 1.5 * (1+33.33\%) / (1+0\%)$$
$$= 2$$

The relative PPP hypothesis is actually more general than this simple illustration implies. Unlike the hamburger example, it does not assume that the starting exchange rate is in PPP equilibrium, so absolute PPP is just a special case in which the starting exchange rate is in fact in equilibrium.

Relative PPP is more in tune with our concerns as investors. We don't have to know whether currencies are at, or close to, absolute purchasing power parity equilibrium, but we are concerned about how currencies will move while we hold foreign assets in the foreign currency. Relative PPP gives us a potential answer, and the hypothesis that Relative PPP holds can be tested historically, since we have histories of exchange rates and inflation rates.

There is a great deal of support for this hypothesis when we look at inflation and currency returns over yearly and longer periods. Using the 19 countries in the DMS dataset, there are 18 currency pairs relative to the USD and 18 relative inflation rates, spanning 111 annual periods from 1900 to 2010. To test this possible relationship, I pooled the data across countries and time, and examined whether the percentage change in exchange rates is a function of relative change in inflation. The time spans are non-overlapping one-, five- and ten-year periods, and in all cases the relationship is highly significant with the predicted sign. Table 9-1 summarizes the results.

The top section of Table 9-1 looks at non-overlapping one-year spans. The coefficient of 0.8256 means that for every 1.0% change in relative inflation as defined above, there is a 0.8256% change in the exchange rate as defined.[2] The coefficient is highly significant, which

---

[2] In the test I wrote that the currencies and relative inflation are defined as being relative to the US. This means that the FX ratio is Foreign/USD, and so if the

Table 9-1:
Annualized Percent Change of FX Rates
as a Function of the Percent Change in Relative Inflation
(Pooled DMS Data for 18 Countries versus the US, 1901 to 2010)

		Value	T-stat	Probability of being 0	Adjusted R-squared
One-year spans	Intercept	0.0182	2.380	1.740%	10.39%
	Coefficient	0.8256	15.093	0.000%	
Non-overlapping five-year spans	Intercept	0.0032	0.868	38.580%	37.38%
	Coefficient	0.8199	15.290	0.000%	
Non-overlapping ten-year spans	Intercept	-0.0017	-0.616	53.860%	69.45%
	Coefficient	1.0362	21.025	0.000%	

means that it is almost certain that this relationship holds and is positive.[3] Moreover the adjusted r-squared of 10.39% means that 10.39% of the variability of the annual percentage change in FX rates is explained by annual changes in relative inflation.

The middle and bottom sections of the table show even stronger results. Over five-year spans the coefficient and its significance are similar to those of the one-year case, but the adjusted r-squared is much higher: 37.38% of the variability of the percentage change in the FX rate is explained by five-year changes in relative inflation. Over ten-year periods, percentage changes in relative inflation explain 69.45% of the movement of country FX rates relative to the USD, and the coefficient is just over 1.0 at 1.03%.

These are very strong results indeed. Over one-year (and shorter) periods, factors other than relative inflation drive changes in exchange rates, but as the period lengthens relative inflation becomes the dominant factor. If RPPP held exactly, the regression coefficient would be 1.0, and in the ten-year case it is very close to that number.

---

percentage change is positive, the USD rises relative to that "foreign" currency, and conversely. Similarly relative inflation is

(1+Inflation Foreign)/(1+inflationUSD) -1.

3 I ignore the intercept term, since in this case it is small although significant, and in the other two cases it is insignificant.

Figure 9-1 graphs the ten-year data along with the regression line of best fit. The clustering of the dots along the line is the visual portrayal of the high adjusted r-squared of 69.45%.

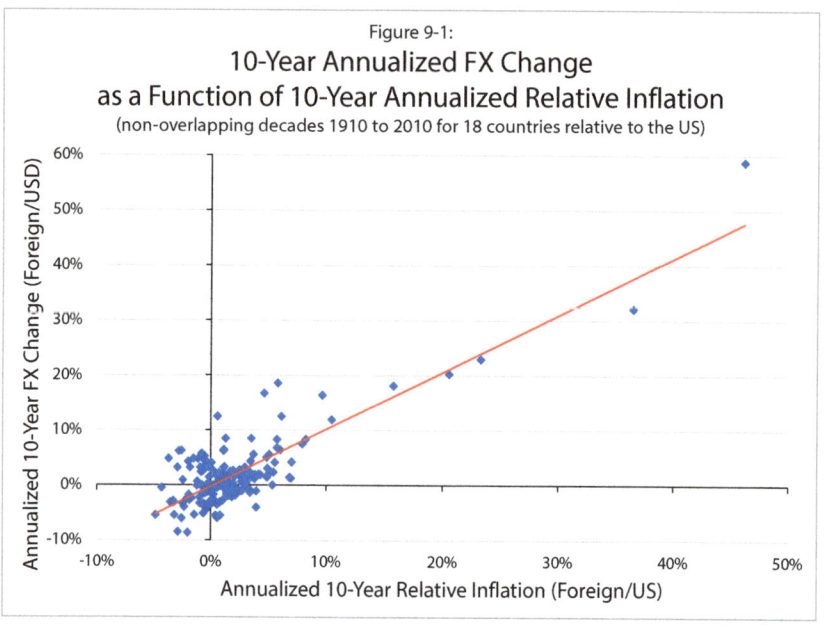

The percentage change in FX that is plotted on the vertical axis is the *nominal return to FX*. Just as real equity returns are the difference between nominal equity returns and inflation, here I define the *real returns to FX* as the difference between the nominal returns to FX and the relative inflation rate — that is, the FX change or movement net of relative inflation. To give the precise definition, using geometric terms:

(9.1) 1+rFX = (1+ rRFX)*(1+ RelInf)

where rFX is the percentage change in nominal FX, defined as home currency per unit of foreign currency
rRFX is the percentage change in real FX; and
RelInf is the percentage change in relative Inflation between the home country and the foreign country, defined as (1+Inflationhome) / (1+inflationforeign) − 1

Or rearranging in terms of the real return to FX:

(9.2) (1+ rRFX) = (1+rFX)/(1+ RelInf)

This relates nicely to the relative PPP theory. You can see that if RPPP were perfectly correct, then the nominal return to FX would equal the change in relative inflation, so that (1+rRFX) would be 1.0 and rRFX would be 0. That is, all the blue dots in Figure 9-1 would fall on the red line, which would have a slope of 1.0 and an intercept of 0.

To give a final perspective on relative PPP and real FX rates, I want to show the dramatic difference between nominal and real FX rates over the long term. In Figure 9-2 below I use the DMS dataset to calculate the percentage annualized nominal FX return[4] (blue bars) and annualized real FX return (red bars) over the whole 111 years in terms of USD/Non-US. The green bars are the relative inflation rates in terms of USD/Non-USD. This means that currency gains or losses are for the non-US currency in each case.

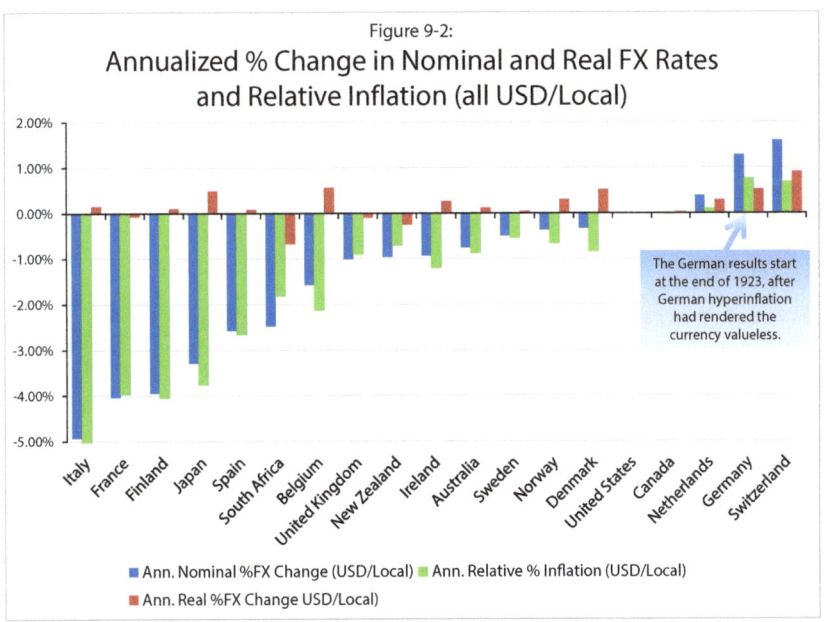

---

[4] Three points should be noted. First, values for the US must be zero by definition. Second, the Canadian values are so close to zero they do not show on the graph. Third, the Deutschmark lost all of its value due to hyperinflation in the early 1920s, and Figure 9-2 only shows values from its new start at the end of 1923, for a span of 87 years. All other country data span the full period.

You can see that annualized relative inflation rate explains almost all of the annualized percentage change in nominal FX rates. That is, the percentage changes in real FX rates, which are the geometric difference between the blue and green bars, are relatively small. In 12 of 18 cases the annualized real FX change was less than +/- 0.30%,[5] and in all cases, less than +/- 1.0%. Taking the cumulative percentage change in nominal FX as a function of the cumulative percentage change in relative inflation, analogous to those in Table 9-1 and Figure 9-1, the linear regression has an adjusted r-squared of 95.45%, while the slope coefficient is 1.0535 with a highly significant t-statistic of 18.35. So over the 111 years almost all of the variability of nominal FX rates is explained by the change in relative inflation.

The final task in this chapter is to integrate the concept of foreign exchange gains and losses into the analysis of equity returns that was developed in Chapter 7. Given the definition of rFX, where FX is defined as the ratio of home/foreign currency, the return of an asset denominated in foreign currency is translated into returns in the base or home currency as:

$$1+TR_{home} = (1+TR_{foreign}) * (1+ rFX)$$

and

$$1+RTR_{home} = (1+RTR_{foreign}) * (1+ rRFX)$$

Most of the time I will drop the "home" and "foreign" nomenclature, assuming that currencies will be properly identified in practice. But just for the record I will generalize equations (7.4) and (7.6) by adding the foreign exchange component as follows:

(9.3) $1+TRH_g = (1+DY_{F_g})*(1+DG_{F_g})*(1+r\Delta DY_{F_g})*(1+rFX_{H/F_g})$

(9.4) $1+RTRH_g = (1+DY_{F_g})*(1+RDG_{F_g})*(1+r\Delta DY_{F_g})*(1+rRFX_{H/F_g})$

where H means home or base currency and F means foreign currency.

Equations (9.3) and (9.4) are general enough to apply to home currency return components as well, since in that case the FX

---

[5] The case of Canada is barely perceptible on the graph, with the return to real FX of 0.03% annualized and the return to nominal FX of 0.01% annualized.

component drops out: the percentage change in the real or nominal FX rate is 0, and the last component (1+ rFX) or (1+ rRFX) is 1.

You can also add the rFX component to the approximations (7.7) and (7.8), by adding in the percentage change to foreign exchange, with the appropriate home and foreign nomenclature understood:

(9.5) $TR_g \approx DY_g + DG_g + r\Delta DY_g + rFX_g$

and

(9.6) $RTR_g \approx DY_g + RDG_g + r\Delta DY_g + rRFX_g$

As a practical matter, investors will seldom focus on inflation in foreign markets, and almost certainly would not think about either real dividend growth from a foreign investor's point of view or about real exchange rates. So equation (9.4) and approximation (9.6) have two components, RDG_{F_g} and $rRFX_{F_g}$ that are difficult to deal with. Fortunately (9.4) and (9.6) can be easily transformed to remove references to foreign real dividend growth and real FX rates, and this will uncover an important fact about real returns to foreign investment from the point of view of the home market.

Starting with equation (9.4) I will substitute the definitions for real dividend growth (1+RDGg) and the percentage change in real FX rates (1+rRFXg). Remember that real dividend growth is nominal dividend growth adjusted for inflation:

$(1+RDG_g) = (1+DG_g)/(1+I_g)$

But let me be pedantic for a moment. Since in (9.4) I referred to the components of foreign market returns, this definition can be clarified as referring to foreign market dividend growth and inflation: foreign market real dividend growth is a function of foreign nominal dividend growth adjusted for foreign inflation, or

$(1+RDG_{F_g}) = (1+DG_{F_g})/(1+I_{F_g})$.

Remember also that the percentage change in real FX rates is a function of the nominal change in FX rates adjusted by relative inflation. Inserting the foreign/home nomenclature this becomes:

$1+rRFX_{H/F_g} = (1+rFX_{H/F_g})/(1+Relinf_{H/F_g})$

Then add in the definition of relative inflation as

$$(1+\text{Relinf}_{H/F_g}) = (1+I_{H_g})/(1+I_{F_g}).$$

When I make the substitutions and reorganize terms, equation (9.4) becomes

$$(9.7)\ 1+\text{RTR}_{H_g} = (1+\text{DY}_{F_g})*(1+\text{DG}_{F_g})*(1+\text{r}\Delta\text{DY}_{F_g})*(1+\text{rFX}_{H/F_g})/(1+I_{H_g})$$

Equation (9.7) says that home market real total returns are a function of foreign dividend yield, foreign nominal dividend growth, foreign return due to a change in dividend yield and change in nominal (home/foreign) FX rates all adjusted by home market inflation. There is no reference to foreign market inflation and real dividend growth from a foreign investor's point of view because the two references to foreign inflation, $(1+I_{F_g})$, associated with RDG and rRFX have cancelled each other out, leaving only references to nominal DG and rFX and to inflation in the home currency.[6] The approximation (9.6) can be similarly rewritten as

$$(9.8)\ \text{RTR}_{H_g} \approx \text{DY}_{F_g} + \text{DG}_{F_g} + \text{r}\Delta\text{DY}_{F_g} + \text{rFX}_{H/F_g} - I_{H_g}$$

I want to emphasize that you cannot ignore foreign inflation on this account, and of course (9.7) is equivalent to (9.4). What (9.7) says is that from the perspective of your home currency, your real returns are nominal returns from any source net of your home inflation, and your foreign nominal returns include all foreign nominal gains *net of the impact of the nominal-foreign exchange rate*. I put it this way because RPPP says that in theory, higher relative foreign inflation should be compensated for by a falling home/foreign exchange rate. So you can see that if you invest in a high-inflation foreign asset, you will reap gains from foreign inflation *to the extent that nominal FX rates haven't fallen as far as relative inflation says they should*.[7]

---

6 The full equation, prior to reorganizing terms, is

$$1+\text{RTR}_{Hg} = (1+\text{DY}_{Fg})*((1+\text{DG}_{Fg})/(1+I_{Fg}))*(1+\text{r}\Delta\text{DY}_{Fg})*(1+\text{rFX}_{H/Fg})*(1+I_{Fg})/(1+I_{Hg}).$$

The two instances of $(1+I_{F_g})$ fall out because one is multiplied and one is divided.

7 And obviously should the nominal FX rate fall further than relative inflation and RPPP would suggest, this would further impair your foreign-based returns.

Equation (9.7) is particularly useful in the analysis or attribution of real returns to foreign investments, especially when we are dealing with multi-currency and multi-country portfolios and indexes. Generally in that case you know the nominal gains and losses to the foreign investment, along with the impact of change to the nominal exchange rate. For example, index provider MSCI provides both "local" (what I call "foreign" in (9.7)) and USD-based indexes for its MSCI EAFE and MSCI Emerging Markets benchmarks.[8] You do not have to compile real dividend and dividend growth data for each country/currency component, as (9.4) might suggest. Rather you can determine nominal dividend and dividend growth for the whole index in local terms.

Table 9-2 shows how this works with two examples using MSCI EAFE and Emerging Markets indexes, from the point of view of an American investor. To focus first on EAFE, for the 41 years since its inception at December 1969 to December 2010, the MSCI EAFE index has generated an annualized total nominal return of 8.71% in aggregate *local* terms and 10.70% in USD (column 1, rows 4 and 6 of Table 9-2). This means that a US investor would have gained 1.83% annualized from aggregate foreign exchange exposures (column 1 row 5, calculated from column 1 rows 6 and 4). Now using EAFE dividend or dividend yield information, a local market attribution of nominal returns can be added in column 2 rows 1, 2 and 3. Note that the 8.64% return from the attribution is very close to the 8.71% local nominal return given by MSCI. It is easy to calculate US inflation over this period, which is 4.36% as shown in column 2, row 7. Finally as equation (9.7) shows, I can calculate the

---

[8] First, local indexes for each country component are calculated daily, and aggregated over time, but USD (and other base currency) versions of each index are also calculated and aggregated over time. EAFE is currently composed of 22 individual markets, aggregated by capitalization every day. The local index version of EAFE aggregates the daily percentage returns from each country in each local currency, while the USD version aggregates the daily USD-based returns for each country component. In both cases they are weighted by capitalization. The Emerging Markets index is calculated in a similar fashion. While the local versions of EAFE or EM are not investable, they are useful for some kinds of analysis, such as the one we are doing here.

Table 9-2:
Total Nominal and Real Returns and Components of Return:
MSCI EAFE 1970-2010; MSCI Emerging Markets 1989-2010

		MSCI EAFE 1970-2010		MSCI EM 1989-2010	
		1 Actual Index	2 Attribution	3 Actual Index	4 Attribution
1	Average DY (Foreign)		2.74%		2.25%
2	Nominal DG (Foreign)		4.76%		25.39%
3	rΔDY (Foreign)		0.94%		1.23%
4	Total Nominal Return (Foreign) (1 + 2 + 3)	8.71%	8.64%	30.12%	29.79%
5	rFX (US/Foreign) (6 - 4)	1.83%	1.83%	-13.17%	-13.17%
6	Total Nominal Return (USD)	10.70%	10.64%	12.99%	12.71%
7	US Inflation	4.36%	4.36%	2.76%	2.76%
8	Total Real Return (USD) (6 -7)	6.08%	6.01%	9.96%	9.68%

Note that all additions and subtractions are geometric

total real US return row 8. Note that rows 1, 2, 3, 5 and 7 are the five elements on the right-hand side of equation (9.7).

Similar calculations are given for the MSCI Emerging Markets index in columns 3 and 4. Since its inception at December 1988 the MSCI Emerging Markets index has generated an annualized total nominal return for the 22 years ending December 2010 of 30.12% in aggregate local terms and 12.99% in USD. Thus the US investor experienced a return of -13.17% due to foreign currency exposures. The rest of the attribution is given, and equation (9.7) shows that the total real return in USD was 9.96% (attributed return of 9.68%) over this period.

When I looked at the historical return and risk properties of global equities in previous chapters, I mostly focused on the characteristics of individual countries, combining the individual country data into a pool of data containing all the countries. But as I continue, and move from examining the past to forecasting the future, I will be focusing on four investable equity assets to illustrate the process. Displaying my home country bias, justified by my hope that some of my readers are Canadian, I will feature the Canadian equity market, along with the more usual US market. For international stocks I will use the MSCI EAFE and Emerging Markets indexes, as these are the most useful and far-reaching indexes that are easily investable and give us global diversification.

So by way of conclusion, Table 9-3 summarizes historical nominal local and US dollar returns, as well as local and US-based real returns for these four assets over the two periods shown in Table 9-2. For interest and for comparison purposes I also add two ten-year spans ending December 2000 and December 2010. The 1990s provide an example of a fairly high-return environment (with the exception of EAFE), while the 2000s provide an example of a lower-return environment (with the exception of the Emerging Markets).

Table 9-3:
Total Nominal Local and USD Returns,
and Total Real Returns for a USD Investor
Based on Equation 9.7

	(1) Total Nominal Return (local)	(2) Local CPI	(3) Total Real Return (local)	(4) Currency Impact (US/For)	(5) Total Nominal Return (USD)	(6) US CPI	(7) Total Real Return (USD)
41 years: Dec. 1969-Dec. 2010							
Canada	10.51%	4.48%	5.76%	0.04%	10.55%	4.36%	5.93%
US	10.15%	4.36%	5.55%		10.15%	4.36%	5.55%
MSCI EAFE	8.71%	4.79%	3.74%	1.83%	10.70%	4.36%	6.08%
MSCI EM							
22 years: Dec. 1988-Dec. 2010							
Canada	9.77%	2.23%	7.38%	0.83%	10.69%	2.76%	7.72%
US	9.48%	2.76%	6.55%		9.48%	2.76%	6.55%
MSCI EAFE	3.91%	2.49%	1.39%	0.93%	4.87%	2.76%	2.06%
MSCI EM	30.12%	51.15%	-13.92%	-13.17%	12.99%	2.76%	9.96%
10 years: Dec. 1990-Dec. 2000							
Canada	14.82%	1.92%	12.65%	-2.55%	11.89%	2.66%	8.99%
US	17.46%	2.66%	14.41%		17.46%	2.66%	14.41%
MSCI EAFE	9.83%	2.50%	7.14%	-1.15%	8.56%	2.66%	5.75%
MSCI EM	32.52%	63.66%	-19.03%	-18.31%	8.26%	2.66%	5.45%
10 years: Dec. 2000-Dec. 2010							
Canada	6.21%	1.97%	4.17%	4.22%	10.69%	2.34%	8.17%
US	1.41%	2.34%	-0.90%		1.41%	2.34%	-0.90%
MSCI EAFE	0.60%	1.88%	-1.25%	3.31%	3.94%	2.34%	1.56%
MSCI EM	15.00%	5.18%	9.33%	1.07%	16.23%	2.34%	13.58%

The first column presents local nominal returns, derived directly from the various historical indexes. The third column presents total real returns in local terms, which are the total nominal returns adjusted by the cumulative local CPI inflation given in the second column.[9] You can see that over the 41-year span, CPI for the three indexes covering developed markets was quite similar, hovering around 4.5% annualized. Over the 22 years since the inception of the Emerging Markets index, CPI for Canada, the US and EAFE has fallen to about 2.5% annualized, but over this period EM CPI has been very high at 51.15%, outpacing total nominal returns by 13.92% annualized. Data for the ten years ending December 2000 confirm this, with EM CPI jumping to 63.66%.[10] The result is that the EM index generated negative local real returns over both periods. Only in the ten years ending in 2010 has EM inflation fallen to levels closer to those of the developed markets, with the consequence that local real returns to the EM countries averaged 10.05% in the decade, outstripping those of EAFE, Canada and the US.

Columns 4 and 5 (the yellow area) transform the local nominal returns from column 1 into US-dollar nominal returns for all of the periods. Finally columns 6 and 7 (the pink area) use equation (9.7) to

---

9 While I mentioned earlier that very few investors will look at foreign (local market) inflation and foreign (local market) real returns, this is especially true when you try to handle multi-country indexes. But it is interesting to see how this works. So for the EAFE and Emerging Markets indexes I created an estimate of their aggregate local CPI: I gathered local annual CPI returns for each member country of the index, covering the years that each member country was included in the respective indexes. Lacking MSCI's capitalization weights that are used in compiling the cross-country indexes, I weighted each country's CPI by its annual US dollar–based GDP.

10 These extraordinarily high levels of inflation are almost entirely due to the hyperinflation suffered by Brazil. From the end of 1988 to the end of 1994, my IMF data show that Brazil consumer prices jumped by 7,544.299 times. Since Brazil was a significant contributor to the total US dollar value of GDP for the EM index countries, its impact on overall CPI was very large. Removing Brazil from the index would have resulted in much more normal CPI numbers for the other emerging markets, as has occurred since. For example, from 1996 to 2010, overall CPI for the EM index countries has averaged 7.1%.

turn nominal USD returns from column 5 into real returns from the US investor's point of view. That is, the nominal US dollar returns are adjusted to reflect US inflation.

You can see that the Emerging Markets index has provided a dramatic example of how equation (9.7) works. For example, in the ten years ending in 2000, local inflation across the EM (what equation (9.7) calls "foreign") was a whopping 63.66% annualized, so that real local returns are negative at -19.03%. But to the US investor, what matters is the local (foreign) nominal return, translated into US dollars and adjusted for US inflation. Since on average the EM FX depreciated by -18.31% per year, much less than the amount that EM inflation rose relative to US inflation, some of the nominal inflationary gains were passed on to the US investor: 8.26% in nominal terms or 5.45% after US inflation. On the other hand, in the decade ending in 2010, EM inflation moderated to 4.49% annually, still higher than US inflation, while average EM FX actually rose by 1.07% annualized relative to the US dollar, the opposite direction to the RPPP forecast.[11] So in nominal terms the US investor received the 15% local return plus an FX gain of 1.07%, for a nominal US dollar gain of 16.23%, or a real return of 13.58% after US inflation.

Canadian investors will be interested in seeing the same local market information that was presented in Table 9-3 from their own perspective in Table 9-4, while non-Canadian investors can see how currency translations can impact returns. Columns 1-3 of Table 9-4 are of course identical to those in Table 9-3, but column 4 shows the impact of the currency translations to Canadian dollars rather than to US dollars. Thus column 5 presents the total nominal returns in Canadian dollars.

Since the US and Canadian dollars performed quite similarly over the full 41-year period relative to other currencies, the net impact is quite small. But over the shorter time spans the impact can be quite significant. For example, as we saw in Chapter 8, the Canadian dollar was rather strong over the 2001–2010 decade,

---

11 That is, since US inflation was still lower than EM inflation, RPPP predicts that the nominal FX return should still be modestly negative.

Table 9-4:
Total Nominal Local and CAD Returns,
and Total Real Returns for a CAD Investor
Based on Equation 9.7

	(1) Total Nominal Return (local)	(2) Local CPI	(3) Total Real Return (local)	(4) Currency Impact (CN/For)	(5) Total Nominal Return (CAD)	(6) CNCPI	(7) Total Real Return (CAD)
41 years: Dec. 1969-Dec. 2010							
Canada	10.51%	4.48%	5.76%		10.51%	4.48%	5.76%
US	10.15%	4.36%	5.55%	-0.04%	10.10%	4.48%	5.38%
MSCI EAFE	8.71%	4.79%	3.74%	1.79%	10.66%	4.48%	5.91%
MSCI EM							
22 years: Dec. 1988-Dec. 2010							
Canada	9.77%	2.23%	7.38%		9.77%	2.23%	7.38%
US	9.48%	2.76%	6.55%	-0.83%	8.58%	2.23%	6.21%
MSCI EAFE	3.91%	2.49%	1.39%	0.09%	4.00%	2.23%	1.73%
MSCI EM	30.12%	51.15%	-13.92%	-13.88%	12.05%	2.23%	9.61%
10 years: Dec. 1990-Dec. 2000							
Canada	14.82%	1.92%	12.65%		14.82%	1.92%	12.65%
US	17.46%	2.66%	14.41%	2.62%	20.53%	1.92%	18.26%
MSCI EAFE	9.83%	2.50%	7.14%	1.44%	11.40%	1.92%	9.30%
MSCI EM	32.52%	63.66%	-19.03%	-16.17%	11.09%	1.92%	9.00%
10 years: Dec. 2000-Dec. 2010							
Canada	6.21%	1.97%	4.17%		6.21%	1.97%	4.17%
US	1.41%	2.34%	-0.90%	-4.05%	-2.69%	1.97%	-4.57%
MSCI EAFE	0.60%	1.88%	-1.25%	-0.87%	-0.27%	1.97%	-2.19%
MSCI EM	15.00%	5.18%	9.33%	-3.02%	11.53%	1.97%	9.37%

relative to most other currencies. So Canadian investors experienced a negative impact from currency exposures in their unhedged foreign investments. On the other hand, Table 9-3 shows that over the same decade, US investors experienced gains from their foreign investment exposures as the US dollar weakened.

Finally, since US and Canadian inflationary experience was rather similar over these time spans, the impact on real returns is also similar in column 7. Tables 9-3 and 9-4 will provide a useful reference as we work through our approach to forecasting in Part 2.

Part 2:

Looking Towards the Future: an Approach to Building Equity Forecasts

Chapter 10:

Economic Growth and Equity Market Returns — Round One

My goal is to motivate and build a framework for directly forecasting future long-term equity returns, but I will begin by exploring the relationship between equity returns and economic growth or success.

> **OVERVIEW**
> The idea that equity returns are linked with economic growth is examined and tested.
>
> Key findings:
> - total returns are not related to contemporaneous or lagged real economic growth;
> - equity returns are linked to *future* real economic growth, but this does not help investors.

I would guess that almost every professional investment review at the total fund level for pension funds and foundations features an "economic outlook" report. I'm sure there are many reasons for this, most of which stem from the fact that this kind of report is a tradition, and everyone feels they have accomplished something by thinking about the economy. While I am sceptical that any investment decision-making is normally based on such economic forecasts, most people have the strong intuition that the fate of markets is closely tied to the fate of the economy.

In particular, it is widely believed that if the economy does well, then the equity market will do well. Conversely, in a poor or weak economy, surely the equity market will do badly. So if you forecast what the economy will achieve, then perhaps that's more or less the same as forecasting what the equity market will achieve. And this seems to makes sense, because isn't "the economy" essentially the sum of all businesses? To say that the economy will do well is to say that business will do well — make strong profits, pay dividends and (for those that trade on stock markets) sell at high (or higher) prices.

Furthermore, you will often hear this line of reasoning as one of the primary justifications for investing in the so-called emerging markets. Since their economies are expected to grow faster than those of the more established "developed" markets, it is often suggested that investors will make more money by overweighting their holdings in those high-growth markets and underweighting the developed markets.

While this all sounds plausible and reasonable, there are actually some serious difficulties with these assumptions. It's not just that accurate economic forecasting is difficult to do well, a problem shared with most kinds of empirical forecasting. It's worse than that: when you study the relationship between economic growth and equity market returns, you will find that there is essentially no correlation between the two.

This is a puzzling result that flies in the face of the common and widely held views that I've outlined. Yet these and similar results have been known for some time, although they are largely ignored and certainly are not well understood. I will work through these issues with some care because in the end there has to be a strong connection between economic growth and the equity market. The real question is whether the relationship that we think must exist is of any use in forecasting equity returns. So first I want to show what the relationship isn't, and then what it might be. When you get this right you can actually understand why the initial idea of a correlation between an economy and its equity market doesn't hold, despite its apparent foundation in common sense.

When people talk about economic growth, they are usually referring to some form of GDP: gross domestic product. This comes in several flavours, much like equity returns. First, economists distinguish between nominal and real GDP, the former including inflation and the latter net of inflation.[1] Given the discussions about inflation so far, you can guess that comparing nominal equity market returns and nominal GDP growth, where both are subject to inflation, will add noise to any analysis,[2] and so I will concentrate on real returns and real GDP as I continue.

A second distinction comes from the fact that overall real or nominal GDP growth includes the effects of population changes. Table 10-1 compares real GDP with real GDP per capita (labeled as GDPPC), which removes the effect of population growth.[3]

Since per capita real GDP reflects period-to-period average real output per person, positive growth of real GDP per capita implies that average productivity has grown in real terms. Table 10-1 shows that for the 19 countries over a 40-year period, 72% of real GDP growth that averaged 2.54% has been due to the effects of productivity increases (1.82% per year), while 28% has been due to population growth (0.72% per year). South Africa is an outlier, which has had a young and fast-growing population, where much more of its real GDP growth has been due to population growth than to productivity improvements. In my analysis I will always remove the effects of population growth, and focus on real GDPPC growth, which serves as a proxy for real growth of productivity in the economy.

---

[1] While I use the terminology "nominal" versus "real", which coincides with how I have categorized investment returns, sometimes economists and government statisticians who collect these data refer to nominal GDP as being based on current prices (meaning prices that are current at each measurement point), while real GDP is said to be stated in constant prices, usually with a reference to a specific "base" year. While both terminologies make sense, I continue to use nominal versus real.

[2] We have seen that when you look across time, inflation can vary dramatically over years and decades.

[3] Data are based on statistics compiled by the International Monetary Fund and contained in their World Economic Outlook dataset. The data are available on the IMF website: www.imf.org and begin in 1980. Earlier history was gathered from OECD statistics and other sources.

Table 10-1:
Annualized Real GDP and Real GDP per Capita
1970 to 2010

	Annualized Real GDP Growth	Annualized Real GDPPC Growth	Geometric Difference
Australia	3.18%	1.74%	1.42%
Belgium	2.25%	1.93%	0.31%
Canada	2.91%	1.71%	1.18%
Denmark	1.89%	1.59%	0.29%
Finland	2.67%	2.28%	0.38%
France	2.29%	1.72%	0.56%
Germany	2.05%	1.92%	0.13%
Ireland	4.49%	3.40%	1.05%
Italy	2.00%	1.71%	0.29%
Japan	2.56%	2.04%	0.51%
Netherlands	2.46%	1.84%	0.61%
New Zealand	2.35%	1.24%	1.10%
Norway	3.10%	2.51%	0.58%
South Africa	2.54%	0.52%	2.01%
Spain	2.85%	2.08%	0.76%
Sweden	2.08%	1.69%	0.38%
Switzerland	1.54%	0.99%	0.54%
United Kingdom	2.16%	1.87%	0.28%
United States	2.89%	1.83%	1.04%
Arith. Average	2.54%	1.82%	0.71%

With these two distinctions in hand, the hypothesis that economic growth drives equity market growth can be refined to say that real GDP per capita growth drives real total equity returns.

In the remainder of this chapter I will focus on the negative point that it is hard to find a direct link between real GDP per capita growth and total real equity returns, while the one link I do find is of little use to investors. In the next chapter I will go a little deeper to show what I believe is a real and useful link between economic growth and market returns, and in so doing will give a potential explanation of the negative results in this chapter.

I present both long-term and short-term data.[4] Figure 10-1 shows the geometric average real returns for each of the 19 DMS countries from 1970 to 2010, ranked from lowest to highest (blue

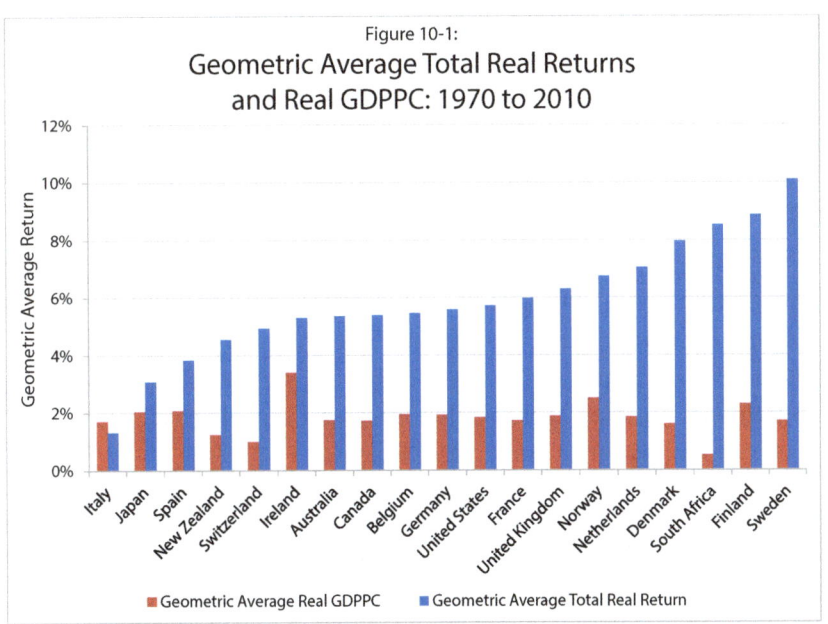

---

4 First, I have a very long historical data set of annual GDP for the US compiled from various sources, including the US Department of Commerce Bureau of Economic Analysis and the useful website http://www.measuringworth.com/. This dataset has been integrated with the monthly Shiller US data to create 140 years of annual returns and growth rates at the total market level for prices, earnings dividends and total returns. Results from this data set will be labelled as Shiller US.

Second, I have a GDP dataset primarily from the OECD, supplemented by the IMF and other sources, spanning 1970 to 2010 and covering the 18 developed markets over this period for which I have data from Morgan Stanley Capital International (MSCI) database. The MSCI data also include monthly market level data for each country for price levels, total returns, earnings and dividends. The OECD GDP data have been integrated with the MSCI dataset to create annual data from 1970 to 2010 for 18 countries.

Third, I have also attached the OECD GDP data to the DMS dataset of 19 rather than 18 countries. However, since the dataset only has total real and nominal equity returns, and does not include prices, dividends and earnings, I only use it in this context for broad summary information as in Figure 10-1. This is called the DMS dataset.

bars). Plotted next to the returns are the geometric average growth rates for each country's real GDP per capita from the OECD (red bars).

There is no obvious visual correlation between the two sets of bars. The correlation is actually negative at -0.11, although it is statistically insignificant (not statistically different from 0). This means that looking across the 19 countries, there is no evidence that GDP per capita or productivity growth was linked to market returns over this total sample span of 40 years.[5]

While Figure 10-1 compares economic growth and real equity returns over a 40-year span, I also compare numbers over a much shorter term. In Figure 10-2 these data are used on a year-by-year basis, with all of the individual yearly real return and real GDPPC growth data "pooled" across all years over a sample that includes 18 of the 19 countries from the MSCI dataset.

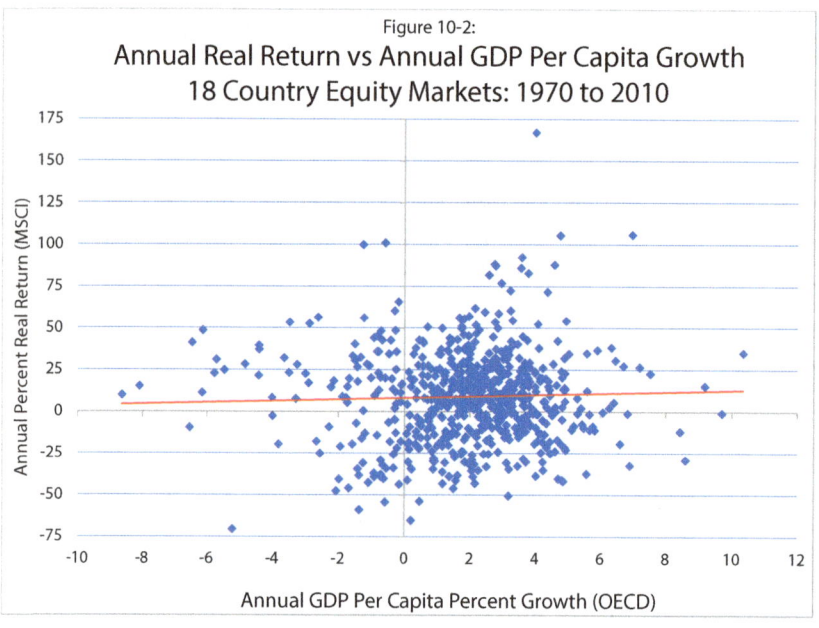

---

[5] Remember that in the discussion of correlation in the Appendix to Chapter 3, I pointed out that while significant correlation relations do not imply causation, causation requires correlation. So if you think that economic growth "drives" market returns, then there should be a significant and positive correlation.

The correlation between annual real returns and real GDPPC growth is slightly positive at 0.038, and the slope of the line of best fit (the regression coefficient) pictured in the diagram is 0.45. However both the correlation and the slope coefficient are insignificant,[6] so there is essentially no evidence of a relationship between real GDPPC growth and real returns on an annual basis.

This result is confirmed by the longer Shiller US dataset, which generates a correlation of 0.017 and a regression coefficient of 0.064 for similar US data. Both the correlation and the regression coefficient are not significantly different from zero.

Perhaps the 40-year time spans are too long (Figure 10-1) and annual time spans are too short (Figure 10-2) to identify a correlation, and I should be examining an intermediate time frame of perhaps ten years. However, using non-overlapping data from the Shiller US dataset and the MSCI global dataset, I find no significant correlations for ten years. Table 10-2 summarizes the results for one-year

Table 10-2:
Contemporaneous Real Equity Returns vs GDPPC Growth

	Shiller US 1871 to 2010	MSCI Global 1970 to 2010
Current 1-year real equity return as a function of current 1-year real GDPPC growth		
Correlation	0.017	0.038
Regression Coefficient	0.064	0.452
T-Statistic	0.201	0.970
Probability of being 0	84.07%	33.26%
Current 10-year real equity return as a function of current 10-year real GDPPC growth		
Correlation	0.151	0.197
Regression Coefficient	0.884	1.691
T-Statistic	0.530	1.608
Probability of being 0	60.56%	11.29%

---

6 The correlation and its associated slope coefficient have the same t-statistic and significance. The t-statistic is 0.970, which implies a 33.3% probability that both the correlation and the slope are 0. I briefly discussed correlation and the line of best fit in the Appendix to Chapter 3.

and ten-year time spans, as I test the contemporaneous relationship between real equity total returns and real GDPPC growth using the Shiller US and MSCI global datasets.

Dimson, Marsh and Staunton also report[7] that for ten-year spans from 1970 to 2009, roughly the same period as Figure 10-1, the correlation between GDPPC real growth and real equity returns was low and insignificant. Their data for this analysis include not only the 19 developed markets but an additional 64 smaller markets.

So despite the strong and prevalent intuition that real GDP growth must be linked with real equity returns, there is little evidence of a *contemporaneous* relationship. But what if the relationship is across time? There are two possibilities: equity markets might be driven by, or at least react to, past real GDPPC growth; or equity market moves might precede or forecast future economic growth.

Think of these questions on two levels. First, I would like to find and understand a connection that might hold between equity markets and economic growth. Second, I would like to be able to forecast equity market returns to make rational investments. Had I found the contemporaneous correlation, I might have been able to use the information as a roundabout way of forecasting real equity returns. The process would have been to: (a) project that past correlations would hold in the future, (b) find a dependable economic forecast of future economic growth, and (c) find a method for applying that future correlation to the forecast of economic growth to project real equity returns. This is complicated even further by the fact that GDP isn't actually reported for several months or more into the next year.

Rather than using past contemporaneous correlations between real returns and real GDPPC growth and then forecasting economic growth, it might be possible to forecast by using relationships that in the past have directly influenced future real equity returns.[8] In

---

7 Dimson, Elroy, Paul Marsh and Mike Staunton, "Economic Growth", DMSW 2010, p. 16.

8 Although projecting past contemporaneous correlations forward, and forecasting something that is correlated with what you are really interested in is a legitimate approach, it has two major disadvantages. First, your forecast will

the case at hand, is past economic growth related to future equity returns? The idea might be that investors pick up on recent economic trends, and bet on the continuation of those trends in the future.

Unfortunately, the story here is pretty succinct and completely negative. I used the Shiller and MSCI datasets to look at the relationship between past one-year and ten-year real GDPPC growth and future one-year and ten-year real total equity returns. The results are presented in Table 10-3. The hope is to find a positive relationship between past GDPPC growth and future real returns. But you can see that in three of the four cases the correlations and regression coefficients are statistically insignificant (there is a high probability that the coefficients are zero), and in the fourth case (one-year GDPPC growth as a predictor of next year's equity returns for the

Table 10-3:
Relating Future Real Equity Returns
to Past GDPPC Growth

	Shiller US 1871 to 2010	MSCI Global 1970 to 2010
Next year's annual real equity return as a function of last year's real GDPPC growth		
Correlation	-0.071	-0.101
Regression Coefficient	-0.268	-1.217
T-Statistic	-0.838	-2.591
Probability of being 0	40.34%	0.98%
Future 10-year real equity return as a function of the past 10-year real GDPPC growth		
Correlation	0.329	-0.067
Regression Coefficient	1.977	-0.654
T-Statistic	1.154	-0.471
Probability of being 0	27.29%	64.00%
pink highlight: significant with the "wrong" sign		

compound the inherent uncertainty related to the correlation with the inherent uncertainty associated with any forecast. Second, you can't keep appealing to correlations, and at some point you need a "direct" forecast of the kind now being suggested. For example, in our case if the economist's GDPPC forecast wasn't direct in this sense, and also appealed to contemporaneous correlations with one or more other factors, the chain of forecasts would become very tenuous indeed.

MSCI global universe), the coefficient and correlation are significant but the sign is negative — the "wrong"[9] or unexpected sign. That is, positive GDPPC growth has been followed by negative market returns, which is opposite to what we were looking for.

In sum, there is no evidence that past GDPPC growth is linked to future real equity returns, and it certainly cannot be used to forecast those returns.

When I turn things around, and look at whether past market returns can predict future economic growth, there is a surprisingly positive answer. This is what is meant when you read in the newspaper or an economic report from a bank or brokerage that the equity markets provide a "leading indicator" of the economy.

Table 10-4 presents results for treating future real GDPPC growth as a function of past real equity returns for one and ten years.

Table 10-4:
Relating GDPPC Growth to past Real Equity Returns

	Shiller US 1871 to 2010	MSCI Global 1970 to 2010
Next year's annual real GDPPC growth as a function of last year's real equity return		
Correlation	0.449	0.440
Regression Coefficient	0.120	0.036
T-Statistic	5.884	12.611
Probability of being 0	<0.001%	<0.001%
Future 10-year real GDPPC growth as a function of the past 10-year real equity return		
Correlation	0.037	-0.374
Regression Coefficient	0.007	-0.034
T-Statistic	0.124	-2.737
Probability of being 0	90.33%	0.88%
yellow highlight: significant with the "right" sign		
pink highlight: significant with the "wrong" sign		

---

[9] Of course there is really no "right" or "wrong" sign from my point of view, because I intend to show you in the next chapter why we should not expect any particular relationship between total real equity returns and real GDPPC growth.

Both the US history and the MSCI global data show extremely strong positive relations between past one-year real returns and next year's real GDPPC growth. However the ten-year relationship is not significant for the US history, and while the MSCI data show a significant relationship, it has the "wrong" or unexpected sign: positive real equity returns over ten years are a negative indicator for economic growth over the subsequent ten years.

This strong link between past one-year real equity market returns and future one-year real GDPPC growth is great for the economist, who is paid to forecast economic growth, because it gives him a potentially powerful tool to help him in his endeavours.[10] Sadly, on the face of things, this doesn't help us much as investors.

---

10 In the case of the long US dataset, the adjusted r-squared of the regression is 19.6%, and for the MSCI dataset the adjusted r-squared is 19.2%. This means that almost 20% of the variability of GDPPC one-year growth has been "explained" by the previous year's real equity returns.

Appendix: past real equity returns and future GDPPC growth — a possible explanation of the relationship

Speculating on why past real one-year equity returns have exhibited a strong positive correlation with future real one-year GDPPC growth may actually teach us a little bit about how markets react to information. I have placed this discussion as an appendix because it is a little peripheral to the main line of thought.

It helps to remember that when we talk about what drives equity returns, we are really talking about the behaviour of investors who are buying and selling equities. Prices rise and returns are positive when there is more demand (to buy) at the current price than supply (to sell) at that price, and buyers are willing to pay increasing prices to fulfill their demand. Conversely, prices fall and returns are negative when selling interest at the current price outstrips buying interest, and sellers are willing to accept lower prices for their stocks.

Investors, and hence markets and prices, react very quickly to real and perceived news and information. So let's suppose that something occurs that investors (and for that matter economists and businesspeople) agree will be good for the economy. You might see an immediate market reaction, certainly within minutes and hours in the very short run, and perhaps with subsequent action over days and weeks. But it might take many weeks, and more likely many months, for such an occurrence to have a measurable impact in the real economy. Thus, if investors and markets react to the information that will eventually have a material positive or negative effect on the real economy, it is pretty clear that the market impact will presage the real economic impact.

A fairly obvious and often-cited example of this is the manipulation of short-term interest rates by central bankers. The basic idea is that the central banks will lower rates with the goal of increasing nominal (and hopefully real) economic growth. The mechanism is roughly that lower rates will increase the money supply, with the hope that credit will ease, so consumers and businesses will increase their spending, which will lead to increased economic activity. Conversely, rates may be raised with the goal of decreasing money supply, dampening credit and spending, and ultimately slowing inflationary (nominal) economic activity, and possibly real growth as well. This is a useful example because we know that investors and markets react very quickly to rate changes, both actual and anticipated. Yet the impact of a rate change may take three to six months before we begin to see tangible economic effects.

This process happens continuously: investors and markets react to and process information that may eventually have an impact on the real economy. By the time the economy itself begins to show the effects of the information or events, the market has long since moved on to new issues.

I have just told a story. Investors like to tell stories about "how things work", but unless there is some kind of evidence to back them up, they remain just that — stories, convincing or otherwise. So let's try to put a little flesh on this story.

I started with annual data: last year's real equity returns are significantly correlated with next year's real GDPPC. But to find support for my story I need to look at shorter time frames within that whole period. That is easy with equities, which can be measured over quarters, months, weeks, days and even shorter periods. But the shortest measure of GDP is quarterly, and even then the reporting lag is roughly an additional month, and historically has been much longer.

Nevertheless, I have set up a small quarterly dataset with GDP data for the UK and the US, spanning the 1970 to 2010 period,

Appendix: past real equity returns and future GDPPC growth

along with market data and related information. Table 1 of this Appendix shows the regression results for pooling the data across both countries, and testing to see whether real quarterly GDPPC growth is a function of quarterly real total equity returns, contemporaneously, or lagged by one, two, three or four quarters. The relationship is insignificant for the concurrent quarter, and for one quarter and four quarters lagged, but is significant for both two and three quarters lagged (highlighted in yellow).

Appendix Table 1:
Real GDPPC Quarterly Growth as a Function of
Real Quarterly Equity Total Returns
Across UK and US Markets, 1970 to 2010

Real Quarterly Equity Total Returns	Coefficent	T-stat	Probability of being 0	Adj. R-squared
Concurrent quarter	-0.0014	-0.200	84.20%	-0.29%
Lagged one quarter	0.0071	1.018	30.96%	0.01%
Lagged two quarters	0.0150	2.171	3.06%	1.14%
Lagged three quarters	0.0207	2.976	0.31%	2.39%
Lagged four quarters	0.0003	0.048	96.16%	-0.31%

(Each regression is univariate)

These results are consistent with the idea that there is indeed a delay between the equity markets processing the information that drives them, and the impact of that information on the real economy. The precise length of this delay is masked when we look at annual data, but comes to light when we look at quarterly data. The lag of two quarters means that the information drives equity returns over the span of four to six months prior to its apparent impact on quarterly GDPPC. The lag of three quarters, which has higher significance, means that information drives equity returns seven to nine months prior to its apparent impact in the real economy.

But to take the story to the next level, I need to find some information that both directly impacts the market in the very short term and then impacts the real economy in the longer term. Equity markets react quickly to many kinds of information, and by hypothesis the delay with respect to the real economy is long and the impact of any one event must be relatively small. But here is one suggestive example: equity markets are very sensitive to changes in interest rates, and it would not be surprising to find that the real economy is too. However, unlike the suggested example above, which discussed short-term rates that are directly influenced by central bank policy, I find stronger relationships based on returns to ten-year bonds.

Over the same measurement period and again pooling the US and UK markets, the first row of Table 2 of this appendix shows that changes in monthly equity returns have a strong positive correlation with last month's return to ten-year bonds: the t-statistic is highly significant and the probability that the coefficient is 0 is just 0.04%.

Appendix Table 2:
Impact of Bond Returns on Future Equity Returns
and on Future Real GDPPC Growth
UK and US Markets, 1970 to 2010

Bond Returns	Coefficient	T-stat	Probability of being 0	Adj. R-squared
1-month Equity Returns as a function of 1-month Bond Returns lagged by 1 month	0.2585	3.546	0.04%	1.28%
Contemporaneous quarterly Real Equity Returns as a function of Quarterly Bond Returns	0.6680	5.905	0.00%	10.21%
Quarterly Real GDPPC Growth as a function of Quarterly Bond Returns lagged by 3 quarters	0.0297	2.021	4.42%	1.02%

The second row of Table 2 shows that over a full quarter of equity returns, the contemporaneous quarterly bond return is highly correlated and extremely significant, with a high r-squared of 10.2%. While this isn't a useful relationship in terms of forecasting, it reinforces the idea that information about local interest rate changes is immediately processed by local equity markets and seems to directly impact its returns.

Finally the third row shows that quarterly bond returns have a significantly positive relationship with real quarterly GDPPC growth three quarters hence (that is, the bonds were lagged by three quarters). Not shown is the fact that quarterly bond returns lagged

Appendix: past real equity returns and future GDPPC growth

by one, two and four quarters have no significant relationship with GDPPC real quarterly growth, and that the concurrent relationship is actually significant and negative.

Table 1 showed that quarterly equity returns lagged by two and three quarters were correlated with future real GDPPC growth. Table 2 is at least suggestive that long-term bond returns provide an example of why this might be: bond returns seem to be an example of a factor that influences the equity market in the very short term (concurrently and within a month) while impacting the real economy in the longer term, three quarters later.

I want to emphasize the term "suggestive". All these results are very sensitive to the breadth of the data used, and further studies with much broader data sets and the ability to examine relationships over multiple time frames such as days and weeks, as well as months and quarters, would be needed to draw any stronger conclusions.

Chapter 11:

Economic Growth and Equity Market Returns — Round Two

While economic growth has very uncertain ties to equity returns as a whole, perhaps further insight can be gained by thinking about the individual components of return that were discovered in Chapters 7 and 9. There I showed that total equity return for an investment period is closely approximated by the sum of the average dividend yield for the period, the average dividend growth over the period, the return due to the change in dividend yield and, for foreign investments, the return due to the change in the FX rate. Since I am examining the relationship between an economy and its own equity market, there is no impact due to changes in foreign exchange rates, and since I am more concerned about real rather than nominal returns, the focus will be on the real return version of the approximation:

> **OVERVIEW**
>
> A deeper analysis finds a relationship between economic growth and equity returns, through the components of the dividend-based model of return.
>
> **Key findings:**
> - real dividend growth is related to contemporaneous and lagged real economic growth;
> - economic growth is not significantly related to the other components of return, which obscures the relationship with total returns.

(7.8) $RTR_g \approx DY_g + RDG_g + r\Delta DY_g$

Of the three components of real total return, the most obvious place to look for a link with economic growth is the middle element, real dividend growth (RDG). Think of it this way: earnings growth, or lack thereof, is a measure of the economic success of a company, so in aggregate, the earnings growth of the market as a whole may be a good representative of the growth of the economy as a whole. Dividends are a payout of some proportion of the earnings, and to the extent that the payout is constant over time, dividend growth mirrors earnings growth.[1]

Remember my working hypothesis from the previous chapter: the lack of correlation between real equity returns and growth in the real economy may be due to the fact that investors process new information about the economy into market prices very quickly, long before the effects of such changes are exhibited in the economy. This is reflected by the first and third elements of approximation (7.8). Dividend yields (DY) will change as prices change: if investors bid up prices, yields will fall, and conversely. And of course these changes in dividend yield generate returns, what I have called the return due to a change in dividend yield (rΔDY). So both DY and rΔDY can be expected to react in the very immediate time frame of market price changes. By contrast dividend growth should not be directly affected by market valuations over the short term. Rather it should be a function of the fortunes of companies in the real economy, and so can be expected to change in the same time frame as the real economy itself.

On the basis of this reasoning I will start with the question: is there a positive relationship between real GDPPC growth and real dividend growth (RDG)? Then if the answer to the first question is positive, can I explain why this relationship is not evident at the level of total returns, as we saw in the last chapter?

Fortunately, the answer to the first question is a straightforward affirmative. Using the Shiller and MSCI datasets once again, I find that one-year concurrent real dividend growth and real GDPPC

---

[1] If the payout ratio is constant, dividend growth is exactly equal to earnings growth. If the payout ratio (Dividends paid /Earnings) varies as it does in practice then the exact relationship is: (1+dividend growth) = (1+earnings growth) * (1 + the percent change in the payout ratio).

growth are significantly positively correlated. Table 11-1 presents the results.

Table 11-1:
One-Year Real Dividend Growth as a Function of Concurrent One-Year Real GDPPC Growth

	Shiller US 1871 to 2010	MSCI Global 1970 to 2010
Correlation	0.246	0.323
Regression Coefficient	0.583	2.195
T-Statistic	2.976	8.783
Probability of being 0	0.340%	<.0001%
Adjusted R-Squared	5.35%	10.27%

The first column shows that for the US Shiller data there is a strong positive relationship, with the probability of the coefficient and correlation[2] being 0 at just 0.34%. The second column looks at the relationship across 18 countries in the MSCI data over the 41-year span from 1970 to 2010. Again there is a strong positive correlation of 0.323, and with an even stronger t-statistic of 8.783. This means that the probability of the correlation and the regression coefficient being zero is substantially less than 0.001%. The adjusted r-squared of 10.27% means that 10.27% of the variability of one-year dividend growth is explained by one-year real GDPPC growth over this period.

I also examined the relationship over non-overlapping five- and ten-year time spans for both datasets, and while the five-year sample for the MSCI data was significant and positive, neither the ten-year results for MSCI nor the US five-year and ten-year results were significant.

To take this one step further, I looked across time to see whether one-year real GDPPC growth is predictive of next year's real dividend growth as well. Table 11-2 shows this for both datasets.

Compared with the contemporaneous relationship shown in Table 11-1, these results are slightly less robust, not unexpected for

---

[2] The correlation and the coefficient of the linear regression have the same t-statistic.

Table 11-2:
One-Year Real Dividend Growth as a Function
of Previous One-Year Real GDPPC Growth

	Shiller US 1871 to 2010	MSCI Global 1970 to 2010
Correlation	0.170	0.220
Regression Coefficient	0.402	1.494
T-Statistic	2.015	5.753
Probability of being 0	4.590%	<.001%
Adjusted R-Squared	2.17%	4.71%

a relationship across time. However, the relationship shown by the US data is positive and significant, and the relationship shown in the MSCI global data is also positive and extremely strong, with a highly significant correlation and a substantial r-squared. Longer-term relations were again insignificant.

So there is a positive answer to the first question: the hoped-for link between real GDPPC growth and real market returns turns out to be a positive correlation between real annual GDPPC growth and both concurrent and one-year ahead real annual dividend growth. However, I want to be very clear here that a longer-term relationship between real GDPPC growth and real dividend growth, even on a purely contemporaneous basis for ten-year spans, has not been found. Although perhaps not at all surprising,[3] the lack of evidence for a longer-term contemporaneous connection will disappoint many investors.

I can now answer the second question, as to why the positive short-term relationship that has been found does not show at the total returns level. As I have already explained, the other two

---

3 Of course you might wonder if part of the problem could be a lack of data. To properly test a ten-year contemporaneous relationship, you need non-overlapping data. That gives us 14 data points for our 140-year US data, and just 4 (and in some cases fewer) data points for each of our 18 MSCI countries. On the other hand when you think about this, why should positive GDPPC growth over the past five or ten years forecast future positive real economic growth or real dividend growth over a subsequent long period such as five or ten years? Good stretches are just as likely to be followed by bad periods, aren't they?

components of approximation (7.8), DY and rΔDY, are essentially a function of prices. But we know that price changes are not related to concurrent real GDPPC growth, so we should expect no positive relationship between these two factors and real growth.[4] Not surprisingly, Table 11-3 shows this.

Table 11-3:
Dividend Yield and One-Year Return
Due to the Change in Dividend Yield as a
Function of Concurrent One-Year Real GDPPC Growth

	Shiller US 1871 to 2010	MSCI Global 1970 to 2010
1-year DY as a function of concurrent 1-year real GDPPC growth		
Correlation	-0.069	-0.179
Regression Coefficient	-0.024	-0.153
T-Statistic	-0.815	-4.751
Probability of being 0	0.417	<.001%
Adjusted R-Squared	0.00%	3.13%
1-year rΔDY as a function of concurrent 1-year real GDPPC growth		
Correlation	-0.130	-0.232
Regression Coefficient	-0.581	-3.729
T-Statistic	-1.531	-6.140
Probability of being 0	0.128	<.001%
Adjusted R-Squared	0.96%	5.23%

In all four cases the concurrent relationship between one-year GDPPC growth and each of the two factors is negative. The relationships are not significant in the US cases, but are highly significant for the MSCI global data.

You might think of it this way. If the market has correctly foreseen that GDPPC growth will be strong, prices will tend to have risen already, driving dividend yields down, which in turn will have produced prior positive returns due to change in dividend yield.

---

4 Indeed since the market has a small but statistically significant ability to predict real future GDPPC growth, we should expect the changes in DY and rΔDY to be predictive as well. Although I will not show these results here, this is supported empirically, with lower DY (implying positive price change) and positive rΔDY both predicting positive real GDPPC growth in the next year.

This likely occurs long before the growth materializes either in the real economy or as real dividend growth.[5] What happens to DY and rΔDY concurrently with one-year GDPPC growth is unrelated, as those two factors are reacting to new information on a continual basis.

To summarize, I have found strong backing for the original and widely held intuition that economic growth has to be linked with market returns: the link is through the component of real dividend growth. But in addition, we can now understand why this link with real economic growth is obscured at the level of total returns. Let's refer back to approximation (7.8). On the one hand real GDPPC growth is positively correlated with concurrent one-year RDG, the second factor of return, which means that it tends to have a positive impact on real equity returns through this factor. But real GDPPC

---

5 While the strength of the negative relationship between both DY and rΔDY on the one hand, and real GDPPC growth on the other, is surprising in the MSCI global data, we can easily confirm that the price movement has taken place in the prior period. The relation between DY lagged one period and real GDPPC growth is significant and strongly negative, meaning that dividend yields fell as prices rose prior to positive future GDPPC growth, and conversely. Similarly the relationship between rΔDY and future real GDPPC growth is significant and strongly positive, again meaning that investors tend to drive prices higher prior to positive real GDPPC growth, and conversely. These results are shown in the following table, for a linear regression that expresses future real one-year GDPPC growth as a function of all three return components simultaneously, lagged by one year. Of course this is consistent as well with the result from Chapter 10, that real equity returns are strongly and positively linked with next year's real GDPPC growth: all three components below contribute to this.

One-Year Real GDPPC Growth as a Function of
DY, RDG, and rΔDY all Lagged by One Year
(MSCI Global Data 1970 to 2010)

	Regression Coefficient	T-statistic	Probability of being 0
Constant	2.259	11.820	<.001%
DY lagged one year	-0.175	-3.756	0.02%
RDG lagged one year	0.031	4.826	<.001%
rΔDY lagged one year	0.022	7.926	<.001%
Adjusted r-squared	15.02%		

growth is not positively correlated with either DY or rΔDY, the first and third components, and may indeed be negatively correlated with them. This means that these additional factors tend to have either a neutral or negative impact on real returns when real GDPPC is positive.

So this should be a cautionary lesson for investors. Let's suppose that you are correct in forecasting that, for example, emerging markets will exhibit very strong real GDPPC growth over the next year or two, and that consistent with the analysis here, this economic growth will indeed translate into robust real future dividend growth. However, strong real dividend growth will translate into higher real returns for your portfolio only if, at the point at which you make your investment, *the markets have not already reacted to the information that leads you to expect this future higher growth.* If markets have reacted, then higher prices, lower DY, and positive gains to rΔDY may have already occurred, and higher returns will not accrue to you despite your successful forecast of higher levels of real dividend growth. The forecasting approach I am developing in the following chapters will take this into account.

For the record, I also checked the correlation between real dividend growth and real GDPPC growth over the longest available time span in the MSCI data for the 18 countries. These data are reflected in Figure 11-1: most of the data span 40 years between 1970 and 2010, but six of the countries have dividends only for shorter periods, which are noted.

In this sample real GDPPC growth averaged 1.82%, real dividend growth averaged 1.38%, while real earnings growth (not pictured) was roughly half way between the two at 1.61%. However, the correlation between real GDPPC growth and real dividend growth is -0.347 (although not quite significant), and removing some of the obvious outliers of dividend growth only makes the correlation more negative.[6]

---

6 In their article "Economic Growth", p. 15 (DMS 2010), Dimson, Marsh and Staunton present similar results using data covering 1900 to 2009. They find a negative correlation of -0.30. Moreover in my dataset real earnings growth has a

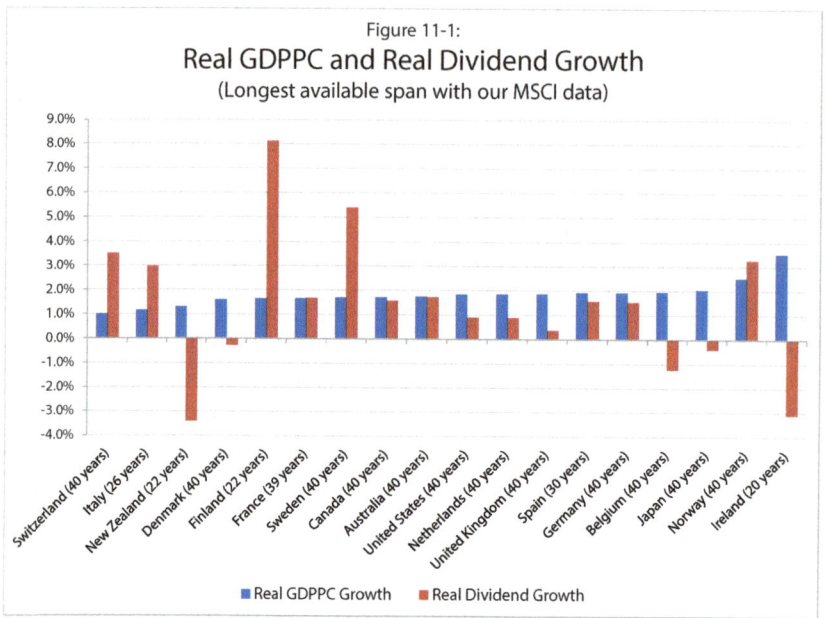

Figure 11-1:
Real GDPPC and Real Dividend Growth
(Longest available span with our MSCI data)

So while there is a link between the economy and real dividend growth over a one-year time span, there is no substantive evidence of a longer-term link. And for those who want to use economic growth as a signal for longer-term equity positioning, I find no evidence to support such an approach.

---

negative correlation with real GDPPC growth of -0.394, slightly worse than with dividend growth.

Chapter 12:

Does the Future Simply Repeat the Past?

How can you make the huge leap from examining history to formulating expectations about the future? As I mentioned in the introduction, many investors, including institutional pension consultants and retail investment advisors, like to skirt around the issue. One of the oldest tricks used for long-term asset allocation decisions is to take the longest history you have for each of your potential investments and project the average historical return forward as your expectation of the "long-run" future.

> **OVERVIEW**
>
> **Long-term historical cumulative returns have often been used as forecasts of future cumulative returns. Both conceptual and empirical difficulties with this approach are shown.**
>
> **Key findings:**
> - **long-term past returns provide no information about 10-year, 20-year or 30-year future returns.**

I find this approach to be troublesome both from a practical empirical standpoint and from a conceptual point of view. I will mostly look at the empirical side here, but let me begin with what I understand the conceptual view to be. I'm guessing there are several steps, beginning with the idea that measuring historical returns provides an estimate of the historical "risk premium" for holding equities. The risk premium is the return that investors *expect to receive* or *require* in order to justify the risk of holding equities,[1] and I have seldom seen or heard justification

---

1 Properly speaking, the risk premium is the expected return in excess of the risk-free rate, usually short-term government treasury bills. Since government

for linking what actually happened to what investors expected to happen. But here's a plausible argument. What actually happened, historical returns, are a function of the historical expected returns of investors *plus or minus random "surprises"*. If expected returns are unbiased, then the surprises should average 0%, and historical actual returns would be a good estimate of historical expected or required returns.

You need to make some kind of claim like this, linking past actual returns with past expected returns, otherwise the long-term historical return is just an arbitrary number, one of a myriad of possible outcomes, important because it actually happened but for no other reason. As just one of an infinite number of possible outcomes, what compelling reason is there to think that future returns should match the actual past? It has an additional special status only if you go on to say that actual past returns are an estimate of past expected returns. This seems to be what many people have believed, and what they have acted on.

As a practitioner who is not a financial economist, it is this first step that I find difficult. But given this premise, the rest is fairly easy. If you assume that investor preferences and risk tolerances haven't changed, then past expected returns (the returns required for holding equity risk) should equal future expected or required returns.

Here's my problem with the first premise. I endorse the idea that past actual returns can be understood as the sum of past expected returns plus surprises. I'll even accept the idea that the *expected* value of the average surprise is 0%. But without some hypothesis about the structure of expected returns, how much history is needed before it is reasonable to assume that the surprises have summed to 0%?

The DMS history in Chapter 5 showed that from 1900 to 2010 an Italian investor would have received real cumulative annualized

---

t-bills are assumed to be risk free, it is only the return in excess of bills that compensates for holding equity or other risks. Theoreticians prefer to discuss risk premia rather than total returns, and some kinds of analysis require this distinction. But for my purposes, it is much more straightforward to focus on total nominal or total real returns, and treating t-bills as an investable asset class.

Does the Future Simply Repeat the Past? 141

returns of 2.01%, while the Australian investor would have received 7.43%. The American investor, whose history we see most often in academic and commercial research, received a comfortable 6.45%. Did the Italian investor only *expect* a real return of 2.01%, while the Australian investor expected a return 5.42% higher? Probably not. Going forward does the Italian investor expect just 2.01%? Probably not. I'm certainly tempted to think that over the 111 years of history that have been examined, the Italian investor probably experienced all sorts of negative surprises, while the Australian investor probably experienced many positive surprises, but how can I say that without hypothesizing a structure to expected returns?

While I'm sure that financial economists would have an answer here, the facts I've pointed out make me wonder whether the relatively stable, positive and well-known US history, combined with the relative obscurity of other market histories, hasn't made the first premise a little more comfortable to accept than would otherwise have been the case.

Turning to the empirical or practical point of view, I hope that you have seen enough examples of long-term volatility to at least question this approach to forecasting. For example, Table 4-1 gave the standard deviation of the 30-year nominal US return sample at 2.3%. At various points in time investors faced a subsequent 30-year return of more than 2.3% below the mean return, which generates a huge shortfall in terms of cumulative wealth. While you can just shrug your shoulders and believe that such a potential divergence is simply part of the risk of forecasting, is this really a sound approach?

Figure 12-1 expresses my concern in pictorial form. Every point of the red line shows the annualized cumulative real return[2] for US

---

[2] I am going to continue to focus on real returns, first because achieving positive real returns is a primary investment goal, and second, because I don't want to entangle the issues by worrying about inflation. However, I want to be clear that our previous discussions of inflation should suggest that we can't ignore it just by saying we will focus on real returns. For example, we saw that in high inflation regimes (say higher than 15% or 20% a year), it was not clear that equities would produce positive real returns. In particular, real growth rates will almost certainly lag when inflation is high and economy stops functioning smoothly. To

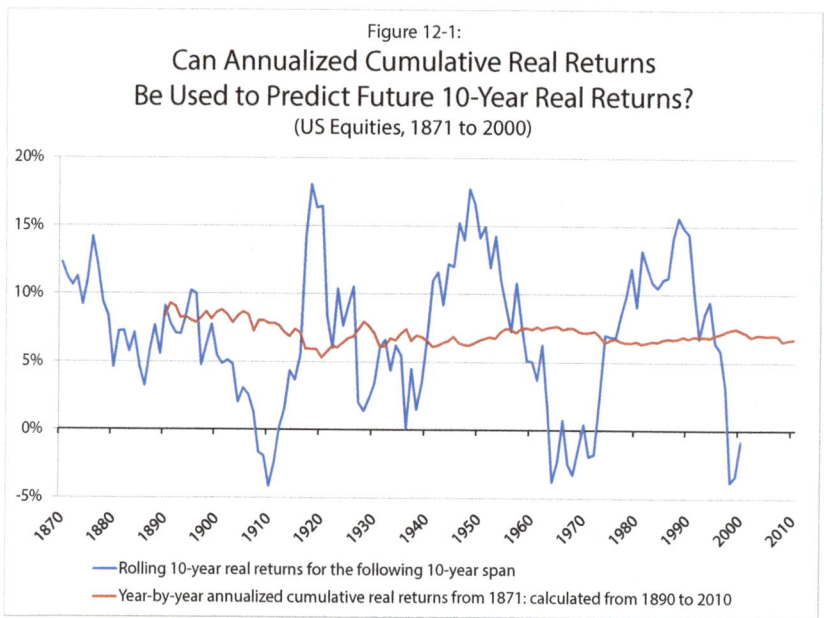

equities up to that time, as calculated from the US Shiller dataset. Remember the concept that I am exploring: can history, in this case cumulative annualized real returns, be used as a reasonable estimate of future long-term returns? The more volatile blue line depicts annualized ten-year real returns, but the line has been moved so that the ten-year return coinciding with a point on the red line is the subsequent ten-year return *from that point*.[3] That is, for any annualized cumulative real return point on the red line, the subsequent ten-year real return is the point on the blue line that is either directly above or directly below it.

It is immediately apparent that the red cumulative real return line is much more stable than the blue rolling ten-year real return line. Since 1915 the cumulative real return has ranged from 5.3%

---

the extent that we are willing to bet that the financial system will keep inflation under reasonable control, perhaps we can set this issue to one side. But it is a risk that needs to be noted and monitored. We will mention this issue again when we pull our forecasts from multiple asset classes together in Part 4.

3 You can see this because at the right-hand side the blue line stops ten years before the end, and in the beginning at the left, the first ten-year return is dated 1871, the beginning of the first subsequent ten-year period.

Does the Future Simply Repeat the Past?

to 7.9%, ending in 2010 at about 6.7% annualized. However, if you thought that cumulative returns were a useful forecast of subsequent ten-year returns you might want to think again. To give two examples using more recent data points, you can see that the forecast of 7.4% in 1998, based on the cumulative real return, vastly overstated the subsequent ten-year real return of -3.4%. Conversely, the forecast of 6.7% based on the cumulative real return to 1988 vastly understated the subsequent ten-year real return of 15.6%. Had you been more optimistic in 1988 you would have benefited from investing more heavily in equities, and had you been less optimistic in 1998 you might have benefited from investing less.

When I look at the picture and think about it for a moment, forecasts based on the cumulative real returns portrayed by the red line remind me of the broken clock that is "right" twice a day. That's one way of saying that cumulative historical returns explain very little, and are poor predictors of future ten-year returns.

Perhaps a ten-year investment horizon is too short to be considered "the long run". But it would still be useful for an investor to make better ten-year forecasts than the red line in Figure 12-1 suggests. Nevertheless, let's look at 20- and 30-year return spans. Figures 12-2 and 12-3 work just the same as Figure 12-1, and indeed the red line is identical. It looks more volatile in each subsequent figure because the vertical scale is more compressed. Figure 12-2 shows 20-year subsequent returns, with the last data point ending in 1990, and Figure 12-3 shows 30-year returns, with the last data point ending in 1980.

The story is very much the same in both the new examples: subsequent 20- and 30-year returns are usually very far from the cumulative return measured at the start of the period. I encourage you to inspect both graphs carefully, but I will just point out two more examples from Figure 12-3 and the 30-year subsequent returns. You can see that an investor in the early 1960s saw a cumulative historical real return of about 7.5%, but his subsequent 30-year return hovered around 5% or below, a huge shortfall of more than 2.5% annualized. Conversely, an investor in 1974 saw a historical cumulative real return of about 6.4%, but this vastly underestimated his subsequent 30-year return of 8.9%.

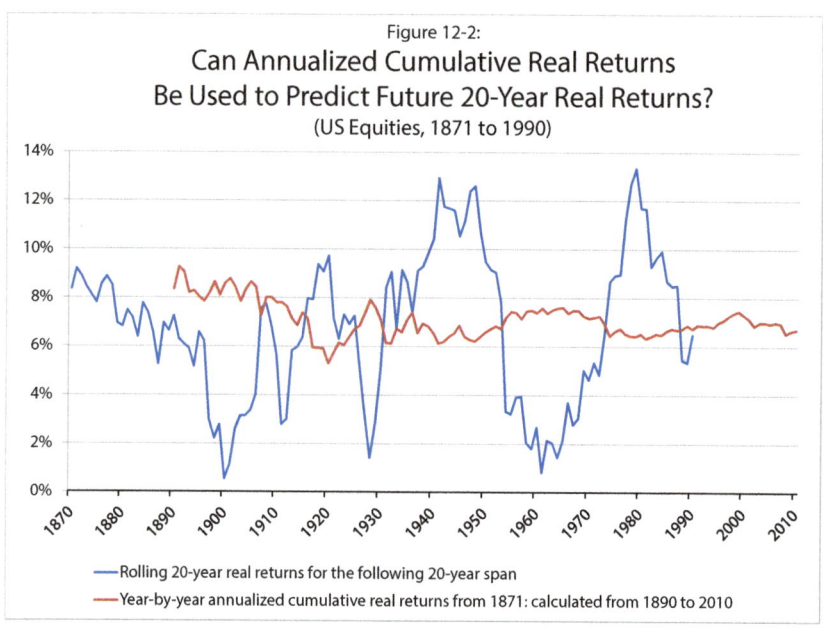

Figure 12-2:
Can Annualized Cumulative Real Returns Be Used to Predict Future 20-Year Real Returns?
(US Equities, 1871 to 1990)

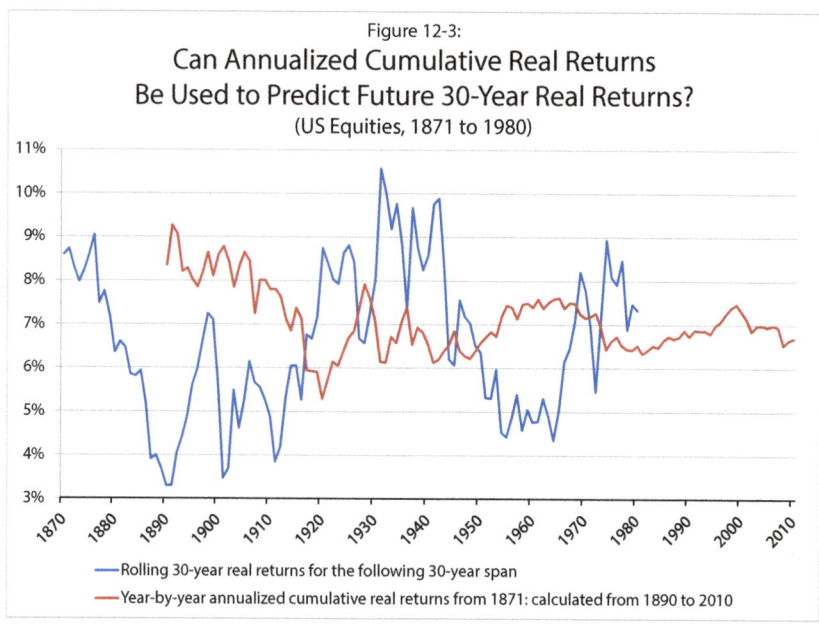

Figure 12-3:
Can Annualized Cumulative Real Returns Be Used to Predict Future 30-Year Real Returns?
(US Equities, 1871 to 1980)

Does the Future Simply Repeat the Past? 145

You can also look at these results statistically. Using non-overlapping future returns, the US data show a negative but insignificant relation between cumulative real returns and subsequent real 10-year, 20-year and 30-year returns.[4] The DMS data show a significant negative relationship for the 10-year data across 19 markets, and insignificant relations for 20- and 30-year data. If past cumulative real returns provided information about future 20- or 30-year returns, you would expect a positive relationship with statistical significance. These results confirm the visual impressions given by Figures 12-1 through 12-3 that cumulative historical returns, simply extrapolated forward, provide no information with respect to forecasting future long-run returns.

Of course someone might argue that even 30 years isn't "the long run" either, and I acknowledge that pension funds, foundations and some large pools of private capital may have multi-generational investment time frames. Even so, I don't think that the leap from *the longest cumulative average of the past* to *a forecast of the indeterminately long-term future* is very useful, and it is certainly hard to see how it could ever be justified by empirical methods, even if we could compile a great deal more data than we have now. Think back once again to the wide range of real long-term returns spanning 111 years from our global DMS data (Table 5-1). Specific circumstances led to real returns ranging from 2.01% at the low end (Italy) to 7.43% at the high end (Australia). Would investors of 100 years ago have any reason to think that Australia's prospects would be that much better than Italy's over the next century? Specific circumstances matter even for the "long run" of 100 or more years. And while investors with multi-generational horizons need estimates of long-run real returns to estimate the feasibility of meeting their long-term obligations, I am going to suggest that we can do at least a little better than that.

As of the end of 2010, US annualized real returns were 6.67% over 140 years (Table 1-1) and were 6.25% for the 111 years of

---

4 As in Chapter 6, I am making a compromise for spans of longer than ten years by calculating 20- and 30-year returns every decade. Thus 20-year spans overlap the previous and next span, and 30-year spans overlap two previous and two future spans.

the DMS dataset (Table 5-5), while the World index return was 5.48% over the same period. These are still very robust levels of return. Yet there is lots of anecdotal evidence that over the past decade, institutional investors have lowered allocations to public markets in general and equities in particular, substituting non-liquid assets ranging from direct ownership of real estate, regulated and unregulated infrastructure investments, private equities, and so on. If they actually thought that real returns of between 5.5% and 6.5% were available in global equities over the long run, would long-term allocations be changed? Perhaps the paradigm of using long-term equity returns as a best estimate of future long-run returns has begun to lose its grip on investors.

In the following chapters I am going to develop a simple approach to modeling expected returns, with results that differ widely from historical averages. Once it becomes clear how expected returns can be generated in a fairly consistent, objective manner, I hope that the attraction of using historical averages will wane.

Chapter 13:

Future Returns and the Components of Return

> **OVERVIEW**
>
> Just as our attribution model explains past returns, it will describe future returns as well. The idea of forecasting future returns by potentially forecasting each of the components of return is suggested.

Anyone who tries to make forecasts of financial markets would be wise to start from the premise that this is an extremely difficult enterprise. Not only did I show that long-term past real returns give very little information as to what we might expect over the next 10, 20 or 30 years, I reminded you that investors in "developed" markets have realized very different returns over the past 100 years and more. Yet to make a potentially long-term investment allocation decision you need to make a forecast to justify the risk that you embrace when you make investments. Is there a better approach?

Let me put the problem this way: in the face of market volatility I am looking for traces of information that I think of as threads that weave through that volatility. This information will never explain more than a tiny proportion of that volatility, but it may give me at least a small edge over a generic forecast based on past historical averages.

Where do I look for that edge? Past returns can be explained by looking to the dividend-based components of return: geometric average dividend yield, geometric average dividend growth, the return due to any change in dividend yield and for foreign investments the return due to the change in FX rates. The useful approximations developed in Chapters 7 and 9 were given as:

(9.5) $TR_g \approx DY_g + DG_g + r\Delta DY_g + rFX_g$

for nominal returns, and

(9.6) $RTR_g \approx DY_g + RDG_g + r\Delta DY_g + rRFX_g$

for real returns.

Obviously (9.5) and (9.6) will also explain future returns once they occur. But the more interesting point is that if I could estimate or forecast the components of the approximations, the elements on the right hand side, I would have a forecast of future returns. Perhaps I can gain that small edge I am looking for by forecasting some or all of the individual components of return.

To capture this idea I will restate (9.5) and (9.6) in terms of *expectations*: expected total return is approximately the sum of expected geometric average dividend yield, expected geometric average dividend growth, expected geometric return due to the change in dividend yield and expected geometric return due to the change in FX. In symbols:

(13.1) $E(TR_g) \approx E(DY_g) + E(DG_g) + E(r\Delta DY_g) + E(rFX_g)$

for nominal returns, and

(13.2) $E(RTR_g) \approx E(DY_g) + E(RDG_g) + E(r\Delta DY_g) + E(rRFX_g)$

for real returns. Of course using the precise form we have

(13.3) $1+E(TR_g) = (1+E(DY_g)) * (1+E(DG_g)) * (1+E(r\Delta DY_g)) *$
$(1+ E(rFX_g))$

and

(13.4) $1+E(RTR_g) = (1+E(DY_g)) * (1+E(RDG_g)) * (1+E(r\Delta DY_g)) *$
$(1+ E(rRFX_g))$

for expected nominal and real returns respectively.

While I would never suggest that the future will mirror the *average* of the past, I certainly believe that the future has to relate

Future Returns and the Components of Return

to the past in some way. At the very least, given enough history we can expect that *most of the time* future returns will lie within the bounds of past returns. For example, it is plausible that almost all future annual US equity returns will fall within the bounds set by the maximum and minimum annual returns shown in Figure 3-1. But in addition, I hope to find some kinds of relationships that have held in the past and that might reasonably be expected to continue to hold going forward.

Since I want to continue to focus on real returns, I will begin by comparing the historical return and volatility of each of the components on the right-hand side of (13.2), and comparing that to the volatility of real total returns on the left-hand side. Combining these data with some of the information already gleaned may help me begin the process of finding some of the "threads of information" I am looking for.

Table 13-1 presents arithmetic averages and standard deviations for non-overlapping samples of one-year, five-year and ten-year data for the US market (1871 to 2010). Since no other markets

Table 13-1:
Average Returns and Standard Deviations
Components of Return for US Data 1871-2010

	(1) Real Total Returns	(2) Average Dividend Yields	(3) Annualized Real Dividend Griowth Rate	(4) Annualized Return due to Change in Dividend Yield
One-Year Data				
Average	8.40%	4.48%	1.85%	3.16%
Standard Deviation	18.69%	1.70%	11.84%	22.44%
# of Observations	140	140	140	139
Five-Year Non-Overlapping Data				
Average	6.95%	4.48%	1.28%	1.26%
Standard Deviation	7.49%	1.46%	5.21%	7.54%
# of Observations	28	28	28	27
Ten-Year Non-Overlapping Data				
Average	6.85%	4.48%	1.20%	0.78%
Standard Deviation	6.12%	1.38%	3.37%	4.43%
# of Observations	14	14	14	13

are involved, there is no real return due to changes in the FX rate. Column 1, which shows the averages and standard deviations of real total returns for the three samples, is consistent with the earlier work on volatility. You can see that as time extends from one year to ten years, annualized volatility falls from 18.69% to 6.12%. Remember that this is not because equities are less risky as time extends, but rather this is an expected consequence of the intrinsic annual risk, as variance grows over time (see Chapter 4). Columns 2 through 4 show a similar drop in volatility for each of the components of return as the time span is increased.

In column 2 you can see that the standard deviation of the one-year dividend yield is 1.7%, which is less than one-tenth the volatility of one-year real returns of 18.69%. Look back at Figure 7-1 which shows the US dividend yield from 1871 to 2010. While it hit a year-end low of 1.12% in 2000, and spiked to a year-end high of 10.1% in both 1917 and 1931, almost all of the points lie between 2% and 6%, which is consistent with the standard deviation measure of 1.7%. By contrast, Figure 3-1 shows that one-year US equity returns ranged from a high of more than 50% to a low of less than -40%. For ten-year spans the standard deviation of dividend yields falls to just 1.38%.

I also observed that in Tables 7-2 and 7-3, dividend yield is a very large percentage of longer-term returns. Combine this with the additional fact that dividend yield has by far the lowest volatility of the components of return, and there is some hope that dividend yields can be exploited as I try to forecast longer-term returns.

Column 3 shows that the standard deviation of one-year real dividend growth is 11.84%, substantially higher than that of dividend yields, but still only about 60% of the variability of real total returns. Volatility drops by two-thirds for the ten-year sample, to just 3.37%. In Chapter 11, I showed that not only is real dividend growth linked contemporaneously with real economic growth through real per capita GDP, it is linked to the previous year's real per capita GDP growth as well. While there is no evidence of a longer-term relationship between real GDPPC and real dividend growth, it is at least possible that real dividend growth may be usefully forecast using some other approach.

Moreover I also suggested that real growth should be quite independent of short-term price movements in the equity market. That is, stock price movements and overall market movement should not directly affect either real economic growth or the real earnings and dividend growth of companies. So despite the fact that real dividend growth displays more volatility than dividend yield, we might be helped by the fact that dividend growth is largely unconnected with price volatility.

Finally, column 4 shows the variability of the third component, returns due to change in dividend yield. One-year volatility is 22.44%, noticeably higher than the volatility of total real returns. Volatility drops dramatically as the time span increases, and the volatility of the ten-year data is 80% lower at just 4.43%, which is also much lower than the variability of ten-year real total returns.

Return due to a change in dividend yield isolates the part of price movement driven solely by a change in valuation or market sentiment. This component contains most of the volatility that we see in markets day-to-day, month-to-month and even year-to-year. How it is treated will depend on one's views about valuation and changes in valuation. To summarize very briefly, if you are inclined to believe that at any point in time pricing is "fair", then changes in pricing or valuation are probably random and unpredictable. On the other hand if you think that at least some of the time equity markets are "cheap" (undervalued) or "expensive" (overvalued), then you might hope to be able to forecast this component of return. This is such an interesting component that I will show you several approaches to handling it.

In the following chapters I will examine each of these three components of return, along with a discussion of how one can handle foreign exchange, and present some simple but useful ideas about formulating expectations of return. None of the discussions will be about forecasting returns over the next few years, which in this context is the short term,[1] because in the short term, volatility swamps average return. The main focus will be on expectations for the longer term, which I will nominally assume is a ten-year time span, especially when I look to "test" relationships. Ten years is quite long relative to normal standards, but certainly not "the long term". I will also occasionally cross-check results over 20- and 30-year spans, although as you have seen these data are very limited.

In addition, you have seen the underlying volatility of each of the components of return, and I want to emphasize again that we are trying to discern threads of information that might be visible in the volatility. I am searching for an approach that is at least a little bit better than simply using historical long-term average returns as a predictor of long-term future returns. Each component that is forecast will have lots of error, and as a consequence so will the total forecast. In the end, each investor will have to judge whether this approach has enough information to make it useful enough to act on.

---

1 Of course for most market commentators, journalists and even many advisors, what I am calling the short term would be very long term indeed. These days most discussion is focused on weekly, daily, or even shorter spans, and while earnest commentators try to parse the "reasons" for market moves up and down hour by hour and day by day, in the end most of that movement is pure volatility or noise.

Chapter 14:

Expected Dividend Yield

The first component of our model of expected equity return is expected average dividend yield, symbolized as E(DY$_g$). How should we go about forming expectations for either the next specific period (say ten years) or over "the long term"? You might be surprised that a very good answer, and perhaps one of the very best answers, is by using today's dividend yield. Of course you may come up with other approaches to forecasting future average dividend yield, but I will show you that using the current dividend yield as an estimate of future average dividend yield has worked fairly well.

As usual, I begin by looking at some history. The blue line in Figure 14-1 plots current U.S. dividend yield for every year-end over time, exactly as in Figure 7-1. The red line is the future ten-year (arithmetic) average dividend yield that starts at each year-end — you can see that the last point on the red line is year-end 2000, as the final red point captures the final ten-year average from 2001 to 2010.

> **OVERVIEW**
>
> The first component of expected return is expected average dividend yield E(DY$_g$).
>
> Key findings:
> - current DY has been an excellent forecaster of future average DY;
> - current DY has also been useful as a direct forecaster of future long-term real returns, although we will not use it in this fashion;
> - any tendency for DY to revert to longer-term average DY will enhance its predictive power.

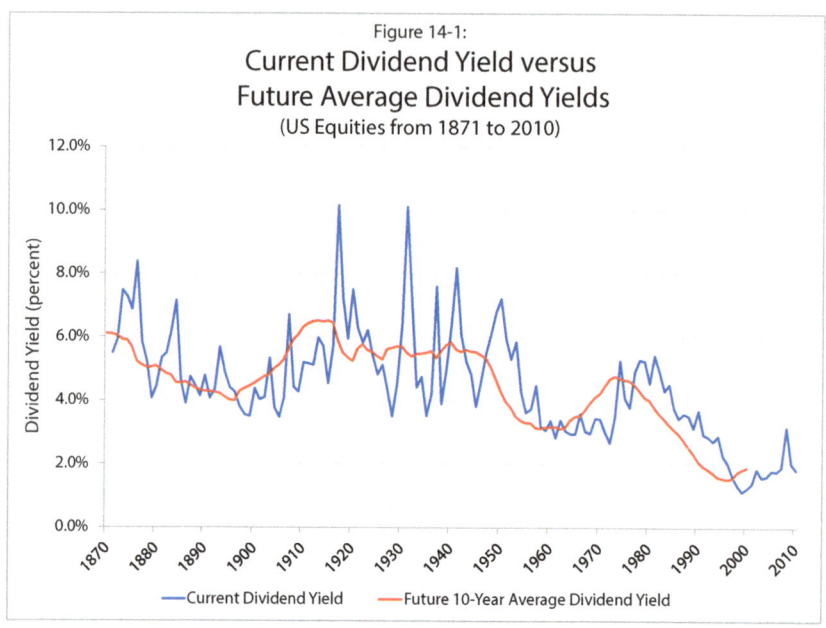

The blue line, representing individual yields, is clearly more volatile than the red line, which represents averages. At its peaks the blue line overstates the subsequent average dividend yield, captured by the red dot directly below it, while in valleys the blue line understates the subsequent average dividend yield, captured by the red dot directly above it. Yet the current dividend yield gives a reasonable estimate of future yields. You can measure this statistically: when non-overlapping future ten-year average dividend yields are tested as a function of the current yield, the relation is positive with a t-statistic of 3.47, meaning that the probability that the coefficient is 0 is just 0.5%. In addition, the adjusted r-squared was 47.9%, meaning that 47.9% of the variability in future ten-year average dividend yield was explained by current dividend yield.

This point is confirmed by the 18-country global MSCI dataset from 1970 to 2010. Figure 14-2 shows non-overlapping data for future ten-year average dividend yields as a function of current dividend yields across all countries. The regression coefficient is even more significant at the 0.1% level (so there is just a 0.1% probability that the coefficient is 0), and current dividend yield explains 34.7% of the variability of future ten-year average yields (adjusted r-squared).

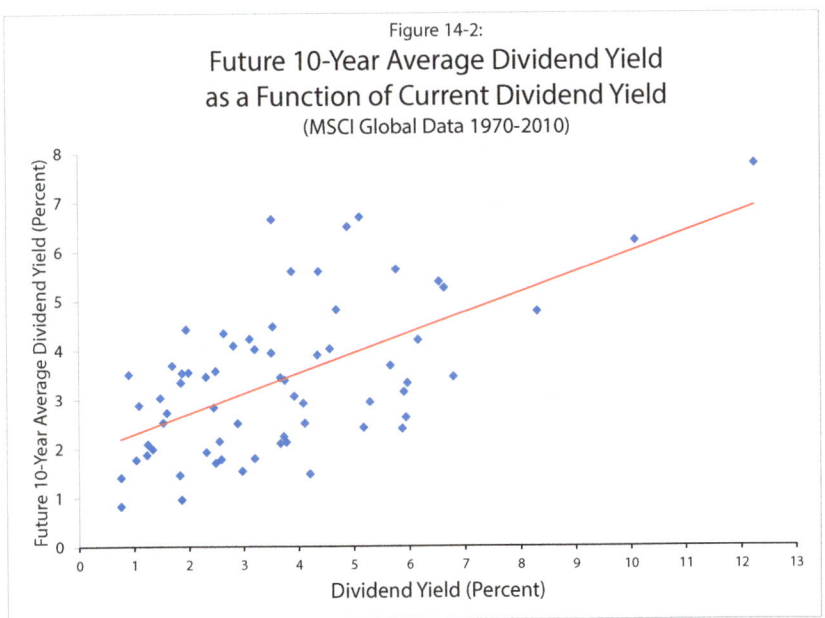

But current dividend yield is not only very good at explaining future average dividend yield, which is the first component of forecasting equation (13.1), it also has some ability to directly explain future real *returns*. I use the global MSCI dataset to plot future non-overlapping ten-year real returns as a function of current dividend yield in Figure 14-3. The regression coefficient is highly significant at the 0.2% level, and current dividend yield explains 12.9% of future real returns (adjusted r-squared).

I'm sure that many people will find it incredible that the simple current dividend yield can be a useful forecaster of future returns. This incredulity will be highest for those who observe and trade the equity markets on a daily basis, and deal with short-term volatility that is an order of magnitude higher than current yields. But remember that I am not talking about forecasts spanning days, weeks, months or even a few years. For example, I happen to be writing this on Wednesday August 10, 2011, on which the S&P500 fell 4.4%, preceded by a gain of 4.7% on Tuesday and a decline of 6.66% on Monday. However, this daily volatility will be at most a dim memory by the time you are reading this, and generally such volatility in the short term has very little impact when we look ten years or more to the future.

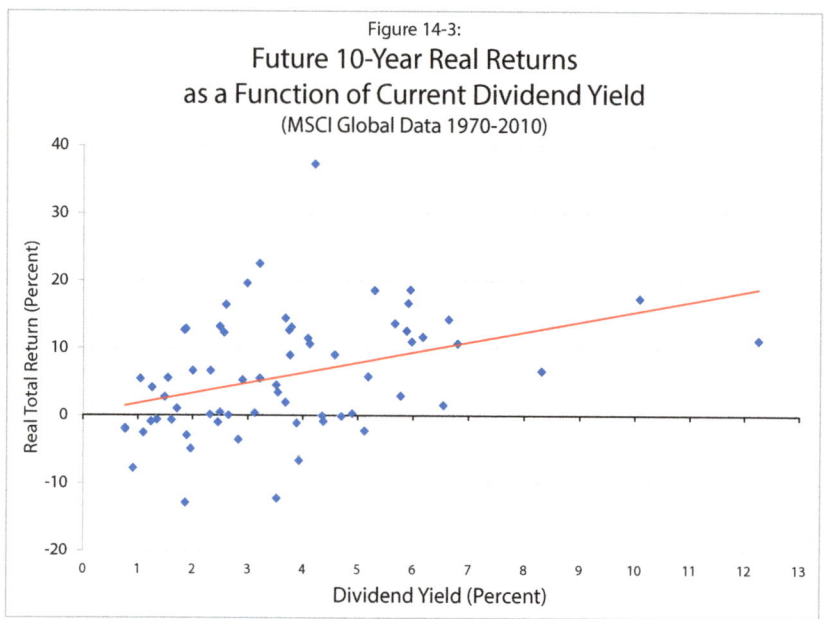

Moreover as the investment time frame extends, the forecasting results from dividend yields look even better. Figure 14-4 shows current US dividend yields as they relate to future 10-, 20- and 30-year returns. I'm not going to give you summary statistics because the returns shown on the graph are overlapping, but the chart is very suggestive. You can see that as the time span increases, the total future returns get closer to the level of starting dividend yields: the mauve line representing future 30-year returns closely tracks both the movement and the general level of current dividend yield. As an aside, look at the right-hand side of the chart and take a moment to think about the possible implications of the current dividend yield on future returns.

In support of these empirical results, I want to show you a reason why, when yields are low, future returns will be low *even if yields rise in the future* and return closer to their historical levels. Conversely, when yields are high, returns will tend to be high *even if yields fall in the future* and return closer to their historical levels. The reasoning is a little bit complicated, but it has to do with the interaction between two of the three components of return.

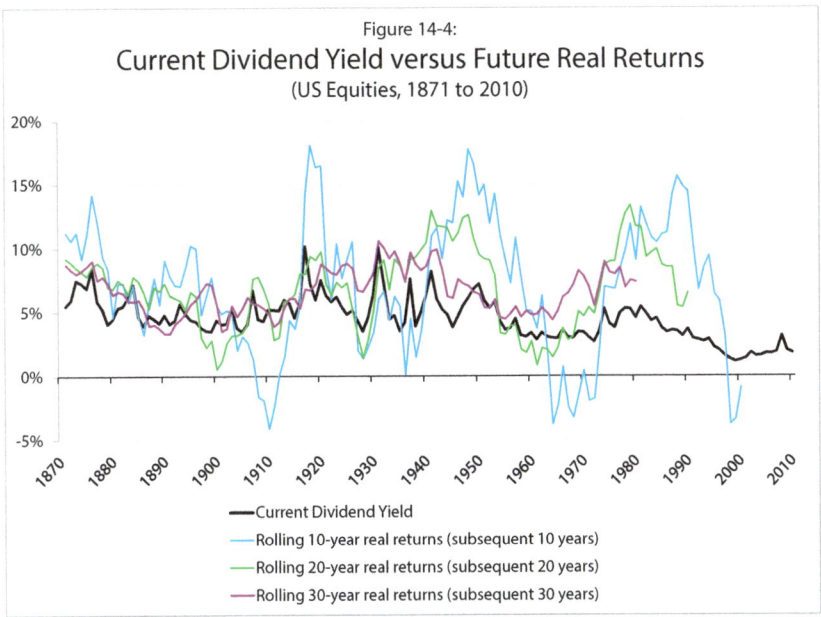

Figure 14-4:
Current Dividend Yield versus Future Real Returns
(US Equities, 1871 to 2010)

I have already argued that real dividend growth (RDG) will be independent of either dividend yield (DY) or return due to a change in dividend yield (rΔDY). While the latter two components are a direct function of current prices and are unconnected with real economic growth,[1] RDG is related to growth in the real economy rather than to changes in current prices, and so I will set RDG aside for now. But DY and rΔDY are clearly linked. If dividend yield doesn't change over any investment period, then rΔDY is 0%. However, if dividend yield rises over an investment period then rΔDY will be negative, since the price per unit of dividend income is falling. Conversely, if dividend yield falls over an investment period then rΔDY will be positive, since the price per unit of dividend income is rising.

So here is my point. Suppose that dividend yield is low relative to history, say 2% or lower as it has been for some time in the US market. Then if the yield doesn't change over my investment period, the 2% current yield will be a very good forecast of the DY component of future returns, as well as of total return itself. But what if

---

[1] In Table 10-3 we saw that DY and rΔDY were actually negatively correlated with real economic growth

dividend yields rise in the future, and move up closer to historical average yields, won't the 2% current yield understate returns because average yields will generate higher returns? The answer is *no* in many cases and over most time frames, because while it is true that average yields will rise, the negative impact of rising yields on return, captured by the return due to change in dividend yield (rΔDY), is so large that it overwhelms the gains due to higher yields. The converse argument will hold for starting dividend yields that are substantially higher than average.

I can put numbers to this very easily. For the sake of argument let's say that US dividend yields are now 2% (July 31, 2011). Using my forecasting approach this means that over the next period, say ten years or perhaps more, I can expect to receive 2% annually from dividend yields. But suppose 2% understates what will actually transpire, and over the forecast period, yields turn out to average 3%. That is, on average I receive 3% per year from dividend yield, which is an improvement of 1% per year over the starting yield. Let's also assume, conservatively, that at the end of the period the yield will be at 3%.[2] This means that while I pay $50.00 for each $1.00 of dividends at the start of the investment (a 2% yield), by the end of my holding period I would receive $33.33 for each $1.00 of dividends (a 3% yield). This is a gross loss of -33.33% per dollar of dividends due to revaluation.[3] So while by hypothesis I receive 3% from the average yield, I will lose money on the revaluation of dividends.

For example, if my forecast period is ten years, the -33.33% loss due to revaluation would amount to an average of -3.97% per year, so my return would be 3% from average DY and -3.97% from rΔDY, for a total return of -1.09%[4] ignoring dividend growth. This is summarized in the first row of Table 14-1 below, with the geometric sum of DY and rΔDY in column 7.

---

2 You might expect that the ending yield will be even higher, to account for an average yield of 3% over the period. We'll consider that in a moment.

3 That is, ($33.33/$50.00)-1= -33.33%.

4 That is, (1+3%)*(1–3.97%)–1= –1.09%

Expected Dividend Yield

Table 14-1:
The Interaction of DY and rΔDY
over Various Time Frames: Rising Yields

(1) Starting DY	(2) Average DY	(3) Ending DY	(4) Span in Years	(5) Gross rΔDY	(6) Annualized rΔDY	(7) Return before RDG	(8) Annualized RDG *	(9) Real Total Return
Stylized examples: rising yields with only the time span changing								
2%	3%	3%	10	-33.3%	-3.97%	-1.09%	1.00%	-0.10%
2%	3%	3%	20	-33.3%	-2.01%	0.93%	1.00%	1.94%
2%	3%	3%	30	-33.3%	-1.34%	1.62%	1.00%	2.63%
2%	3%	3%	40	-33.3%	-1.01%	1.96%	1.00%	2.98%

* 1% RDG assumed for stylized examples

The second through fourth rows of Table 14-1 mirror the first: the starting yield is 2% in column 1, the average and ending yields are 3% in column 2 and 3. The only difference is a change in the investment holding period shown in column 4, which stretches from ten years in the first case to 40 years in the fourth case. In all four examples the unannualized or gross rΔDY is -33.3% as noted in column 5, with the annualized return to rΔDY given in column 6. Column 7 shows the geometric sum of the average yield and the rΔDY. For completeness, column 8 adds in a value of 1% for real dividend growth (RDG), while column 9 gives the total real forecast return.[5]

You can see that as the time span lengthens, the annualized rΔDY becomes less negative as the gross rΔDY is "amortized" over a longer period. So over the 40-year investment period, the rΔDY has risen to -1.01% per year, roughly balancing the rise of 1% return due to the higher average dividend yield. So in this simple case, for periods of less than 40 years the hypothesized increase in yield adds less than the impact of the negative rΔDY.

Had the final dividend yield in column 3 been made higher than the average dividend yield, the impact of rΔDY would have been even more negative. So to summarize, when DY is much lower than

---

5 Columns (7) and (8) are added "geometrically", using (13.4) or (7.6) rather than the arithmetic approximations (13.2) or (7.8).

average, any tendency to move back towards its historical mean will actually hurt prospective returns more than the benefits of increasing dividend yields over the investment period.

Now I can make the converse argument more succinctly. If dividends are relatively high at the start of an investment period, you can easily see that even if dividends were to fall during the investment period, it is likely that the positive impact of rΔDY due to falling yields will outweigh any negative impact of future lower yields. I will start with an actual example in the first row of Table 14-2.

Table 14-2:
The Interaction of DY and rΔDY
over Various Time Frames: Falling Yields

(1) Starting DY	(2) Average DY	(3) Ending DY	(4) Span in Years	(5) Gross rΔDY	(6) Annualized rΔDY	(7) Return before RDG	(8) Annualized RDG *	(9) Real Total Return
Actual example: year-end 1980 to 2000 including actual DG of 1.36%								
4.54%	3.05%	1.23%	20	268.2%	6.73%	9.99%	1.36%	11.48%
Stylized examples: falling yields with only the time span changing								
4%	3%	2%	10	100.0%	7.18%	10.39%	1.00%	11.50%
4%	3%	2%	20	100.0%	3.53%	6.63%	1.00%	7.70%
4%	3%	2%	30	100.0%	2.34%	5.41%	1.00%	6.46%
4%	3%	2%	40	100.0%	1.75%	4.80%	1.00%	5.85%

* 1% RDG assumed for stylized examples

At the end of 1980 the dividend yield of the S&P500 was 4.54%, so my simple forecast from current yields would peg subsequent return, before dividend growth and the return due to a change in valuation, at about 4.5%. In fact over the next 20 years the average dividend yield was 3.048%, and the ending yield in the year 2000 was dramatically lower at 1.232%. So while an investor received much less than 4.5% from dividend yield alone — the average dividend yield of roughly 3% — he gained from the huge revaluation of dividends. That is, in 1980 an investor paid just $22.04 for $1.00 of dividends, but in 2000 he would have received $81.15 for each $1.00 of dividends, a rise of 268.2% unannualized, or 6.73% annually for the 20-year buy-and-hold investor. Adding in the actual real dividend growth for the period of 1.36%, the total return is calculated at 11.48% annualized. This is very close to the actual real total return of 11.69%, the main difference being due to an understatement of the actual geometric average dividend yield in Table 14-2.[6]

The bottom section of Table 14-2 shows a case of falling dividends, and just as in Table 14-1, the effect of a changing holding period is examined. I've varied the example a little by making the ending yield lower than the average yield over the investment period. You see that even at 40 years the starting yield of 4% understates the return of 4.8% before real dividend growth is added in.

In sum, if there is any tendency for high dividends to fall towards the historical average dividend yield, and if there is any tendency for low dividend yields to rise towards historical average levels, then the impact of the implied rΔDY will reinforce the idea that higher dividend yields will tend to be followed by higher returns, and lower dividend yields will be followed by lower returns. And of course if yields remain the same, then the current dividend is an excellent forecast of returns.

I want to be very clear here that I am not using dividend yield as a *valuation measure*, and certainly the forecasting model of return does not imply this. That is, I am not saying that when DY is high or higher than average, stocks are "cheap", or when it is low or lower than average, they are "expensive". Rather I am using current DY as a proxy for (or forecast of) future average dividend yield, which is the first component of the forecasting model. The forecasting model says that expected returns are higher when expected average dividend yields are higher, not because equities are cheap per se, but *because a higher average dividend flow is expected*. Conversely the forecasting model says that expected returns are lower when expected average dividend yields are lower, not because equities are expensive, per se, but *because a lower average dividend flow is expected*.

---

[6] The calculation of actual average DY is the arithmetic average of the 20 subsequent year-end yields, not the true geometric average of the dividend yields of the monthly data used to calculate the index.

This model can work for an investor who is completely agnostic about market valuation, or for someone who believes that markets are always fairly priced. I will return to the idea of market valuation when I discuss the third component of expected return.

Table 14-3 presents dividend yields for December 31, 2010, as well as dividend yields and subsequent ten-year average dividend yields at the beginning of each of the previous four decades. I have included Canadian equities, along with US equities, the MSCI EAFE equity index and the MSCI Emerging Markets equity index. MSCI EAFE is currently composed of 22 developed markets from Europe, Asia and the Far East (excluding Canada and the United States), while the MSCI Emerging Markets Index is currently composed of 21 markets, of which China and India are the largest.

Table 14-3:
Selected Dividend Yields
From Selected Markets and Indexes

As of Year-End	Canada		United States		MSCI EAFE		MSCI Emerging Markets	
	Current DY	Subsequent Avg.10-yr DY	Current DY	Subsequent Avg.10-yr DY	Current DY	Subsequent Avg.10-yr DY	Current DY	Subsequent Avg.10-yr DY
1970	3.50%	3.94%	3.41%	4.22%	4.30%	4.02%		
1980	3.67%	3.44%	4.54%	4.01%	4.26%	2.31%		
1990	3.73%	2.24%	3.66%	2.09%	2.27%	1.79%	3.71%	1.88%
2000	1.25%	2.09%	1.23%	1.87%	1.56%	2.85%	2.14%	2.52%
2010	2.29%	?	1.79%	?	2.96%	?	2.08%	?

I will refer back to these yields as we progress in the following chapters. The year-end yield at the beginning of each decade can be viewed as my forecast for average dividend yield over the following decade. I have highlighted in yellow the cases where the subsequent ten-year average yield has diverged by more than 1%. As of December 2010, starting yields for the coming ten years are low, but not as low as those at the beginning of the previous decade for all except the Emerging Markets index.

Chapter 15:

Expected Real Dividend Growth

The second component of our model of expected equity return is *expected real dividend growth*, which I have symbolized as $E(RDG_g)$. The historical analysis of the US market suggested that real dividend growth was the second most important component of real return after dividend yield, with an arithmetic average ten-year growth rate of 1.2%[1] and a geometric average growth rate of 1.15%.[2] However real dividend growth can vary considerably, depending on the market and the time span.

> **OVERVIEW**
>
> While long-term dividend growth is difficult to forecast, I outline a simple framework that links long-term dividend growth with long-term real GDPPC.
>
> The framework provides a mechanism for adjusting expectations relative to GDPPC forecasts and the cyclical nature of dividend growth.

The DMS data showed[3] that over the long term from 1900 to 2010, real dividend growth ranged from a low of -2.39% annualized for Japan to a high of 1.77% annualized for Sweden. The average real dividend growth rate across all 19 markets was negative, at -0.11%, with 8 cases of positive real growth and ten cases of negative real growth, and so real dividend growth actually detracted from real equity returns. For the capitalization-weighted World index in USD, real dividend growth was positive at 0.83%, due to the very large

---

1 Table 13-1.
2 Figure 7-2.
3 Table 7-3.

weight of the United States. Even for the long term the range of experience is wide.

Finding a satisfying approach to forecasting real dividend growth is difficult. While I showed you a link between short-term real GDP per capita growth and real dividend growth in Chapter 11, I did not find any link between longer-term GDPPC and real dividend growth. This does not mean that there are no *other* relationships that might help us forecast real dividend growth over the longer term. But while I have found interesting relationships within particular markets such as the US, I have not been able to usefully extrapolate these ideas across a broader spectrum of markets, at least with these limited datasets.

So how can we forecast longer-term real dividend growth here? A fall-back approach is to use long-term past dividend growth as the best estimate for future dividend growth. Unfortunately, this kind of forecast estimate is open to some of the same kinds of objections that I raised against using past long-term real return history as your best estimate of future expected real returns.

You can observe this informally in Figure 15-1. The black line shows cumulative annualized real dividend growth from 1871 to 2010, with the first cumulative data point in 1890 after the first 20 years. The other lines show RDG over 10-year, 20-year and 30-year spans, adjusted so that each point above or below the black line denotes the RDG for the future time span starting at that point. Higher levels on the black cumulative RDG line seem to line up with lower levels on the other lines, and conversely, meaning that cumulative RDG is a poor forecaster of future RDG.

The one counter-point might be that over the past 60 years since 1950, the future RDG seems to be closer to the cumulative RDG than in earlier times. This is because the volatility of RDG has fallen, and whether or not RDG continues to be less volatile going forward is at least open to debate.

This assumption of lower RDG volatility probably makes the most sense either for a very large and diversified market such as the United States, or for a large and diversified global index such as the

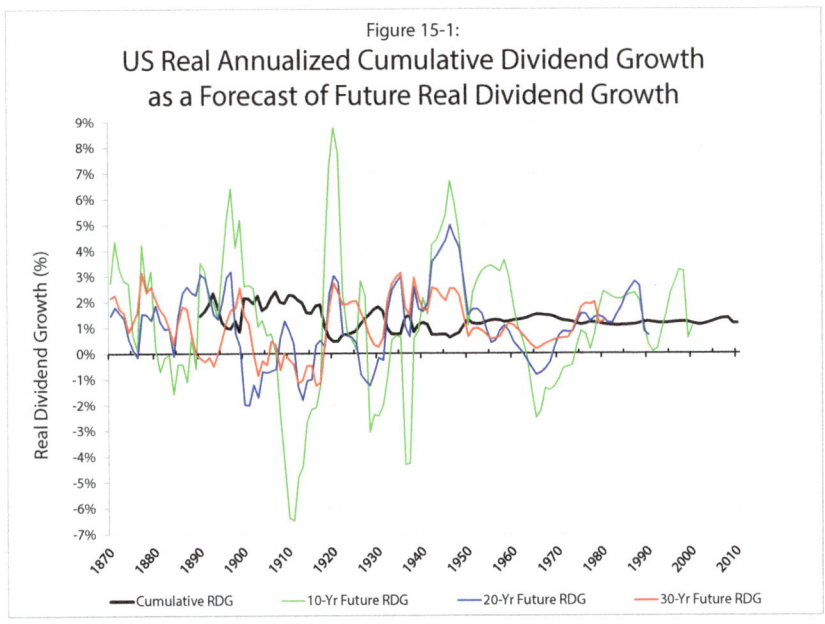

DMS World Index or MSCI EAFE in USD. If I assume that lower volatility will continue, and extrapolate future RDG from the past cumulative level, this would place expected US RDG at just over 1%, and World RDG in US dollars at just under 1%. But when you narrow your focus either to individual markets or across shorter time spans the obvious volatility of real dividend growth becomes more problematic. Providing better estimates of RDG is certainly one of the areas where economists and professional money managers can try to add value.

In the absence of those professional resources, I want to develop a simple framework that both defaults to a forecast of historical cumulative average dividend growth, but allows for, and perhaps encourages, an ongoing questioning of that position. Despite the fact that I have not uncovered a powerful statistical relationship between longer-term RDG and GDPPC, I want to tie the two concepts together. Following the approach taken by Arnott and Bernstein,[4] I will lay out some parameters or guidelines for formulating expectations for long-term dividend growth.

---

4 Arnott and Bernstein, 2002: pp. 70-72.

Arnott and Bernstein make the salient starting observation that over the very long term we should not expect real dividend growth to outpace real GDPPC growth. Remember that real GDPPC captures the productivity growth of an economy. In a broadly diversified economy the real dividend growth of businesses as a whole (adjusted for changes in the payout ratio) cannot grow faster over the long term than increases in productivity, without hidden return of capital to investors. For example, over the 140-year history of our US database, real GDPPC grew by 1.96% annualized, real earnings grew by 1.73% annually, and real dividends grew by 1.15% annually. Real dividend growth fell short of real GDPPC growth by 0.81% annually, obtaining just 57.8% of real GDPPC growth.

Arnott and Bernstein argue that not only should real GDPPC be the upper bound of RDG, *you should expect RDG to fall short of real GDPPC growth,* as in the US case. They suggest several interesting reasons for this, all of which also support the original idea that real GDPPC is a natural upper bound for real dividend growth over the long term. One key point is that in a growing economy, a significant part of growth comes from the creation of new enterprises. By definition, this aspect of growth is not captured by an existing market portfolio. For an existing investment portfolio to gain exposure to this growth, it must wait until companies are mature enough to sell shares to the public, and then some existing holdings must be sold to generate cash for the new investments. In this model, market portfolios will lag the broader growing economy, and in particular their dividend growth will not reflect the increased productivity growth of private companies.

A second idea revolves around what Arnott and Bernstein call "pirate capitalism": in poorly regulated markets majority shareholders issue shares to themselves in good times, diluting dividend growth to existing outsiders. The issuance of underpriced share options to insiders during the recent tech bubble can be viewed as a modern version of this.[5]

---

5 As does any corporate action that generates huge fees to insiders and service providers. In my view the real scandal of the income trust debacle in Canada was not its ignominious ending at the hands of the government in search of

Expected Real Dividend Growth

A third element might be termed "corporate hubris". Managers like to retain earnings to grow their empires, but often fail to generate returns commensurate with those available outside the corporation, and so earnings and dividend growth may fall short of real GDPPC growth. A study by Arnott and Asness[6] shows that when the US market has a lower payout ratio and a higher level of retained earnings, subsequent ten-year earnings growth has been lower; and conversely if the payout ratio is higher, subsequent earnings growth has been higher. This is the reverse of what you might expect if management could make good use of retained earnings. Many readers will be aware of large companies in their home markets that have a reputation for repeatedly squandering retained earnings on bad investments.

This shortfall is confirmed by other long-term data sources. Dimson, Marsh and Staunton present a chart[7] showing that over the period 1900 to 2009, only Sweden, out of their universe of 19 markets, had real dividend growth that slightly outpaced real GDPPC growth. Moreover while real GDPPC growth was positive, apparently averaging close to 2%,[8] the average real dividend growth across all markets in the dataset was -0.11%, as shown in Table 7-3.

In addition, Table 15-1 shows real GDPPC, real dividend and real earnings growth for the 18 developed markets from our MSCI database for the period 1970 to 2010.[9] This was a buoyant period for real GDPPC growth in the developed world, with average growth of

---

tax revenues. Rather it was the rapacious money grab by insiders, the golden handshakes, fees, old options redeemed and new options generated by the legal "change of control" during the transition from corporation to income trust, where the same insiders ended up running the new entity.

6 Arnott and Asness, 2003 use market data. I have confirmed similar results with individual stock-level data in the Canadian market.

7 DMS 2010, p. 15.

8 An estimate from visual inspection of the chart, since a number for the average real GDPPC is not reported.

9 While most of the dividend and earnings data span this 41-year period, GDPPC data are less extensive. So for each country the data are constrained by the span of the GDPPC data, and the length of each data series is shown in parentheses after each country name.

Table 15-1:
Real GDPPC, Dividend and Earnings Growth
(MSCI Data 1970-2010, or sub-periods)

	Real GDPPC Growth	Real Dividend Growth	Real Earnings Growth
Switzerland (40 years)	0.99%	3.49%	2.23%
Italy (26 years)	1.15%	2.95%	4.29%
New Zealand (22 years)	1.30%	-3.41%	-6.09%
Denmark (40 years)	1.59%	-0.29%	2.15%
Finland (22 years)	1.63%	8.11%	5.20%
France (39 years)	1.65%	1.66%	1.89%
Sweden (40 years)	1.69%	5.38%	6.08%
Canada (40 years)	1.71%	1.56%	2.32%
Australia (40 years)	1.74%	1.72%	1.16%
United States (40 years)	1.83%	0.89%	2.55%
Netherlands (40 years)	1.84%	0.87%	1.15%
United Kingdom (40 years)	1.87%	0.37%	0.48%
Spain (30 years)	1.91%	1.56%	5.51%
Germany (40 years)	1.92%	1.52%	2.35%
Belgium (40 years)	1.93%	-1.23%	0.73%
Japan (40 years)	2.04%	-0.41%	0.18%
Norway (40 years)	2.51%	3.26%	2.77%
Ireland (20 years)	3.52%	-3.10%	-5.97%
Average	1.82%	1.38%	1.61%
Standard Deviation	0.53%	2.68%	3.17%

1.82% and 12 of 18 countries growing between 1.5% and 2% and a low standard deviation of just 0.53%. But you can see that average real dividend growth and real earnings growth were both lower at 1.38% and 1.61% respectively, although with five to six times more variability. This means that real dividend growth fell short of real GDPPC growth by 0.44% annually.

The previous points argue to the conclusion that real earnings and dividends can be expected to grow more slowly over the long term than the real economy. But we might find the opposite result in specific cases, especially in small countries with small and less diversified equity markets, as well as for shorter time frames in any market. For example, the time frames in Table 15-1 are short enough that for six of the eighteen markets, dividends grew faster than real GDPPC. Moreover in some cases one or two large companies, perhaps with global sales tied to international economies, may dominate a small country stock market: an oil company in Norway, a phone company in Finland, a bank in Iceland, and so on. In such an environment, real dividend growth for the local market may outstrip local real economic growth for extended periods, although in bad circumstances the reverse can happen. This is another way of saying that real dividend growth is likely to be more volatile than real GDPPC growth.

Taking into account all of these considerations, my working approach to making an estimate of real long-term dividend growth for a market (or market index) is to treat RDG as a function of real GDPPC growth, roughly along the lines of Arnott and Bernstein.[10] The essence of the approach is very simple, although executing it well may be much more difficult than a first glance would suggest. Given the discussion of real GDPPC as a long-term upper bound to real dividend growth, a simple model to forecast real dividend growth over a period is (1) forecast real GDPPC growth, and (2) forecast a dividend shortfall factor and subtract it from (1).

By way of example, Figure 15-2 summarizes the historical numbers for the US market over the 140 years from the beginning of 1871 to 2010, some of which have been mentioned in the text. Real GDPPC growth was 1.96% endpoint to endpoint, while real dividend growth was 1.15%, for a shortfall of 0.81% relative to real GDPPC. The trend growth numbers (represented by the fitted straight lines) were 1.98% and 1.06% respectively, for a shortfall of 0.92%. Rounding to one decimal, this gives 2% long-term real GDPPC growth, a real dividend shortfall factor of 0.9%, and real dividend growth of 1.1%.

Obviously if you forecast real GDPPC growth of 2% mirroring the long-term historical average over the database period, and assume a shortfall of 0.90%, you will just be forecasting future real dividend growth equal to the long-term historical dividend growth number, which I have suggested as a default forecast. This "model" only gives you new information content if one or both of the two inputs varies

---

10 Arnott and Bernstein, 2002: pp. 71-73.

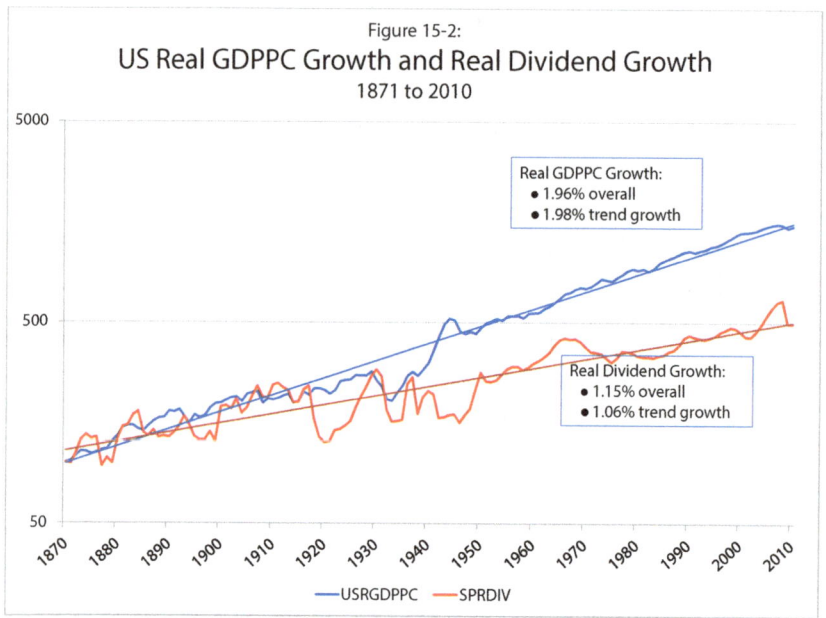

from history: your forecast of real GDPPC growth, or your forecast of the dividend shortfall factor. To put it another way, this simple model provides a mechanism for thinking about why real dividend growth may differ from the long-term average.

I suspect most people will focus on the first step, the forecast of real GDPPC, which I actually think is very difficult. The very long-term investor might want to adjust historical average growth rates if, for example, he believed that over the longer term, real productivity gains would shift from the currently developed markets to the emerging markets. Or he might be concerned about current conditions, such as recent weak or strong economic growth, that might influence future performance, say over the following ten years.[11]

---

[11] But this is tricky. From the perspective of the end of summer 2011, with indications that at least the US and Europe could be heading back into recession, would you want to forecast lower-than-average real GDPPC growth over the next 10 years because of these lowered growth prospects? But by early 2012 the US was reporting some positive economic indicators, that suggest to some that there will be a fairly rapid return to more normal growth.

I've actually found that when working with ten-year horizons rather than the longer term, there may be some benefit to working with the second step, the dividend shortfall factor. So even if you decide that you don't have reason to depart from long-term real GDPPC growth trends, when you acknowledge that dividend growth over spans such as ten years have been volatile at times, you can account for recent growth experience by adjusting the shortfall factor. For example, after a ten-year period of weak real dividend growth you might lower the shortfall factor (making it less positive or perhaps even 0 or negative), to reflect a forecast of higher real dividend growth over the next ten years, while maintaining long-term real GDPPC at its current level.

This simple model works best for very diversified individual markets such as the US, and for diversified multi-market indexes such as the MSCI EAFE and MSCI Emerging Markets indexes. Even very long-term history is more problematic if you want to forecast growth for a market such as Japan or Germany that has had historical discontinuities such as hyperinflation (Germany) and disruptive wars (both countries). If you believe those disruptions are not going to be repeated, then you will almost certainly believe that the whole historical record is not relevant, which means that choices must be made. For example, you might decide that for Japan, Germany, and the rest of Europe, a better indicator of future prospects would be to look at cumulative real GDPPC growth from 1950 on, rather than their full history. So even the idea of basing your forecast on history requires an informed decision on exactly *which* history is relevant.

I want to be clear that I am not recommending a specific formulaic approach to estimating future dividend growth. Rather I am outlining a framework that could be adapted and used, but that needs to be modified depending on what exactly your purpose is. A good forecasting approach should foster questions, insights and alternatives. So while you could do worse than starting with the idea that dividend growth will continue at its historical pace, the technique of using a GDPPC growth forecast for your investment horizon, adjusted for the dividend shortfall relative to real GDPPC growth, gives you a little more flexibility.

I ended Chapter 14 with some information on dividend yields for Canada, the US, EAFE and Emerging Markets, to summarize the historical perspective and provide current yields that can be used for forecasting dividend yield. Table 15-2 provides similar information for real local dividend growth along with real local GDPPC. I estimated EAFE and EM GDPPC data by aggregating data across the countries included in the respective indexes.[12] Data for the US, Canada and EAFE cover the 40-year span back to 1970, while the Emerging Markets data is much shorter, spanning 22 years, since the index only dates back to December 1988. I also added data for the two ten-year spans ending December of 2000 and 2010.

Table 15-2:
Real Local Dividend Growth and GDPPC
Over Various Time Spans

	(1) Real DG (local)	(2) Real GDPPC (local)	(3) DG Shortfall (local)
40 Years: Dec. 1970-Dec. 2010			
Canada	1.56%	2.06%	0.50%
US	0.89%	1.83%	0.94%
MSCI EAFE	-0.03%	1.29%	1.31%
MSCI EM			
22 Years: Dec. 1988-Dec. 2010			
Canada	3.34%	1.19%	-2.15%
US	1.05%	1.40%	0.36%
MSCI EAFE	2.63%	1.40%	-1.23%
MSCI EM	-17.04%	4.37%	21.41%
10 Years: Dec. 1990-Dec. 2000			
Canada	-1.36%	1.86%	3.22%
US	0.31%	2.16%	1.84%
MSCI EAFE	1.30%	1.57%	0.27%
MSCI EM	-24.95%	3.88%	28.83%
10-Years: Dec. 2000-Dec. 2010			
Canada	8.37%	0.80%	-7.57%
US	0.97%	0.60%	-0.37%
MSCI EAFE	2.39%	0.81%	-1.58%
MSCI EM	6.56%	5.10%	-1.46%

---

12 I aggregated the data across countries using US dollar GDP weights since I do not have a history of EAFE and EM market capitalization weights for each country.

Notice how stable the US data have been. For the full 40 years real dividend growth has been 0.89% and for the past 22 years it was 1.05%. In the 1990s it fell to 0.31%, but rose back to 0.97% in the 2000s, close to its average historical average levels. US GDPPC has also been fairly constant, outpacing real dividend growth in all but the last ten years, in which it trailed by 0.37%. The real dividend growth shortfall of 0.94% relative to real GDPPC over the whole 40 years is very close to the long-term average shortfall of 0.90%.

By contrast, real dividend growth in the other markets has been more volatile. For example, Canada, with its less-diversified market and economy that is highly concentrated in resource industries and finance, shows real dividend growth of 8.37% in the last decade, far outstripping its real GDPPC of just 0.80%, while in the previous decade it experienced negative real dividend growth, falling far behind very positive real GDPPC growth. Similarly EAFE and the EM showed strong dividend growth over the past decade, again outstripping real GDPPC, in contrast to the previous decade.

I will give only the most general outline of how I might go about generating real dividend growth (RDG) forecasts for the coming decade, limiting myself only to considerations of real GDPPC growth and real dividend growth. I start by cataloguing the host of financial and structural problems within both the Eurozone and the United States. This leads me to believe that the economies of developed markets will struggle to match historical real growth, and so I assume that real GDPPC for Canada, the US and EAFE countries will be below longer-term historical averages for the next ten years at 1.0%, although slightly ahead of real GDPPC growth over the last decade.

Longer-term historical growth of real GDPPC for countries in the Emerging Markets index has been much higher at 4.37%, and was 5.1% over the past decade. Accepting the common assumption that these countries will continue to exhibit higher growth than the more developed world, I will peg real GDPPC growth at 4.25%, lower than that of the past decade but close to its long-term historical average. These forecasts are presented in column 1 of Table 15-3.

Table 15-3:
Dividend Growth and GDPPC
10-Year Forecasts in Real USD

	(1) Real GDPPC (local)	(2) Real DG Shortfall	(3) Real DG (local)
10-Year forecast			
Canada	1.00%	0.25%	0.75%
US	1.00%	0.25%	0.75%
MSCI EAFE	1.00%	0.25%	0.75%
MSCI EM	4.25%	0.25%	4.00%

Since real dividend growth in the past decade has outpaced real GDPPC for all four markets, the shortfall factor was negative. I assume that the shortfall factor is likely to turn back to a small positive number, and that dividends will not outpace real GDPPC growth. The shortfall factor is in column 2, and the resulting forecasts for real dividend growth are in column 3. The results show relatively modest but positive real dividend growth for developed markets, and continued higher real dividend growth for the emerging markets.

Again my point is not to justify a particular set of forecasts, but rather to show you a simple approach to making such forecasts. You will be able to read volumes of reports on economic growth prospects, and can make your own best guess as to future real GDPPC. You can then relate dividend growth to your underlying view of the economy, taking into account recent past dividend growth.

Chapter 16:

Expected Return due to the Change in Dividend Yield

I will discuss two very different approaches for handling the third component of expected return, the expected return due to a change in dividend yield, $E(r\Delta DY_g)$. These two approaches are based on diametrically opposed views of markets. On the one hand, if you believe either that markets are efficient, or less strongly, that investors cannot dependably evaluate whether markets are cheap or expensive at any point in time, then you must argue that the *expected* return to this component is 0%. This is not to say there will be no return to it, it's just that you believe that the return is unpredictable. On the other hand if you believe that it is possible that equity markets can be valued, and that such valuations may differ significantly from today's pricing, then at least some of the time you may have a non-zero forecast for this component.

> **OVERVIEW**
>
> Two approaches to forming expectations for the return due to the change in dividend yield $E(r\Delta DY_g)$ are discussed. The first assumes a *no forecast* approach, while the second assumes that equities can be *valued*.
>
> The consequences of both approaches are explored, and several issues are raised.
>
> I adopt the no valuation approach, but monitor valuations on an ongoing basis. They serve as a sounding board against which I can test my forecasts.

Although I have some sympathy for the second camp, and certainly do not believe that markets are fully efficient, I also don't believe that it is easy for investors to consistently exploit market inefficiencies and to outperform the market over the long term. In particular I don't believe that it is easy to value the market at any time, especially if you have an expectation that your valuation will "come true" within a specific time frame.[1] So as a practical matter I am unlikely to provide forecasts of $r\Delta DY_g$, in most circumstances, and I believe that this is a sensible point of view for many investors.

I will begin by showing the consequences of the *no valuation forecast* view, after which I will present an alternative approach that shows how one can add a market valuation component. However I will also point out some of the very serious difficulties with a true valuation approach, and for me these difficulties reinforce my preference for staying with the no valuation approach.

Remember that when I discussed expected dividend yields I emphasized that this component of expected return was not a valuation measure, but rather a forecast of what an investor's return would be, due to the average dividend yield received over his investment period. Add to that a forecast of expected dividend growth. Given the additional stance of *no forecast* for the third component, return due to changes in valuation, I now have a complete forecast of local returns. In the case of the US or Canadian market these would be appropriate for home market investors, but of course EAFE or EM investors, as well as non-local investors in the US or Canada, still have to account for currencies, which I will do in Chapter 17. Table 16-1 presents a set of local market real return forecasts from the end of 2010, using the then-current dividend yields (from Table 14-3) and the dividend growth forecasts (Table 15-3).

You may think that these are very modest forecasts for real returns, especially in light of the much higher levels of historical average real returns. I will focus on the US case, at least in part because that market is so heavily followed, but also because it is the lowest and most unusual forecast. The historical overview of the US

---

[1] By this I mean that if you think a market is cheap (or expensive) at a point in time, the market might keep getting cheaper (or more expensive) for many years. It might also take many more years to reach the fair value level you were predicting. Were you "right but early" or "wrong"? If you had to reverse your position before it reached your perceived fair value, the "right but early" claim gives no satisfaction. None of this includes a consideration of opportunity costs.

Expected Return due to the Change in Dividend Yield

Table 16-1:
10-Year Local Market Equity Real Return Forecasts
as of December 2010 with a No Valuation Forecast

Dec 31 2010	Canada	United States	MSIC EAFE	MSCI Emerging Markets
Current DY	2.29%	1.79%	2.96%	2.08%
Forecast RDG	0.75%	0.75%	0.75%	4.00%
Forecast rΔDY	0%	0%	0%	0%
Forecast Real Return	3.06%	2.56%	3.74%	6.16%

market in Chapter 1 showed historical real returns at 6.67%, more than two and a half times higher than the real return of 2.56% that I am suggesting in Table 16-1. Can I seriously present such a low forecast?

Let's compare this US market forecast with the breakdown of the real long-run total return of 6.67% in Table 7-2. First, the geometric average dividend yield over history was 4.57%, with a starting yield of 5.86% in 1871. Second, real dividend growth was 1.15%. And third, return due to change in dividend yield was 0.84% annualized over the 140 years, as yields fell from 5.86% to 1.81%. Even if you increased my forecast of RDG from 0.75% to the historical average rate of 1.15%, you would only add 0.40% to the forecast for a total of 2.96%. Of course here I am forecasting 0% return due to the change in dividend yields, rather than the 0.84% annual return actually received historically, but is that unrealistic given that the starting yield is just 1.79%? I am assuming a *no valuation forecast* approach for the moment, but if you are looking ahead and thinking that forecasting valuation might be a good idea after all, would you actually have a good reason to assume that yields will fall significantly lower over the next ten years, the requirement if this component is to generate positive returns?[2] The remaining difference is the dividend

---

[2] To match the historical gain of 0.84% annualized over ten years, the ending yield would have to fall from the starting yield of 1.79% to 1.646%. To receive 2% annualized return from a change in valuation, yields would have to fall to 1.469%. It's not that these ending yields are so hard to imagine, given the previous 20 years of low dividend yields, but rather that investors would continue

yield itself: at 1.79% it is 2.78% lower than the geometric average dividend yield experienced, and a staggering 4.07% lower than the starting dividend yield back in 1871.

So yes, while this forecast may turn out to be wildly wrong, I am indeed serious. By far the largest difference between my US market forecast in Table 16-1 and the historical long-term actual real return is that very large difference in dividend yield. Remember that if you assume that yields will rise to their long-term levels, then any gains from running yield will be swamped by losses from the change in valuation, which I currently hold at 0%. The only factors that can make my forecast higher are (1) a significant increase in expected RDG to well above historical average levels, or (2) further decreases in dividend yield, leading to capital gains. While I might be persuaded that my forecast of RDG is too low, I don't think that I would want to bet my investing future on gains from dividend revaluation.

The other forecasts are fairly self-explanatory, and the main bone of contention is whether expected RDG should be significantly different. In the end, that aspect of the forecast is the one in which the most discretion and judgment will be placed. But you can see that adjustments to the RDG rate are likely much smaller than the differences between the current DY and long-term values, at least in the US market.

Now I will turn to the second approach to $r\Delta DY_g$ and think about forecasting returns based on a change in valuation. What do I have to believe in order to make a non-zero forecast for $r\Delta DY_g$? Since this component is the return due to a change in dividend yield, on the face of things I have to be willing to predict whether dividend yields will rise or fall.[3] If I predict that dividend yields will rise, I am saying

---

to be content with such low yields if market and economic turmoil continues for another decade.

3 I say "on the face of things" because in this framework, any price change that is not caused by dividend growth must be a consequence of a change in dividend yield. That is the implication of the algebra in Appendix 2 of Chapter 7. However, an investor can forecast returns beyond the change due to dividend growth without explicit reference to dividend yield change, and I will show you an example of this. But any direct forecast of such price change can then be

that today's market is expensive: investors are paying too high a price for dividends today and will eventually insist on a lower price for each dollar of dividends. Conversely if I predict that dividend yields will fall, I am saying that today's markets are cheap: investors will be willing to pay higher prices for each dollar of dividends than they do today. While at first glance this concept of *valuation* — judging that an asset is cheap or expensive — may seem to be quite obvious and straightforward, I actually think that it is a difficult notion to clarify. I will elaborate this point step by step.

So far my forecasts have been based on expected dividends and dividend growth, without direct reference to pricing and valuation. Given any set of forecasts, such as those in Table 16-1, I can take a second step and compare them. When I also consider their potential riskiness, I might decide that some of the alternative investments are *more attractive* than others. For example, given the roughly comparable risk levels for each of Canada, the US and EAFE, I might think that the low expected return for the US market makes it unattractive — it seems to be "expensive" — and that the higher expected returns of the other markets make them more attractive — they seem to be "cheaper". But in making a relative evaluation of this kind, I am not thereby suggesting what the valuation *ought to be*. In the case of the US forecast, I might lament the low expected return, and I might re-examine my stance several times to try to understand why so many other investors apparently do not share such a view.[4] But the fact that *I* believe that the prospects are unattractive because of my calculation of a low expected return does not imply that I think today's value is somehow *wrong*, or that I should have a positive or negative forecast for $r\Delta DY_g$.

---

translated into a change in dividend yield, consistent with this framework: because the investor forecasts a price rise beyond that implied by dividend growth, the dividend yield must fall, and so on.

4 That is, in early 2011 investors were piling into the US market, and even during the ongoing Eurozone crisis of 2011, investors continued to look for every possible justification to push markets higher whenever the negative news let up for a moment.

This idea of comparing investment alternatives based on my expectations of return and risk is essentially what I will be doing as I examine portfolio construction in Part 4. But many investors want to take a further step. When they say that a market, or any particular security, is cheap, they are saying that its price is low *and should rise*, presumably to a level higher than that implied by expected dividend growth. Conversely when they say that the current market is expensive, they mean that its current price is too high *and should fall*. This implies that they have a view of what its price ought to be, what its *fair or intrinsic value* is.

The idea that there is an objective fair value or "correct price", that is or can be different from actual consensus market prices at any point in time, is the gripping vision behind security valuation in its fullest sense. You can think of this as a philosophical realism as opposed to the previous instrumentalist or subjective view that I prefer to adopt. Part of this realism is not only that true or fair value exists, but that the analyst can *know* what that value is. Very few analysts who work on security or market valuation base their work on a clear theory, and with rare exceptions the role of fair value is either implicit or is relatively unmotivated and unjustified.[5] Yet many investors find this approach compelling, and so by way of illustration I will use an example that is both relatively easy to explain and for which data (at least for the US market) are readily available. This is the Cyclically Adjusted Price-Earnings ratio (CAPE) popularized by Robert Shiller, and often referred to as *Shiller PE ratios*.[6]

CAPE compares real (inflation-adjusted) prices to trailing ten-year average real (inflation-adjusted) earnings, which are a robust measure of real profitability. As in most of my previous analysis the

---

[5] One prominent exception is Andrew Smithers. In his recent book Wall Street Revalued (Smithers, 2009), he proposes a theory of markets that is based on the idea of an objectively defined fair value around which prices rotate. He offers this as a replacement to efficient markets theory, and importantly sets out criteria which a replacement theory should meet (p.69).

[6] Shiller 2005. I have already mentioned the data source as http://www.econ.yale.edu/~shiller/data.htm. Historical and recent CAPE calculations are presented in an updated spreadsheet, along with the other data.

noise from inflation is removed, in this case from both denominator and numerator. In addition, using a ten-year average smooths the short-term volatility of real earnings associated with the business cycle, hence the term "cyclically adjusted". Figure 16-1 shows the history of US CAPE. Since its average value is 16.38 as indicated by the horizontal red line, this means that on average investors paid $16.38 for each dollar of cyclically adjusted real earnings.

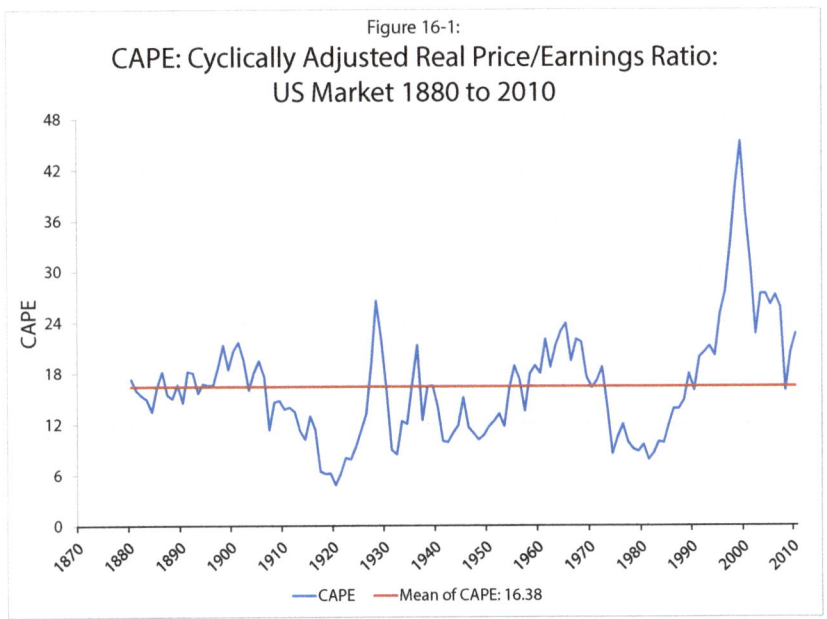

Proponents of CAPE as a true valuation measure will say that Figure 16-1 shows that the cyclical P/E *revolves around its average*, and has a *tendency to revert to that average* after straying from it. As a consequence the average value is a measure of fair value. Thus the extremely high levels in 1999 and 2000, with investors paying as much as $45 for each $1.00 of real (cyclically adjusted) earnings, should have told any observer that markets were overvalued, and that prices relative to real earnings would eventually fall towards the mean (fair value) level of $16.38 per $1.00 of earnings. While this description is somewhat persuasive, and I certainly agree that this measure does have some predictive power,[7] it is possible to raise many questions about this kind of measure.

But before I do so, let's see how CAPE can be used to forecast the valuation component of return. At the end of 2010 I calculated a value for the CAPE ratio of 22.08. While nowhere near the levels of 1999 and 2000, this is still almost 35% higher than the long-term average level of 16.38. The first thing is to make a direct calculation of the price change required to bring 2010 CAPE back to average or "fair" levels, assuming that this occurs over a specific time frame. The move from its December 2010 value of 22.08 ($22.08 for each $1 of real earnings) to the long-term average of 16.38 ($16.38 for each $1 of real earnings) is a loss of 25.8%. If I assume a ten-year time frame, this is -2.94% annualized. In other words, if you think that "fair value" will be reached within ten years, you will believe that the impact of declining CAPE will be -2.94% per year on real returns. This number could be used as a ten-year forecast for $r\Delta DY_g$, along with your forecasts of DY_g and RDG_g.

You can see that if you accept a measurement of fair value, then using it to generate forecasts for $r\Delta DY_g$ can be fairly straightforward. However, there are many difficulties with this approach, and the search for an objective fair value may be more difficult than it appears.[8] First, what does it mean to say that CAPE "revolves about its mean" and has a tendency to "revert to fair value" in Figure 16-1? While many samples *look* as though they revolve around their mean,

---

7 For example, using non-overlapping data, and using the CAPE measure to predict future ten-year non-overlapping real returns, the t-statistic of the coefficient is significant at the 5% level, with an adjusted r-squared of 25.2% (despite the fact that there are just 13 data points for the US history).

8 The best approach I have seen is Andrew Smithers' complex justification. In addition to outlining the economic justification for CAPE, perhaps more importantly he shows its high correlation with another fundamental concept, a variant of Tobin's q ratio, in this case the market value of non-financial equities divided by their net worth at current replacement cost. While there is much to debate in his exposition, I tend to believe that some of the attractiveness of the data-oriented arguments may be influenced by the long-term stability of the one case for which we have long-term data, the US market.

when I ran the statistical test[9] on the data in the graph, it showed only a modest mean reversion.[10] You can see this because the CAPE ratio has stayed above or below the average level for 10, 20 or even 30 years.

A second and more important point is that the mean from this particular data sample from 1880 to 2010 has little to recommend it as an estimate of fair value, as distinct from the mean of any other data sample. For example, in Figure 16-2 I divided the data into two halves, and show the averages of each half.[11] Clearly the average for the first half (mauve line) is much lower, with a CAPE ratio of 14.41, than in the second half where the CAPE ratio is 18.37 (green line). Why does it make sense to say that the true fair value is 16.38, when in the first 66 years the average CAPE was generally below this (as yet

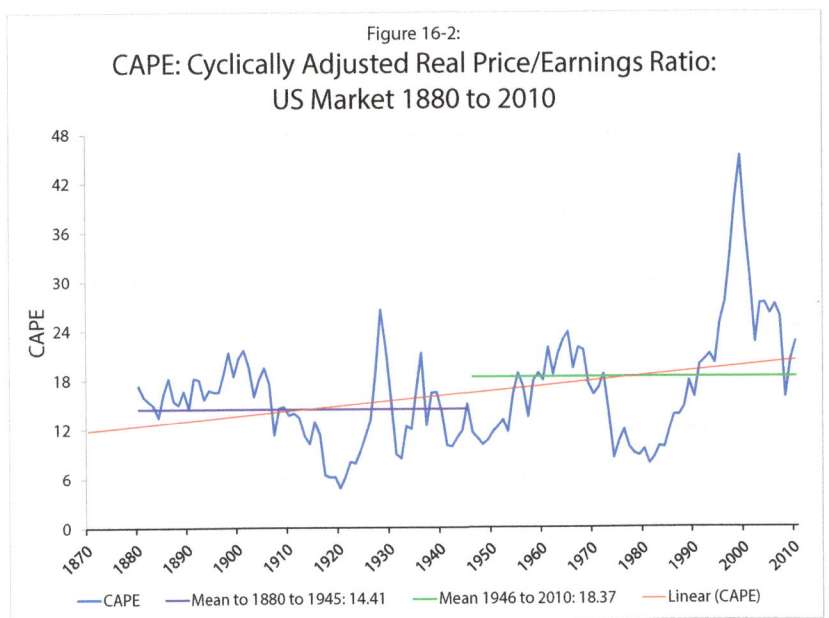

9 The test is called the Augmented Dickey-Fuller test.

10 Using the data from the graph, which are overlapping in the denominator, mean reversion is rejected at the 8.7% level, hence "modest" evidence of mean reversion. When I ran the test on non-overlapping samples, the test for mean reversion failed at the 19.7% level, and so mean reversion is not supported.

11 Since the first value of CAPE is 1880, the first half ends with 1945. This gives 66 observations in the first half, and 65 in the second half.

unknown) average, as were many of the individual data points, while in the second half CAPE tended to be above it?

Moreover the upward-sloping light red line is the linear regression (trend) line of best fit. While it is not being proposed as a third representation of fair value, it indicates that as time has passed, the average CAPE ratio has generally increased.[12] This suggests to me that investors have tended to "revalue" the US market at higher levels over the 20th century, perhaps because they perceive the market to be less risky than in the past. It's not that I think this possible upward revaluation can continue forever, but it is consistent with the idea that prospective returns to equities may be lower than in the past. So what is "fair value" now in 2011? I certainly don't think that there is an answer to this question. But you can see from Figure 16-2 that if you want to use CAPE as your valuation tool, the shorter the history you use, the closer current CAPE will be to fair value, given the recent high levels of CAPE.[13]

A third point is that if it is difficult to pinpoint fair value for the relatively stable case of the US market, remember how different market returns and dividends have been across markets.[14] I suspect that once researchers create longer histories of earnings and dividend data beyond the US market, they will find major differences with

---

12 Of course the linear regression line fits the data better than the simple arithmetic average in Figure 16-1, since by definition it is the best linear fit.

13 By way of an afterthought, as I was winding up the last sections of the book in June of 2012 I came across a small article by John Campbell in the Financial Times: "Stocks may be the best of a bad bunch", Financial Times, June 13, 2012. Campbell, a professor of economics at Harvard, has worked extensively with Robert Shiller on the empirical work behind CAPE and other valuation measures. He writes: "Despite the intense fear and financial stress created by the global financial crisis in 2008 and 2009, even at the trough the CAPE fell only slightly below its historical average. This suggests that changes in the economy and financial system – for example, the decline in real interest rates and the expansion of stock market participation through mutual funds and retirement savings accounts – may have permanently altered the CAPE's average level."

14 In Table 7-3 DMS reported that the average dividend growth over their 19-country sample was -0.11%, compared to the very positive earnings growth of the US and their cap-weighted World index. This suggests that dividends (and likely earnings) have behaved very differently outside of the US market.

earnings, real earnings and CAPE across markets as well. If average CAPE or fair value is relative to market history, then — it is indeed a relative measure and falls short of any true model of fair value.

The more you think about these issues, the more clearly the concept seems to be somewhat arbitrary and very much data-dependent. But I want to emphasize that the real problem is not simply a lack of data that could possibly be rectified by painstaking historical research. As I mentioned, there is a reasonable chance that obtaining more data for more countries and indexes will show wide historical differences, which may just raise more questions. So I am inclined to believe that the search for fair value will never end with a truly "objective" standard, but will always amount to a subjective opinion as to *what investors ought to require* in order to hold equity risk.

No matter what view you end up holding about market valuation, as a practical matter the lack of long histories for earnings outside of the US means that it is very difficult to add a similar valuation component for the other three market indexes (Canada, EAFE and EM) for which I have been building forecasts. I only have earnings data back to the beginning of the MSCI indexes in December 1969 for Canada and EAFE, and to 1991 for the EM. Just for interest I have calculated CAPE averages for the three additional indexes, and Table 16-2 shows the results for these small samples. CAPE for

Table 16-2:
Average CAPE Over Various Time Spans

	Canada	United States	MSCI EAFE	MSCI Emerging Markets
Average CAPE:				
1881-1945		14.41		
1881-2010		16.38		
1946-2010		18.37		
1978-2010	20.36	20.53	21.42	
2001-2010	24.59	24.22	21.01	15.8
Year-end				
2010	21.25	22.08	13.53	16.4

Canada and EAFE can be calculated for the 33 years from 1978 to 2010, while for EM, CAPE can only be calculated for ten years.

I suspect that most people would agree that the EM data are too limited to be useful, but I also suspect that the 33-year time span is too short as well. Just consider the fact that the CAPE averages for the US, Canada and EAFE are quite similar over this period, but the US value is much higher than its longer-term history. If you are willing to use just the last 33 years of data, so you can compare CAPE values over the same time period, you are throwing away 100 years of US history, and CAPE becomes more clearly a shorter term comparison measure, and far from any deep-rooted concept of "fair value".

Despite my questions about defining fair value, there is a real benefit derived from understanding and tracking different proposed valuation measures. While I will not formally include a valuation component in my equity forecasts, I monitor CAPE on an ongoing basis, and use it as a sounding board against which to judge my forecasts, as well as those of others. For example, even during 2011, I have seen many Wall Street analysts and managers insisting that US equities are fairly valued or even cheap. When you examine such a view from the perspective of CAPE, you can see that they are probably using data only from the last 30 years or less. The point is that such a perspective on markets implies a very short-term evaluation period, and gives you some context in which to evaluate their claims.

There is a crucial further question that is usually not discussed by proponents of valuation in the strong sense. In the case that markets are at fair value according to whatever measure they use, what is the expected return? Earlier I showed you how you might calculate an expected return when a valuation measure such as CAPE differs from its assumed fair value, and you want to look at the impact of its return to fair value. But I did not discuss what returns to expect when it matches fair value.

I very much doubt that the suggestion in 2011 by Wall Street analysts that the US market is at fair value or even cheap is meant to imply low expected returns of the kind I am suggesting

Expected Return due to the Change in Dividend Yield

in my forecast: 2.56% real (from Table 16-1), or 3% if we bump up expected real dividend growth to historical averages. I would guess that most investors suppose that fair value implies expected real returns similar to the long-term real return of 6.67% (nominal 8.88%), or perhaps the higher real annualized return for the last 30 years of 7.33% (10.71% nominal). Very likely the assumption is that at the neutral or fair value position, future returns are expected to match historical average returns for the period over which fair value has been calculated,[15] although it's also fair to say that few proponents of valuation ever explicitly make this point. Isn't it interesting that a valuation approach may be based on assuming that past long-term average returns will equal future long-term average returns.

I will again briefly raise the question of what investors might expect to receive at "fair value" in Chapter 18, as I review some of the interesting applications of our attribution and forecasting framework.

---

15 So for example, the long-term historical average CAPE of 16.38 is calculated over the full US history for which real return was 6.67%. If I run a regression explaining future ten-year real returns as a function of a constant plus the distance CAPE is from its average (CAPE–Average CAPE), the constant is 6.30%, very close to the real annualized return of 6.67%.

Chapter 17:

Expected Returns to Foreign Exchange

My approach to forecasting expected real foreign exchange returns, $E(rRFX_g)$ is straightforward. I showed you empirical evidence that over the longer term, relative levels of inflation have driven nominal FX changes, so that *real* exchange rate movements, the difference between nominal returns to FX and relative inflation, are small. This is in line with relative purchasing power parity theory, which predicts that real returns to exchange rates are 0%. Given this perspective, many long-term investors, especially multi-generational pension funds and foundations, are willing to assume that the best forecast for real exchange rate movements over the long term is 0%, and I generally follow this approach as my fallback or default position.

While this forecast is very simple, its consequences may not be. Most obviously, like any forecast, it is made with uncertainty. Table 9-1 of Chapter 9 showed that while there was a great deal of statistical support for RPPP, even at ten years the strong adjusted r-squared of 69.45% means that 30.55% of the movement

> **OVERVIEW**
>
> **Given the evidence in support of RPPP over the long term (Chapter 9), my preferred default position assumes that expected returns to real FX $E(rRFX_g)$ are 0%. But the underlying point is that expectations about relative inflation have to be consistent with your expectations about returns to FX.**
>
> **Key consequences:**
>
> - if $E(rRFX_g)$ is 0%, then nominal returns to FX $E(rFX_g)$ can only be 0% if expected inflation differentials are 0;
> - conversely if you assume that nominal returns to FX are 0, then real returns to FX may not be.

of nominal exchange rates is *not* explained by relative inflation, and in Figure 9-1 many of the blue dots are far from the line of best fit. As you shorten your actual holding period, the potential for divergence from our forecast will increase.

But you also have to remember that the relationship between real and nominal FX returns *does not imply that nominal FX returns will be 0%*, even if real FX returns were actually 0%. Equation (9.1) defined nominal return to FX as a function of the real return to FX and relative inflation. Filling in the definition of relative inflation yields:

(17.1) $1+rFX_{H/F_g} = (1+rRFX_{H/F_g}) * (1+IH_g)/(1+IF_g)$

You can see that if the real return to FX is 0%, then the nominal return to FX is a function of home market inflation versus foreign inflation, which is unlikely to be 0%. To put this another way, if I *forecast* home and foreign inflation to be the same, so that the relative inflation ratio will be 1.0, then my forecast that $rRFX_{H/F_g}$ (real return to FX) is 0% does indeed imply that rFX_{H/F_g} (the nominal return to FX) will be 0%, *but in no other case*.

Table 17-1 gives a simple example. First, in row 1, I show my inflation forecasts. In line with inflation levels of the last 20 years or so (see Table 9-3), my forecast of inflation for Canada, the United

Table 17-1:
Relating Forecasts of Real and Nominal Return to FX to Forecasts of Relative Inflation

Dec 31 2010		Canada	United States	MSCI EAFE	MSCI Emerging Markets
1	Forecast foreign (local market) inflation	2.50%	2.50%	2.50%	4.50%
2	Forecast home country (Canadian) inflation	2.50%			
3	Forecast real FX return	0%	0%	0%	0%
4	Implied nominal FX forecast return from a Canadian perspective	0.00%	0.00%	0.00%	-1.91%

States, and EAFE[1] is the same at 2.5%. But my forecast for Emerging Markets inflation is higher at 4.5%. For although EM inflation has been much higher than that historically (Table 9-3), it fell to 4.49% for the decade ending in 2010, and I suggest that it will continue at that rate for the coming decade. Real FX returns are all forecast as 0% as shown in row 3. Using equation (17.1), I calculate nominal FX return in row 4, taking the perspective of the Canadian investor as the home market.

Since the forecast inflation differential between Canada, the US and EAFE is 0%, the forecast for nominal FX between both the US and EAFE with Canada is also 0%. But the forecast inflation differential between the EM markets and Canada means that equation (17.1) *requires* that my forecast nominal return to FX is -1.91%, to compensate for that inflation differential.

To summarize, if I am willing to say that my best forecast for real returns to FX is 0%, in accordance with RPPP, and I can make this forecast for every currency to which my portfolio is exposed, I might be tempted to forecast a 0% return to nominal FX as well, perhaps in part because I have no idea what will happen to nominal currencies. But the only consistent way I can do this is if I implicitly forecast that inflation rates for every currency, including my home market, are the same. If I believe, as in Table 17-1, that Emerging Markets will have higher inflation, then at least in that case I cannot consistently assume a 0% nominal currency return forecast for EM.

The reality is that most investors do not start with a return forecast for real FX, and indeed most investors never even think about real FX rates and returns to them. If they think about foreign exchange at all, it is about nominal FX rates and returns, and unless they make an explicit forecast of nominal FX returns, then the implicit consequence is that their forecast of nominal FX returns is 0%. This is not inconsistent, as long as they have not also assumed a 0% return to real FX rates, and it is unlikely that they have done so.

---

[1] Of course when referring to inflation or currencies for EAFE or EM, I am referring to a weighted average inflation or currency return for the markets in the indexes.

There is nothing theoretically wrong with forecasting that nominal FX returns are 0%, I just think that it, and its consequences, need to be made explicit. My preferred fallback approach that starts with a 0% forecast of *real* returns to FX is based on the theory of relative purchasing power parity, along with its empirical support. The approach of having a 0% forecast for *nominal* returns to FX is not based on a theory, but (if made explicit) is probably based on the view that nominal returns cannot be forecast.[2] In tone this is not so very different from my *null forecast approach* for the third component of expected return, $E(r\Delta DY_g)$, although I think such a view ignores the evidence that I have shown in favour of RPPP.[3] Of course some professional currency managers are in the business of making specific forecasts for nominal FX rates and returns, but that's another story, and normally their time frame is focused on short-term trading.

While I base my currency forecasts on the view that long-term real currency returns should be 0%, and others may base their views on the view that the nominal currency returns should be 0%, neither forecast approach speaks to the fact of currency risk. In the case of equities, we invest because we believe there is a positive expected return, a risk premium for holding equity risk. I have identified at least a core estimate of that expected return as a function of expected dividend yield and expected dividend growth. But there is no obvious similar risk premium for holding currency risk, and assuming RPPP with the consequence that expected real currency returns are 0% confirms this. So unless you forecast positive returns in particular cases, when you invest in foreign assets with a 0% forecast for real or nominal currency returns, you are taking on currency risk without any compensation for that risk. You can view this risk as a cost of investing in foreign markets.

---

2 Just to refresh your memory, think back to Chapter 9, and Figure 9-2 in particular. While returns to real FX were quite close to 0% over the 111-year history shown there, returns to nominal FX were much larger in magnitude, and do not give the impression of being centred around 0%, for reasons we discussed.

3 That is, the evidence in favour of RPPP indicates a very strong relation between the nominal change in FX rates and relative inflation.

Expected Returns to Foreign Exchange

In Chapter 8, I demonstrated the dramatic impact that foreign exchange can have on the returns and volatility of foreign investments over a period of one to ten years and more. I pointed out that currency interacts with foreign investments in one of four ways. In the best case, currency exposures both enhance returns and lower overall volatility, as the foreign currency rises relative to your home currency, and interacts with the underlying foreign investment so as to reduce volatility. This is a clear win. Unfortunately the exact opposite can happen, with the foreign currency both falling and interacting with the underlying investment to increase overall volatility, a clear loss. The other two cases, with returns and volatility both rising, or returns and volatility both falling, are of indeterminate benefit. You might or might not find that in a particular case, enhanced realized returns justify the higher volatility, or lower returns are compensated for by lower volatility. In sum, currency exposures add a level of uncertainty no matter what the actual outcome turns out to be.

Figure 17-1 gives two examples of the effects of currency exposures in a more general way than the very specific examples in Chapter 8. The blue bars give the performance of 10 foreign currencies (as USD/Foreign) from the point of view of a US dollar investor

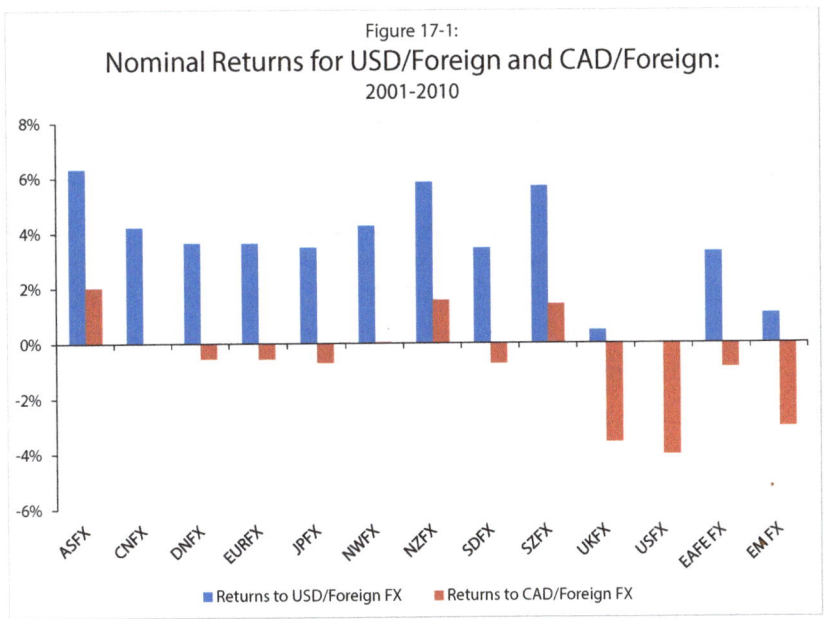

over the ten years ending December 2010. This is compared with the red bars, which present the performance of the same currencies from the point of view of a Canadian dollar investor (currencies are CAD/Foreign) over the same period. Both USD and CAD are shown relative to the baskets of EAFE and EM currencies to the right.

The most dramatic point is that all ten individual currencies shown rose relative to the USD over this period, with gains averaging more than 3% per year, while the EAFE currency basket rose by 3.3%. Only the EM currency basket and the UK pound rose by noticeably lower amounts. This means that US investors benefited significantly from foreign currency exposures over the decade. By contrast, only four individual currencies rose relative to CAD, while the rest fell. In particular the USD fell by 4.05%, EAFE currencies fell by 0.87%, and EM currencies fell by 3.02%. Thus on average Canadian investors were hurt by foreign currency exposures over this period, and in the case of US investments this harm was very large and sustained. This is just a reminder that even over ten years we should expect that currency exposures will have a significant impact on investment returns.

The forecasts I am developing are only for returns, and I will discuss the topic of integrating those return forecasts with risk forecasts in Part 4. But in Chapter 8, I mentioned the concept of hedging currency exposures. Hedging should be understood as removing or undoing the return and volatility impact of the foreign currency exposure, whether harmful or helpful, at the cost of the currency hedge. Remember that this is *not* the same as saying that hedging currencies always reduces realized volatility, the erroneous view held by those who think that currency hedging is a "free lunch".[4] But it does raise the question as to whether or not it is worthwhile to remove the uncertainty of currency exposures by using currency hedges.

A detailed and technical exploration of this topic is beyond the scope of this discussion. But I will lay out a range of considerations to think about, and I will also outline a practical approach that I think

---

4 See Chapter 8.

Expected Returns to Foreign Exchange

makes sense for many investors. The following discussion is meant to apply to your whole portfolio, although the actual examples I am using here relate to equities.

The first point is that your starting position matters. As a Canadian investor I need to understand that my home equity market is very small and under-diversified, at just 3% of the global equity universe. Even assuming a substantial home market bias, common sense would suggest that a majority of investment opportunities must lie outside Canada, and hence significant equity exposures in foreign currencies may be needed. By contrast, the US investor lives in a home market that constitutes roughly 50% of the global equity universe, including many companies that have global exposures themselves. Common sense suggests that a US investor will require smaller foreign equity exposures in order to capture diversification and investment opportunities. The obvious point here is that the smaller the foreign exposures that you require, the less likely it is that the currency component of those exposures will significantly harm your returns.

A second point relates to how diversified your currency exposures actually are. The broader and more diverse the range of currencies, the more likely it is that there will be some offsetting effects or diversification benefits between the currencies themselves, as they potentially move at different rates and in different directions. My expectation is that the broad currency diversification should lower the risk of currency exposures. Figure 17-1 shows this as a possibility, though by no means a certainty. For example, the Canadian case (the red bars) shows some modest benefits from currency diversification: despite the strength of CAD against the USD, the overall impact of currencies on the EAFE basket (which does not include the US market) was only moderately negative. On the other hand, currency exposures from the US point of view (blue bars) show little benefit from diversification, as the USD declined relative to all the individual currencies shown in this graph, meaning that USD investors benefited almost regardless of the investments they chose. While in this case the benefit accrued to the US investor, the opposite case, a sharp rise against every currency, is also possible, with the opposite effect on realized return.

A third point relates to the inevitable lack of currency diversification from US dollar investments for non-US investors. Given the size and breadth of the US equity market, exposure to the US dollar can often be very large, and so the consequences of a bad outcome are significant. For example, Figure 17-1 showed that Canadian investors faced a loss of -4.02% annualized on their US investments over the decade ending 2010, a substantial penalty indeed. But the point would hold for any single large currency exposure generated by investment decisions.

So I have two basic rules of thumb which can be followed, especially when forecasts for $rRFX_{H/F_g}$ or rFX_{H/F_g} are 0%, and on the assumption that currency hedging is feasible. First consider hedging all or part of large single currency exposures, such as large USD exposures taken on by non-US investors. Second, consider hedging at least part of baskets of currency exposures such as those from EAFE indexes. As a general rule it is not feasible for even large investors to hedge Emerging Market currencies, but the positive aspect of these is that they are the least likely to be correlated with those of your own and other developed markets.

As I will discuss in a little more detail in Part 4, smaller Canadian investors are fortunate to have many opportunities to invest in relatively low-cost USD-hedged ETFs that invest in aspects of the US equity and fixed-income markets. I almost always take advantage of these as the first rule of thumb suggests, although I am careful to weigh the costs of the embedded currency hedge.[5] Canadian investors can also hold EAFE-focused ETFs that offer currency hedging, and so again all or part of EAFE currency exposure can be hedged.

By way of summary, I will integrate currency forecasts with the local market forecasts that I have already given. Most people will find

---

5 An explicit cost is that management fees are higher. A second cost is that due to imperfect hedging and the outright cost of hedging, the currency hedged portfolio will tend to trail its currency hedged benchmark by more than the unhedged portfolio will trail its unhedged benchmark due to hedging costs and mismatches.

the local market portion — dividend yield, real or nominal growth, and the return due to the change in dividend yield — relatively straightforward. But applying currency forecasts adds potential complexity that we are less used to and less comfortable with.

Let me start with my base forecast that real long-term returns for CAD/Foreign currencies will be 0%. In this case my local market[6] real return forecasts in Table 16-1 are re-stated as rows 1-4 of Table 17-2 below. With long-term forecast real returns to FX of 0% in row 5, the foreign/local market real return forecasts have the same numerical values as my home market real return forecasts in row 6. This is a direct application of equation (9.4).

Table 17-2:
10-Year Real Equity Forecasts from a CAD Base
as of December 2010

		Canada	United States	MSCI EAFE	MSCI Emerging Markets
1	Current DY	2.29%	1.79%	2.96%	2.08%
2	Forecast RDG	0.75%	0.75%	0.75%	4.00%
3	Forecast rΔDY	0%	0%	0%	0%
4	Forecast Real (foreign or local) Return (1+2+3)	3.06%	2.56%	3.74%	6.16%
5	Forecast Real Return to FX (CAD/Foreign)	0.00%	0.00%	0.00%	0.00%
6	Forecast Home (Canadian) Real Return (4+5)	3.06%	2.56%	3.74%	6.16%

Please note that additions are geometric.

There are several ways I can go about forecasting nominal returns in my home market currency. But I will choose perhaps the most natural way, which is to first create *local nominal* forecasts for equities in each currency. To do this, I could change my forecast of real dividend growth to one for nominal dividend growth in the second row, or I could explicitly add a forecast of inflation. I will do the latter, using the forecast of inflation from Table 17-1. Then I

---

[6] Just to remind you, "local market" forecasts are the forecasts for each (foreign) market from the point of view of the local investor in each market.

translate the nominal total return forecast in the foreign currency into a nominal forecast of total return in the home currency, by using the nominal forecast of currency returns, again from Table 17-1. Table 17-3 below shows this, with both nominal total return forecasts highlighted in pink.

Table 17-3:
10-Year Nominal and Real Equity Forecasts from a CAD Base as of December 2010

	Dec 31 2010	Canada	United States	MSCI EAFE	MSCI Emerging Markets
1	Current DY	2.29%	1.79%	2.96%	2.08%
2	Forecast RDG	0.75%	0.75%	0.75%	4.00%
3	Forecast rΔDY	0%	0%	0%	0%
4	Forecast Real (foreign or local) Return (1+2+3)	3.06%	2.56%	3.74%	6.16%
5	Forecast (foreign or local) Inflation (Table 17-1)	2.50%	2.50%	2.50%	4.50%
6	Forecast (foreign or local) Nominal Return (4+5)	5.64%	5.12%	6.33%	10.94%
7	Forecast Nominal Return to FX: CAD/Foreign (Table 17-1)	0.00%	0.00%	0.00%	-1.91%
8	Forecast Home (Canadian) Nominal Return (6+7)	5.64%	5.12%	6.33%	8.82%
9	Forecast Home (Canadian) Inflation	2.50%			
10	Forecast Home (Canadian) Real Return (8-9)	3.06%	2.56%	3.74%	6.16%

Please note that additions and subtractions are geometric.

I hope that you can follow through the transformations. Rows 1 to 4 are duplicated from Table 17-2, the real return forecast for each foreign or local market, while row 5 is my inflation forecast for each market's local inflation from Table 17-1. Row 6 is the (geometric) sum of rows 4 and 5, and gives the forecast nominal return for each local market. Row 7 shows my forecast of nominal return to FX from Table 17-1, which is derived from my forecast of 0% for real returns to FX combined with my forecasts of the inflation differentials. You can see that in row 6 the forecast nominal local or foreign market return to EM markets jumps because of higher inflation, and then it falls again in row 8 because of the negative forecast nominal return to the basket of EM currencies due to the inflation differential.

If what you are aiming for is a set of compatible nominal return forecasts from a Canadian perspective, the job is done. But the circle is completed in row 10, as I return to my home country forecast of real total returns by adjusting all forecasts for home country inflation in row 9. This is essentially an application of equation (9.7) which we know is equivalent to (9.4), and so the final row of Table 17-3 equals the final row of Table 17-2.

While this may seem very complicated, I hope that the general relations make sense. For example, if you start with Table 17-2, which transforms local real return forecasts for each of the equity markets into home country real return forecasts, you can turn them into nominal home country forecasts directly by adding local expected inflation — essentially working backwards from row 10 to row 8 in Table 17-3. This is shown in rows 7 and 8 of Table 17-4. Here rows 1 to 6 duplicate Table 17-2, and my home country inflation forecast in row 7 is added to my home market real return forecasts in row 6

Table 17-4:
10-Year Nominal Equity Forecasts from a CAD Base as of December 2010

		Canada	United States	MSCI EAFE	MSCI Emerging Markets
1	Current DY	2.29%	1.79%	2.96%	2.08%
2	Forecast RDG	0.75%	0.75%	0.75%	4.00%
3	Forecast rΔDY	0%	0%	0%	0%
4	Forecast Real (foreign or local) Return (1+2+3)	3.06%	2.56%	3.74%	6.16%
5	Forecast Real Return to FX (CAD/Foreign)	0.00%	0.00%	0.00%	0.00%
6	Forecast Home (Canadian) Real Return (4+5)	3.06%	2.56%	3.74%	6.16%
7	Forecast Home (Canadian) Inflation	2.50%			
8	Forecast Home (Canadian) Nominal Return (6+7)	5.64%	5.12%	6.33%	8.82%

Please note that additions are geometric.

to generate nominal return forecasts in row 8. These are the same as row 8 in Table 17-3, but are derived differently.

Finally, I can change the assumption that real returns to FX are 0% in all cases. For example, historically EM currencies have not depreciated quite as far as their higher local inflation would imply. Just to put in a number, let me use a nominal forecast of 0% for EM FX, in line with the nominal forecasts for the other currencies. Table 17-5 shows the changes that take place, highlighted in yellow. You can compare this directly with Table 17-3. The nominal forecast of 0% for CAD/EM currencies in row 7 means that in row 8, the Canadian nominal forecast for EM rises as the higher EM inflation filters through to the Canadian investor as the nominal exchange rate does not fall. This also affects the Canadian home market real return forecast in row 10.

Table 17-5:
10-Year Nominal and Real Equity Forecasts from a CAD Base Assuming all Nominal Forecast FX Returns are 0%

	Dec 31 2010	Canada	United States	MSCI EAFE	MSCI Emerging Markets
1	Current DY	2.29%	1.79%	2.96%	2.08%
2	Forecast RDG	0.75%	0.75%	0.75%	4.00%
3	Forecast rΔDY	0%	0%	0%	0%
4	Forecast Real (foreign or local) Return (1+2+3)	3.06%	2.56%	3.74%	6.16%
5	Forecast (foreign or local) Inflation (Table 17-1)	2.50%	2.50%	2.50%	4.50%
6	Forecast (foreign or local) Nominal Return (4+5)	5.64%	5.12%	6.33%	10.94%
7	Forecast Nominal Return to FX: CAD/Foreign (Modified)	0.00%	0.00%	0.00%	0.00%
8	Forecast Home (Canadian) Nominal Return (6+7)	5.64%	5.12%	6.33%	10.94%
9	Forecast Home (Canadian) Inflation	2.50%			
10	Forecast Home (Canadian) Real Return (8-9)	3.06%	2.56%	3.74%	8.23%

Please note that additions and subtractions are geometric.

Expected Returns to Foreign Exchange

The lesson here is that while it is reasonable that most investors will forecast 0% returns either for real or nominal long-term returns to FX, it is important to work out the consequences of those forecasts, in light of the potential inflation differentials between countries or groups of countries. In the case of Tables 17-3 and 17-5, the changing assumptions about real and nominal returns to FX for emerging markets has a material impact on your home country forecast for EM equities.

Chapter 18:

Equity Forecasts: How do you get There from Here?

To conclude this discussion of equities and forecasting returns, I would like to review some aspects of the analytical framework I have developed, and show some additional uses. The framework was first derived as an attribution tool to analyze historical returns. It can be applied to any time span that you like, and in Table 7-2 it was applied to the 140-year US history, and in Table 7-3 it was applied to the 111-year DMS data for each country and for the World Index. In Part 2 it has been extended as a framework for creating expected returns.

One benefit of using the attribution framework as a tool of historical analysis is to illustrate the idea that at different times, and over different time periods, returns have been generated in very different ways. To give one simple example, I will divide the US history into two subsets, and compare US equity returns over the last 30 years from 1981 to 2010, a period that is often referred to for "historical analysis" by Wall Street analysts,

> **OVERVIEW**
>
> Several uses of the attribution framework are highlighted.
>
> Key concepts:
>
> - historical analysis of sub-periods shows that returns can be generated in very different ways;
> - the forecasting framework can be used to simulate forecasts that might have been made in the past, to compare them with what actually occurred;
> - comparing historical forecasts to what actually happens gives a perspective on "unexpected" outcomes;
> - the forecasts of others can be easily evaluated.

with the first 110 years of the US dataset from 1871 to 1980. Table 18-1 makes the comparison.

Table 18-1:
United States Returns and Attribution:
Over Two Timespans

		The Last 30 Yrs.: Dec 1980 to Dec 2010		The First 110 Yrs.: Dec.1870 to Dec.1980		Difference
1	Actual Nominal Return	10.71%		8.41%		2.31%
2	Inflation	3.16%		1.77%		1.38%
3	Actual Real Return	7.33%		6.52%		0.81%
	Attribution Analysis of real return					
4	Starting DY	4.57%		5.49%		
5	Ending DY	1.79%		4.54%		
6	Actual Average DY	2.66%	37.9%	4.97%	79.3%	-2.31%
7	Actual RDG	1.20%	17.1%	1.12%	17.9%	0.08%
8	Actual rΔDY	3.17%	45.0%	0.17%	2.8%	2.99%
9	Geometric Sum	7.19%	100.0%	6.34%	100.0%	
	Difference: Actual - Attributed Return					
		0.14%		0.18%		

The top section of the table presents the overall returns. First, while nominal returns were significantly higher over the past 30 years than over the first 110 years, at 10.71% versus 8.41%, a large part of that difference is due to higher inflation (row 2). Real returns were much closer, at 7.33% over the past 30 years versus 6.52% for prior history. The details of the attribution are even more interesting. Of the three components, only real dividend growth was virtually the same, with just a 0.08% difference between the two periods. The first large difference is in average dividend yield: in the last 30 years the average DY was 2.66% providing 37.88% of the real return, while in the earlier period, average DY was 2.31% higher at 4.97%, providing 79.3% of total real return. The second major difference is the return due to the change in dividend yield: 3.17% in the last 30 years which is 45.02% of the return, and just 0.17% in the earlier period which is 2.75% of the total real return.

To summarize, over the first 110 years of our historical returns, the US market achieved 97% of its real return through a combination of dividend yield and dividend growth, with just a tiny portion of return due to capital gains from revaluation. Over the past 30 years 45% of its real return, or 3.17%, was derived from capital gains due to revaluation, with a commensurately lower contribution from average dividend yield. These are large and important differences, and should cause investors to think very carefully about future equity returns. In particular, given today's starting point, is it reasonable to expect to receive a large portion of your future equity returns from a continuing upward revaluation of dividends, that is, from a falling dividend yield?

While the forecasting version of the framework was developed to help us look ahead, I can also apply it to historical situations, to compare what investors in the past *might have expected or forecast* with what actually happened. For example, let me use the data from Table 18-1 to make a forecast as of the end of 1980, using the approach I have shown you. The dividend yield at the end of 1980 was 4.57%, and the cumulative annualized real dividend growth rate up to 1980 was 1.12%. If I use these as my expected DY and RDG values, and assume an expected return due to the change in dividend yield of 0%, then my expected long-term real return is 5.74%, as shown on the left side of Table 18-2.

Table 18-2:
US Equity Real Return Forecast at December 1980
versus Subsequent 30-Year Return and Attribution

	Forecast	Forecast at Dec. 1980	Attribution Analysis	Attributed Return 1981-2010	Unexpected = Attribution less Forecast
1	Starting DY	4.57%	Actual Avg.DY	2.66%	-1.82%
2	Forecast RDG	1.12%	Actual RDG	1.20%	0.08%
3	Forecast rΔDY	0.00%	Actual rΔDY	3.17%	3.17%
4	Total Real Return Forecast (1+2+3)	5.74%	Attributed Real Return (1+2+3)	7.19%	1.37%
5			Unexplained	0.13%	0.13%
6			Actual Real Return	7.33%	1.50%

Note that all additions and subtractions are geometric.

The right-hand side of Table 18-2 shows the attribution analysis for the 1981–2010 period (repeated from Table 18-1), and the green column calculates what was *unexpected* or different from the forecast: the attributed actual return to each component less the forecast for each component. While the annual gain due to revaluation of 3.17% was unexpected, so was the lower average dividend yield. That is, the actual average dividend yield over the ensuing 30 years was 1.85% below the beginning expected dividend yield of 4.57%. The combination of these two unexpected factors, along with a small 0.08% gain from higher dividend growth, explains most of the forecast shortfall of 1.5%. To turn the point around, this amount of 1.5% was almost certainly not predictable, since no investor in 1980 would have forecast that dividend yields would fall to less than 2% at the end of 30 years, and so it should be viewed as an unexpected windfall that is unlikely to be repeated going forward.

Just as I can use historical attribution analysis to evaluate past "forecasts" relative to what actually transpired, I can compare my current forecast to what has happened in the past. Up to now I have treated the process of forecasting as a "bottom-up" or step-by-step process, generating values for each of the four components (including currencies) and then "adding" them up to an overall forecast. Breaking down my forecast into these components helps me get away from the fairly prevalent inclination to blindly accept that future returns should be assumed to equal past returns "over the long term", which is the implicit fall-back position for most investors. But it is also easy to relate each of these components to history, to help understand how and why my current forecast differs from history. Almost any reasonable historical comparison will be useful, but Table 18-3 compares my current (December 2010) US forecast with the past 30 years. I use this more recent history once again because this is the history that Wall Street seems to be most familiar with.

The historical analysis section on the left side of Table 18-3 is based on the analysis for the past 30 years from Table 18-1. The forecasting section replicates my local market US forecast originally given in Table 17-2. Finally, the green column shows the geometric differences between my forecasts and history. Row 6 summarizes the

Table 18-3:
Bottom Up Forecast for US Equities at December 2010
Compared with the Historical Analysis 1981-2010

		Historical Analysis Dec. 1980 to Dec. 2010		vs	Bottom-Up 10-Year Forecast at Dec. 2010		Current minus Historical
	Actual Nominal Rtn.	10.71%					
	Inflation	3.16%					
	Actual Real Rtn.	7.33%					
1	Starting DY	4.57%					
2	Ending DY	1.79%					
	Attribution analysis				Forecast		
3	Actual Avg.DY	2.66%			Starting DY	1.79%	-0.85%
4	Actual RDG	1.20%			Forecast RDG	0.75%	-0.45%
5	Actual rΔDY (from 1 & 2)	3.17%			Forecast rΔDY	0.00%	-3.07%
6	Real Return (3+4+5)	7.19%			Forecast Real Return (3+4+5)	2.55%	-4.33%
7	Historical Inflation	3.16%			Forecast Inflation	2.50%	-0.64%
8	Nominal Return (6+7)	10.58%			Forecast Nominal Return (6+7)	5.12%	-4.94%
9	Unexplained	0.13%					

large difference between my conservative December 2010 forecast of real returns and the real return from the past 30 years: it is 4.33% lower. The differences for rows 3 to 5 show why this is so, with the largest single difference being that I am not forecasting continued gains from falling dividend yields. Falling yields fueled 45% of real returns over the past 30 years, and I don't see how that trend can continue.

When my bottom-up forecast is compared with historical returns over some period, you can see that I could explicitly present my forecast not as a stand-alone "bottom-up" forecast but as a "top-down" forecast, starting with historical returns and then adjusting them component by component to reflect my forecast. Table 18-4 shows this trivial reformulation based on the real return from the past 30 years, as presented in Table 18-3. Historical real returns were 7.33%, but I have to lower future expectations because of a lower starting yield, lower expectations for RDG, and no positive

Table 18-4:
Top-Down Forecast Relative to 1981-2010 History

		History	Adjustments to reflect current circumstances	Top-Down Forecast
1	Historical Real Return	7.33%		
	Components of Return:			
2	Average DY	2.66%	-0.87%	1.79%
3	RDG	1.20%	-0.45%	0.75%
4	rΔDY	3.17%	-3.17%	0.00%
5	Forecast Real Return			2.55%

expectations for rΔDY. You might find this way of presenting the forecast more useful, because it builds in the reference to history, and allows you to see directly how and why the forecast differs from whatever historical comparison you believe is relevant.

I have found that practitioners generally do not like this approach to forecasting, based on dividends plus dividend growth, at least in part because they don't normally think in these terms. But I haven't heard or read any objections that I believe are valid. One of the few published objections that I've actually seen is from Niederhoffer and Castaldo,[1] who comment on the "pessimism" of the Arnott/Bernstein forecasts for US equities in the early 2000s due to the low starting dividend yield. They add:

> We must caution against this dividend based approach, since dividends are under the control of the corporation and practices in dividend policy have changed a lot over time as Ibbotson and Chen pointed out.

Apart from the fact that the pessimism has turned out to be justified, the fact that dividends and hence dividend growth are "under the control" of corporations, as if earnings were not, seems to miss the point.[2] First from a historical basis, the attribution form of

---

[1] Niederhoffer & Castaldo, 2004.

[2] See footnote 10 of Chapter 7 for a brief discussion of the impact of one of the changes in dividend payout policies in the US market: significant share buybacks. Changes in dividend policy are always accounted for in this analysis.

the dividend model is complete. Even if you believe that dividends are more manipulated than other aspects of corporate accounting, the attribution model fully explains past returns over the whole history of returns, as well as over any sub-period.

Second, from a forecasting or expectations perspective, the model would also be accurate if only you could forecast correctly. Given that current dividends are known, and that forecasting dividend growth seems to be a reasonable (if difficult) endeavour, we know where the largest part of the certainty lies: what future dividend yields will be generated by the market. To reject a forecast based on this approach as "too pessimistic", meaning that it is much lower than historical averages, without understanding the reasons for that pessimism, is not very useful. Moreover since the framework is comprehensive, more positive forecasts that you may have must be translatable into this framework: either you must believe that the RDG forecast is too low, or you must expect DY to fall even further, causing additional capital gains. By the way, isn't it actually a good thing that forecasts that are made using this system aren't likely to just be the average of the past?

You can also turn the Niederhoffer/Castaldo point around, and use the framework to evaluate the "optimistic" forecasts of others: you can use it to ask the question *"how do you get there from here?"* For example, a recent Reuters Money Blog,[3] reports that:

> Most state and municipal pension funds assume a long-term rate of return around eight percent, reflecting a portfolio invested in equities, bonds and alternative assets such as hedge funds. That number reflects the approach preferred by actuaries. It's supported by actual investment history, and it's endorsed by the Governmental Accounting Standards Board (GASB)

So 8% is the stated nominal return required to fund public pensions in the US, and this is "supported by actual investment history". Since equities have historically returned more than bonds,

---

[3] "How big is the public pension funding gap?" Reuters Money, March 16, 2011 http://blogs.reuters.com/reuters-money/2011/03/16/how-big-is-the-public-pension-funding-gap/.

the fact that the typical pension fund mix has an expected nominal return as high as 8%, implies that they assume that equities should provide an expected nominal return of *more* than 8%, probably 9% or more. For simplicity I'll assume that they require a 9% nominal return for equities. Then let's ask the question: *how do you get there from here?*

We have already seen why someone can claim that a 9% investment return is "supported by actual investment history". Table 1-1 gave the total nominal return for the US as 8.88% with 2.07% inflation (140 years). Table 18-1 broke returns into two periods: the last 30 years with a nominal return of 10.71% and inflation of 3.16%, and the first 110 years with nominal total returns of 8.41% and inflation of 1.77%. So yes, on the face of things, history supports a nominal return of 9%, or even higher if you focus on the last 30 years. Let's assume a 3% inflation rate going forward, certainly higher than long-term history for the US, but perhaps not out of line given the past 30 years and current concerns about the potential for rising inflation long term. That leaves 6% required real return. But again on the face of things this looks like it is supported by history, because over the whole 140 years real returns were 6.67%, over the last 30 years 7.33%, and over the first 110 years 6.52%. No problem!

Except that there is a problem. Go back to my US forecast in Tables 18-3 or 18-4. With starting US dividend yields of less than 2%, and long-term real dividend growth of just over 1%, this leaves us short of the 6% real return goal by about 3% annualized. How do you get there from here? We know that historically, dividend yields were much higher, and prior to the last 30 years provided 79% or more of real returns. By contrast, in the last 30 years average dividend yields have been much lower, and about 45% of real returns came from capital gains generated by those falling dividend yields. We know that we can't have higher dividend yields going forward without suffering a capital loss due to rising yields.[4] So that missing

---

4 Table 14-1 showed that a 1% increase in average dividend yields over 40 years was offset by an average capital loss per year of roughly -1%, this with the conservative assumption that the ending yield did not rise above the average, and over shorter time frames the net impact was negative.

3% has to be made up from further dividend yield declines or higher-than-average dividend growth[5] — you choose.

The point is, a 6% *or higher* real return assumption for US equities, let alone 5% for pension funds as a whole, is unrealistic, and many Canadian funds have dropped their total fund real return assumptions to 4% or even lower.[6]

This kind of argument applies to your financial advisor as well, who might tell you that he expects your overall "balanced" investment portfolio to return 7% nominal, and perhaps assumes that your equities will return 8%. Or when Wall Street says they are "bullish", and you naturally interpret that word to mean they expect future returns to be higher than historical average returns, you can use our framework to put their assumptions to the test. If nothing else, the attribution and forecasting framework provides a touchstone against which you can evaluate financial commentary.

The appeal to long-run historical returns as determining expected returns is quite explicit in the case of the pension funds cited, and may be implicit in the Niederhoffer and Castaldo complaint that the Arnott and Bernstein forecasts from the early 2000s were pessimistic. I hope that I have helped to make this unquestioning appeal to history seem unattractive, but I would like to add one more point here. I want to suggest that any time you hear a Wall Street (or

---

5 One way that higher dividend growth could be realized is if companies generally decided to raise dividend payouts back to historically higher levels. For example a move from 40% to 60% payout over ten years on real earnings growth of 1% would imply a real dividend growth rate of roughly 5% instead of 1% — an increase that would more than make up the shortfall. Under such a scenario dividend yields could rise modestly and the net effect still could be positive. I'm not sure that this is a realistic idea, but it is possible, if the trend to lower payouts is reversed. I'm not going to speculate about what such a change would have on dividend yields, and consequently on total returns.

6 You might argue that 3% would be a more reasonable total fund return assumption, given current equity and bond expected returns. But you should understand that the lower the "discount" rate or required return, the higher the present value of the liabilities. So pension funds are hamstrung (as are individual investors) by the fact that as expected returns have declined, the present value of their future requirements or liabilities have risen.

Bay Street) analyst claiming that stocks are "fairly valued", they are almost certainly implying that investors should expect long-term future returns equal to long-term historical returns, without taking into account the starting point and how that may impact future returns. For example, in 2011 and 2012 I have read countless suggestions that stocks are fairly valued or even cheap, but I've almost never seen explicit expected return numbers, let alone a mechanism for how they would be achieved. I'm quite sure that they would not accept the low real and nominal return forecasts for the US market that I have suggested. I prefer to avoid playing the fair value card, but those who do should be honest and provide realistic expected return forecasts.

In Part 4 I will use my equity forecasts, in conjunction with forecasts for other assets, to show how portfolios can be built within a return and risk framework.

Part 3:

Diversification, Fixed Income and Other Assets

Chapter 19:

Investment Opportunities and Diversification

In Part 3, I will discuss fixed income investments in some detail, and then briefly describe several other investment vehicles that retail and smaller institutional investors should consider holding. But before I do so, it is important to raise the question "why?" or "why bother?" Given the incredible focus on equities that we see in newspapers and investment reports, what is the point in investing in anything but equities? Indeed I haven't even discussed why it is useful or important to consider investing in equities outside your home market, and so I will give some perspective now.

The key point is that as an investor you should want to multiply your investment opportunities. Given that any particular forecast that you make is subject to error, the more forecasts you make (assuming that your forecasts actually have some positive information content or value) the more chance you have of succeeding. In one sense you could call this *diversification*

> **OVERVIEW**
> **The concept of diversification as risk reduction is introduced. It is a consequence of imperfect correlations between assets.**
>
> **Some key points:**
> - **on average, diversified portfolios within a market tend to have less risk than undiversified portfolios, but they embody the undiversifiable risk of the market itself.**
> - **similarly a diversified global equity portfolio may have less risk than that of an individual market, but it takes on the undiversifiable risk of global equities as a whole.**
>
> **Diversification is not in itself an investment strategy, and expected returns and risks have to be considered when making investments.**

— diversification of forecasts or investments. But the concept of diversification is often introduced and defined in terms of the diversification or reduction of *risk*, with little or no emphasis on expected returns or forecasts. This is where I will begin.

In its most basic sense, *diversifying* or *the process of diversification* means to vary, to give variety, or to spread out. In an investment context this means that I vary or spread out my investments by holding multiple securities. A common exercise in introductory textbooks is to examine the impact of holding multiple securities within an individual market such as the Canadian equity market. Individual stocks exhibit a wide range of risk or volatility, measured by the historical standard deviation of their returns, but the average standard deviation of individual stocks is likely between 40% and 50% annualized. The standard deviation of returns falls dramatically as you add a second, a third, and a fourth security to your portfolio, but as you reach perhaps 20 securities, the incremental reduction to risk becomes quite small. This is illustrated schematically in Figure 19-1, where the average standard deviation of returns for portfolios of 20 securities is just under 22%. From this point the blue line flattens, with the standard deviation of 50-stock portfolios averaging

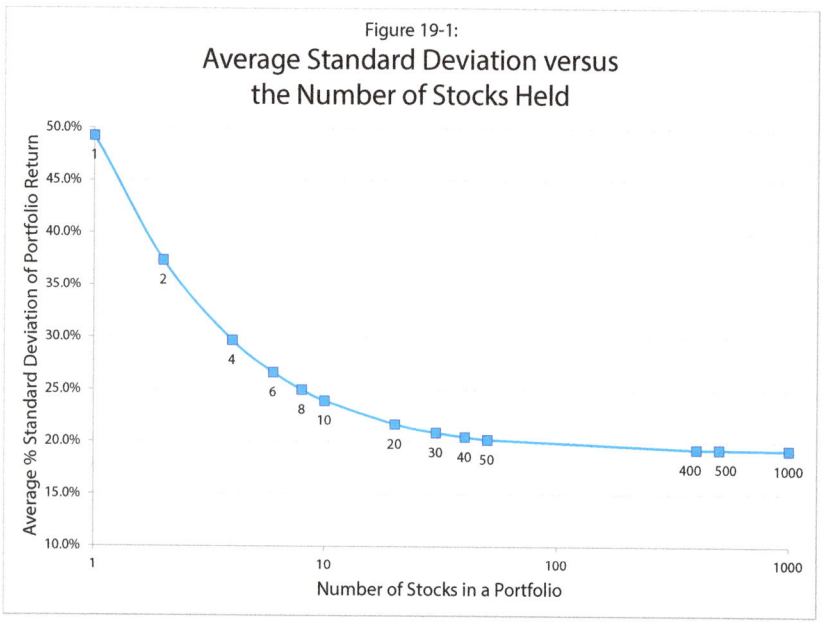

Figure 19-1:
Average Standard Deviation versus the Number of Stocks Held

about 20%, while the standard deviation of 1000-stock portfolio averages about 19%.[1]

You need to understand that the blue line in Figure 19-1 represents the average risk of portfolios of various sizes, and that volatility falls *on average* as you add more stocks. Were you to look at all the possible 50-stock portfolios in this market, as an example, they would be distributed vertically around the average.[2] Note that the blue line can extend to the right until the final portfolio contains all the stocks in the market, and the average risk level of those portfolios is essentially the risk of the market itself, *a risk that cannot be removed by the process of diversification*.

Nothing says that you *must* diversify your portfolio within your home market. Indeed with modern analytical and statistical tools, professional investors may choose to build portfolios that are very different from the market, with a targeted risk level that might be much higher or lower than that of the market. But if you choose to diversify, you are thereby choosing to lower the risk of not being like the market, and are embracing the undiversifiable risk of the market. This means that if the market falls by 50%, holding a broadly diversified portfolio of stocks within that market essentially ensures that your portfolio will fall by about 50% as well. So the idea that diversification reduces risk is partly right — it reduces what can be called *non-market risk* — and is partly misleading — diversification brings a portfolio closer to the risk of the market itself.

---

[1] The example is from a classic simulation of equity portfolio risk by E. J. Elton and M. J. Gruber (E&G 1977).

[2] It's tempting to suggest that 50-stock portfolios are intrinsically less risky than one-stock portfolios, and this is a reasonable idea given sensible practical constraints on the construction of portfolios and the minimum size of each stock holding. But realize that without such constraints, a 50-stock portfolio could have 99.95% of its assets in any one stock, and 0.001% in each of 49 other stocks, and so in extreme cases like this, it would perform just like single-stock portfolios.

Without delving into mathematical details,[3] the basic mechanism that makes the average risk of all the stocks in the market lower than the average risk of a portfolio with a smaller number of stocks, is that individual stocks are not perfectly correlated. This means that they do not move in lockstep, and sometimes will move in different directions or in the same direction to different degrees. Intuitively, the lower the correlation between stocks the more risk reduction that is available.[4]

This concept of diversification due to imperfect correlations applies in a similar fashion across equity markets, and over very long-term history the risk-reducing consequences of diversification have been quite evident. For example, the average correlation between equity markets (in USD) over the whole 111-year period of the DMS dataset from 1900 to 2010 was 0.413, and Figure 19-2 illustrates the impact of this imperfect correlation.

First, the historical US dollar arithmetic average returns and standard deviations of each of the equity markets are plotted on the graph. Second, the average return and average standard deviation of the group of 19 equity markets is plotted as the large black square: the average return was 11.47% with an average standard deviation of 28.1%. But third, the large red square represents a portfolio that invested equally in each country market each year. While its return was still 11.47%, its standard deviation is much lower at 18.7%,

---

[3] Most finance textbooks will have a more technical discussion of correlation and risk reduction, or begin with the Wikipedia article on Diversification (finance).

[4] To give you a sense of the numbers, I calculated ten-year correlations based on monthly returns between pairs of larger capitalization Canadian stocks for the period ending September 2008. The average correlation of the sample was just 0.1327. The average correlation between securities in the broad finance sector was 0.3188, while the average correlation between the six large Canadian banks was 0.5789. Despite the positive average correlation, 15.74% of the correlation pairs had negative values, while the highest ten-year correlations between a stock pair was 0.758.

Daily correlations between stocks in the same industry and over short periods of time can be much higher. For example, over the 125 trading days ending January 31, 2012, the average correlation between Canada's six large banks was 0.796.

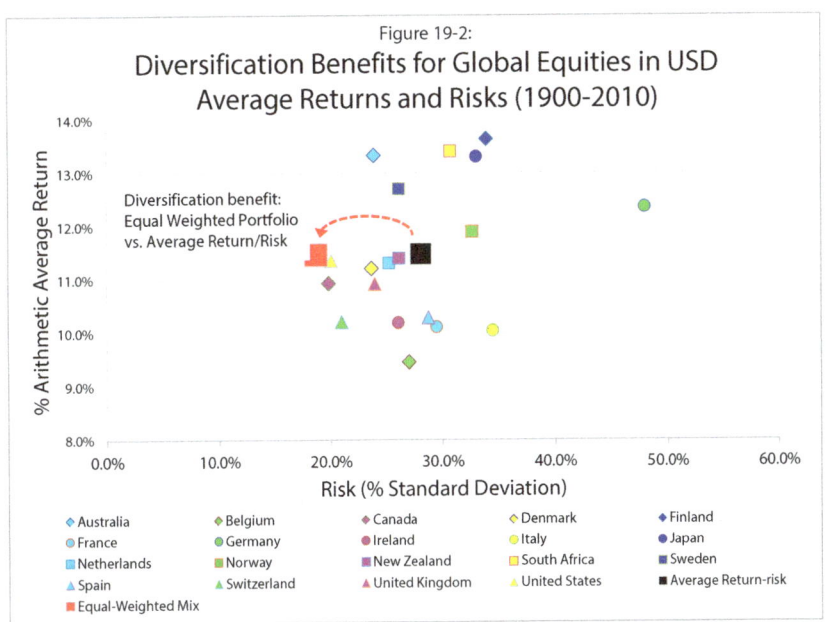

which is just 66.6% of the average risk. This significant reduction of risk is due to the imperfect correlations between markets.

It is noteworthy that in the last half of the twentieth century, correlations began to creep upwards as equity markets became more global and unified. Staying with annual data, the average correlation between country returns rose to 0.612 for the 30 years ending in 2010, and to 0.682 for the last 20 years. The fact of rising correlations is even more apparent using monthly data from our MSCI equity index data. Over the 41 years from 1970 to 2010, the average correlation between country markets in US dollars was 0.594, with correlations over the 11 years from 2000 to 2010 averaging 0.719, rising to 0.813 over the 5 years from 2006 to 2010. As correlations rise, the potential for risk reduction falls. For example, in the 2006–2010 period, with the average correlation rather high at 0.813, the standard deviation of the monthly equal-weighted 19-country portfolio was 24.03%, which is 90.7% of the volatility of the average country market over that period. This is a much lower diversification effect than that provided by the earlier and longer time frames.

The fact of high correlations has led some people to lament that diversification has failed, especially in light of the 2008 credit crisis, during which global equity markets fell together. But sit back for a moment. Remember that diversification within your local equity market removed the risk of being different from the market, and that significant diversification increases the probability that your portfolio will behave like the market itself. You should understand global equity diversification in the same way: the more your portfolio is diversified across equity markets *the more it will behave like the global equity market as a whole*, and the less likely it is that your performance will diverge significantly from it. In other words global diversification guarantees that your equity portfolio will react to global crises just as global markets do, rather than protecting it from them. Of course it can dampen the impact of market crises that are strictly in your local market, to the extent that they exist, since by definition other global markets would not share in them.

I hope it is clear from this that diversification is not in and of itself an investment strategy. The fact that broad diversification in your local market lowers the risk of your portfolio not performing in line with your local market, or that diversifying across global equity markets lowers the risk that your global portfolio will not perform in line with the global equity market, does not in itself give you a reason for *making* such a diversified investment. The discussion of the diversification of risk has not considered the component of expected return: is the risk in question justified by the investment return I expect to receive?

Conversely, focusing on expected returns as I did in Part 2, without evaluating the accompanying expected risks, does not lead to a rational investment decision either. As I discuss in Part 4, the process of building an investment portfolio is essentially the process of finding a desirable trade-off between expected returns and expected risks. Diversification benefits of lower risk from imperfect correlations are part of the evaluation of the expected risk side of the equation.

Since I think most investors should be looking at investing in major asset classes, I will summarize the notion of correlation between equity markets by looking at Canada, the US, EAFE and Emerging

Markets (EM). These are four indexes that a Canadian investor could hold that essentially cover the global equity market.

Table 19-1 presents correlations for the longest history for which I have data for all four assets, beginning in 1988 with the start of emerging markets (EM) data. The left-hand side shows the correlations from a US dollar perspective, while the right-hand side shows the correlations from the perspective of a Canadian dollar investor. You will see that correlations from a Canadian dollar perspective have been lower than those from a US dollar perspective, but remember that this does not tell you anything about whether returns to Canadian dollar-based investors would have been more or less attractive than those achieved by US dollar-based investors.

Table 19-1:

23-Year Correlations
Assets in USD
(Monthly Returns 1988/01-2010/12)

	CN Equity	US Equity	EAFE Equity	EM Equity
CN Equity	1			
US Equity	0.77	1		
EAFE Equity	0.69	0.71	1	
EM Equity	0.70	0.66	0.68	1

23-Year Correlations
Assets in CAD
(Monthly Returns 1988/01-2010/12)

	CN Equity	US Equity	EAFE Equity	EM Equity
CN Equity	1			
US Equity	0.63	1		
EAFE Equity	0.55	0.63	1	
EM Equity	0.60	0.54	0.58	1

Table 19-2 shows the same relationships, but over the five-year period beginning in 2006, during which correlations were substantially higher. Again the Canadian dollar correlations are noticeably lower than those for the US dollar investor.

Table 19-2:

5-Year Correlations
Assets in USD
(Monthly Returns 2006/01-2010/12)

	CN Equity	US Equity	EAFE Equity	EM Equity
CN Equity	1			
US Equity	0.83	1		
EAFE Equity	0.86	0.91	1	
EM Equity	0.90	0.83	0.93	1

5-Year Correlations
Assets in CAD
(Monthly Returns 2006/01-2010/12)

	CN Equity	US Equity	EAFE Equity	EM Equity
CN Equity	1			
US Equity	0.54	1		
EAFE Equity	0.66	0.82	1	
EM Equity	0.80	0.60	0.83	1

To give you a sense of the potential benefits of these imperfect correlations, Figure 19-3 displays the historical returns and risks of each of these four assets.

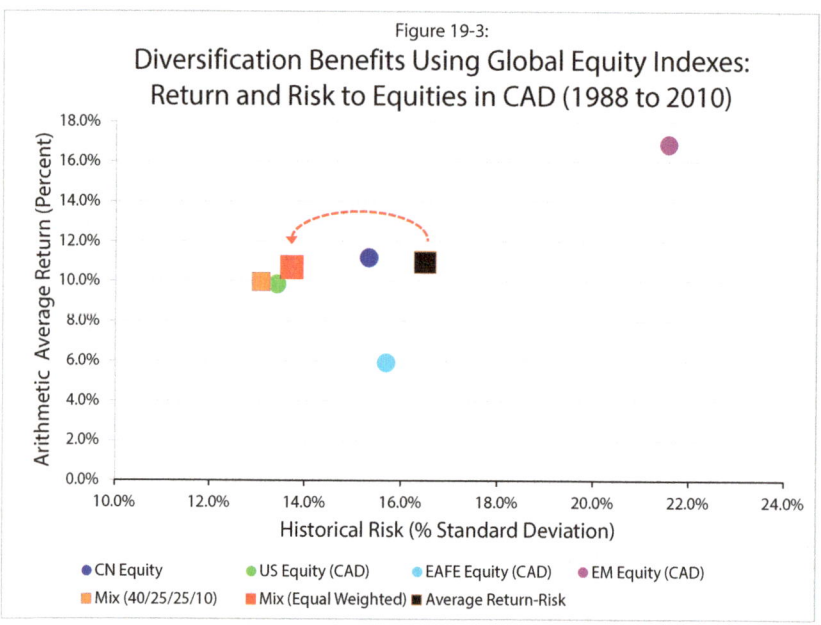

As in Figure 19-2, the larger black square shows the average return and risk of the individual assets, which is compared with the large red square representing a portfolio rebalanced to equal weights at the beginning of each year. This equal-weighted portfolio mix has approximately the same return but noticeably lower risk than the average risk: 13.7% versus 16.5%. The orange square gives a more traditional portfolio mix for a Canadian dollar investor: 40% Canadian Equities, 25% each US and EAFE equities, and 10% Emerging Markets equities. These diversification benefits were maintained even over the past five years ending in 2010, as Figure 19-4 shows.

To come full circle, when an investor searches for investment opportunities there is a tendency to focus on expected returns. But now you can begin to see that the risk dimension is important too. There is at least a possibility that an asset with a lower expected return might enhance your portfolio due to some combination of its

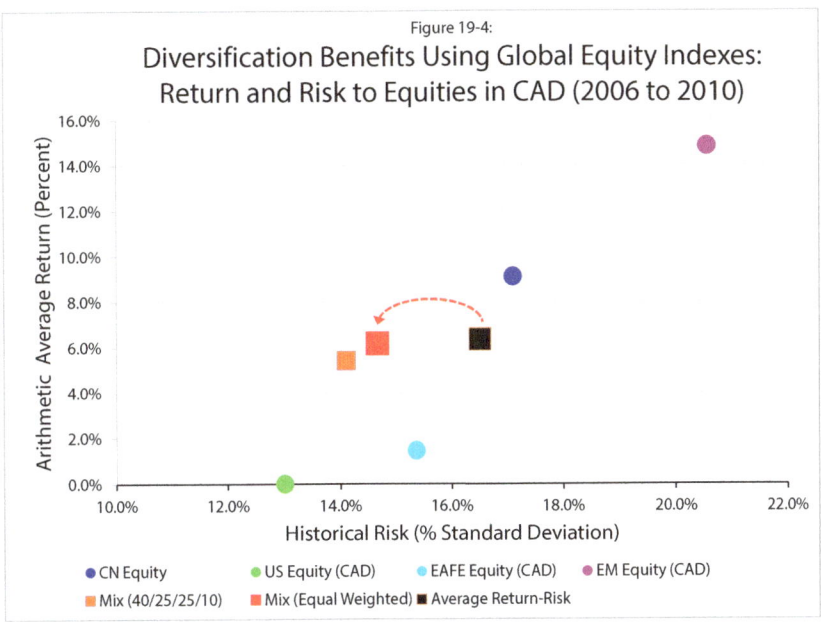

lower risk and imperfect correlation with other assets. And there is also the possibility that the risk level of assets with the highest expected returns might just be too high for your portfolio, although this may depend on the overall level of risk you are willing to bear. Again these issues will be front and centre in Part 4, and in the end you will see that differing risk levels and imperfect correlations will motivate investments across many assets. In the rest of Part 3 I will discuss various fixed income assets, and use this framework to suggest why several other asset classes may be of interest to smaller investors.

Chapter 20:

Historical Returns to Fixed Income

As of 2010 the global market for bonds totalled approximately $95 trillion (USD), almost twice as large as the total global equity capitalization of about $55 trillion.[1] Despite the massive size of the bond or fixed income markets, and despite the fact that most pension funds and foundations have a significant allocation to fixed income, many investors have little knowledge of bonds, their properties, and the role that they may play in a long-term investment portfolio.

Given all the detail and hard work involved in introducing concepts as I outlined the history and described some of the key characteristics of equity markets, the survey of fixed income market history can be substantially streamlined. The two most important sources of bond information are the same as for our equity survey. The first is a 140-year history of US bond yields

> **OVERVIEW**
>
> Historical returns and risks to US and international government bond markets are surveyed.
>
> Key findings:
>
> - over the very long term most bond markets have outperformed inflation;
> - real bond returns have exhibited a negative correlation with inflation;
> - real bond returns have been negative for extended periods; and
> - returns to "cash" or short-term investments have historically kept pace with inflation.

---

[1] Numbers are sourced from the Bank of International Settlements, and cited in an article "Bond Markets", Marko Maslakovic, TheCityUK, July 2011, London UK http://www.thecityuk.com/assets/Uploads/BondMarkets2011.pdf .

from the Shiller dataset (footnote 5, Chapter 1). The second is a 111-year history of longer-term bond returns and the return to "cash" or short-term interest rate instruments for 19 country markets from our DMS dataset. Making some assumptions,[2] the US yield history suggests that over the long term, bonds have outperformed inflation, returning a geometric average annualized return of 4.85% for a real return net of inflation of 2.72%. These numbers, along with a measure of the volatility of returns, are presented in the top section of Table 20-1.

Table 20-1:
Nominal and Real US Bond Returns versus CPI
US data 1871-2010

	Nominal Bond Returns	CPI	Real Bond Returns
Overall: 1871/01-2010/12			
Annualized Return	4.85%	2.07%	2.72%
Annualized Standard Deviation	7.60%	5.86%	9.84%
Divided by Inflation Regime as Defined in Chapter 2			
Period 1 (1871/01-1897/07)	4.85%	-2.55%	7.59%
Period 2 (1897/08-1920/06)	3.07%	5.39%	-2.20%
Period 3 (1920/07-1933/05)	5.35%	-3.84%	9.56%
Period 4 (1933/06-1967/12)	2.35%	2.90%	-0.54%
Period 5 (1968/01-1990/12)	7.76%	6.15%	1.51%
Period 6 (1991/01-2010/12)	7.61%	2.50%	4.98%

Nominal and real bond returns were approximately 4% lower than the nominal and real equity returns for US equities over the same period (see Table 1-1). But the volatility of bond returns was also much lower than the volatility of equity returns: a standard deviation of 7.6% for nominal returns and 9.84% for real returns compared to

---

2 The Shiller dataset provides yields with no related returns, while the DMS dataset provides returns with no related yields. To make better use of the Shiller yield data, I needed to convert them into returns. A sensible way to do this is to assume that they represent yields to maturity of conventional bonds, and since in both cases the bonds are said to be "long", their term should be ten years or more. While choosing a single term for the series is arbitrary and obviously incorrect, I chose 14 years as the average term because that gave the implied returns the same volatility (which suggests the same sensitivity to interest rate changes) as the DMS series over the same period.

Historical Returns to Fixed Income

the standard deviation of both nominal and real equities, which was more than 18% (Chapter 3).

The bottom section of Table 20-1 documents the returns for the various inflation regimes defined in Chapter 2, Table 2-3. The period-by-period nominal bond returns were lower than equity returns, ranging from a low of 2.35% to a high of 7.76%. And while real equity returns were positive in all six regimes, real bond returns were negative in two periods, and ranged from a low of -2.20% to a high of 9.56%.

You can also observe that as with equities, there seems to be a negative relationship between CPI and real bond returns. Table 20-2 helps to show this, comparing real bond and equity returns to CPI over the six regimes, sorting from lowest to highest CPI change. In both cases the correlation is very negative to CPI (-0.88 and -0.87 respectively[3]), while the correlation between real bonds and real equities is strongly positive at 0.72.[4] So both bonds and equities have tended to perform better on a real return basis in low and negative inflation regimes, and worse in higher-inflation periods.

Table 20-2:
Real US Bond and Equity Returns versus CPI
(sorted by CPI regime: lowest average CPI to highest)

	CPI	Real Bond Returns	Real Equity Returns
By Inflation regime ranked from lowest to highest CPI			
Period 3 (1920/07-1933/05)	-3.84%	9.56%	11.88%
Period 1 (1871/01-1897/07)	-2.55%	7.59%	8.26%
Period 6 (1991/01-2010/12)	2.50%	4.98%	6.45%
Period 4 (1933/06-1967/12)	2.90%	-0.54%	8.87%
Period 2 (1897/08-1920/06)	5.39%	-2.20%	2.28%
Period 5 (1968/01-1990/12)	6.15%	1.51%	3.42%
Correlation: vs. CPI		-0.88	-0.87
Correlation: bonds vs. equities			0.72

---

3 Significant at the 0.1% level or better.
4 Significant at the 2.5% level.

Table 2-4 showed that real equity returns were negative in two samples of higher inflation: the nine years from January 1973 to December of 1981, during which CPI averaged 9.22%, and a sample of 26 individual years in which annual inflation was greater than 6%. Table 20-3 compares real bond and equity returns from these two samples. In both cases real bond returns were substantially more negative than real equity returns, posting an average return of -6.52% over the nine-year span from 1973 on, and -8.37% over the sample of 26 high-inflation years. Clearly high inflation has had a negative impact on both stock and bond returns, and long-term bonds are less able to protect investors against inflation than equities. I will show why this is so in the next chapter.

Table 20-3:
Real Bond and Equity Returns when CPI is "High"

	CPI	Real Bond Returns	Real Equity Returns
9-year span from 1973/01 to 1981/12	9.22%	-6.52%	-3.86%
Average of 26 years with CPI Inflation > 6%	10.85%	-8.37%	-3.25%

The international bond dataset generates similar results. Table 20-4 below presents nominal and real bond returns and inflation for the 19 countries, with returns spanning the 111 years from 1900 through 2010. Nominal geometric annualized returns have varied from a low of 2.72% for Germany[5] to a high of 7.19% for Spain. Since inflation has varied significantly, real returns range from a low of -1.91% for Germany to a high of 3.04% for Denmark.

There is no significant correlation between nominal and real bond returns for the whole 111-year span. However, there is a highly significant negative correlation of -0.75 between real returns and

---

[5] As noted in the table, the German data are missing the two years of hyperinflation in 1922-23, during which time bonds essentially lost all of their value. So the German data overstate the actual return to an investor who lost all his investment in 1923, and had to start over again at that point.

Table 20-4:
Real and Nominal Bond Returns
DMS Data: 1900-2010

	Nominal Total Returns			Inflation	Real Total Returns		
	Geom. Mean	Arith. Mean	Std. Dev.	Geom. Mean	Geom. Mean	Arith. Mean	Std. Dev.
Australia	5.36%	5.95%	11.39%	3.86%	1.44%	2.27%	13.19%
Belgium	5.22%	5.66%	9.75%	5.33%	-0.10%	0.62%	11.98%
Canada	5.21%	5.56%	8.80%	3.05%	2.10%	2.61%	10.37%
Denmark	7.05%	7.49%	10.21%	3.89%	3.04%	3.65%	11.65%
Finland	7.06%	7.21%	5.76%	7.32%	-0.24%	1.02%	13.69%
France	7.05%	7.40%	8.70%	7.21%	-0.15%	0.77%	13.01%
Germany***	2.72%	4.95%	13.43%	4.72%	-1.91%	0.76%	15.52%
Ireland	5.16%	5.89%	12.78%	4.26%	0.87%	1.89%	14.85%
Italy	6.65%	7.00%	9.05%	8.45%	-1.66%	-0.37%	14.05%
Japan	5.82%	6.77%	14.39%	7.01%	-1.11%	1.58%	20.11%
Netherlands	4.38%	4.66%	7.70%	2.92%	1.42%	1.84%	9.40%
New Zealand	5.80%	6.16%	8.75%	3.75%	1.98%	2.37%	9.01%
Norway	5.51%	5.88%	8.88%	3.74%	1.71%	2.44%	12.17%
South Africa	6.77%	7.16%	9.34%	4.92%	1.77%	2.29%	10.39%
Spain	7.19%	7.66%	10.38%	5.83%	1.28%	1.95%	11.76%
Sweden	6.10%	6.48%	8.97%	3.57%	2.44%	3.15%	12.41%
Switzerland	4.45%	4.60%	5.71%	2.30%	2.10%	2.49%	9.33%
United Kingdom	5.38%	5.98%	11.84%	3.95%	1.38%	2.23%	13.65%
United States	5.01%	5.33%	8.48%	2.96%	1.98%	2.47%	10.13%
Average	5.68%	6.20%	9.70%	4.69%	0.97%	1.90%	12.46%

*** German data for 1922-23, the period of hyperinflation, have been removed.

inflation.[6] This is readily seen in Figure 20-1, which compares real bond returns (ranked in ascending order from the left) with inflation. Clearly the lower real returns towards the left were associated with higher levels of average inflation, while higher real returns to the right were associated with lower levels of inflation. Note that 6 of 19 countries experienced negative cumulative real returns to bonds over the whole 111-year period, although just one country, Italy, experienced negative arithmetic average annual real returns.

While the bond returns are generally based on fixed income instruments with maturities of ten years or more, short-term

---

[6] The t-statistic is -4.80, which means that the probability is less than 0.02% that the correlation is not in fact negative.

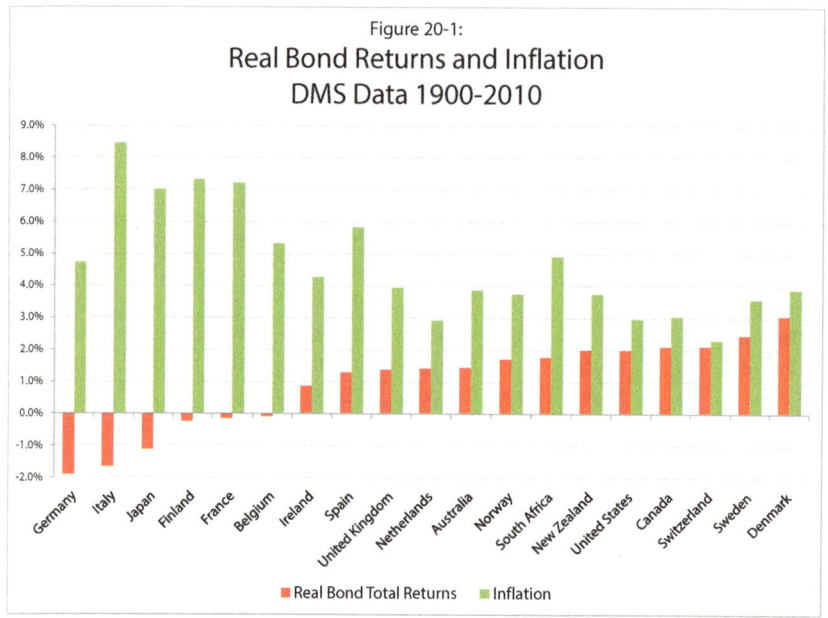

instruments are usually defined as having a maturity of less than one year. Table 20-5 shows the estimated nominal and real returns to short-term interest-rate instruments, often called "cash" instruments in investment jargon. You can see that returns are generally lower than bond returns. Once again six countries experienced negative cumulative real returns over the whole 111-year period, with four of those experiencing negative average real returns.

A good way to put these returns in perspective is to compare the historical returns of short-term and long-term fixed income investments with equity returns. But to make this more meaningful, Figure 20-2 plots real average returns for all three asset classes against their historical risk, the standard deviation of historical real return.[7] Equities are green triangles, bonds are red squares, and short-term

---

[7] I have mentioned that arithmetic average returns rather than annualized returns are more properly compared to standard deviations of return. Both arithmetic average and geometric annualized returns are shown in the tables.

Historical Returns to Fixed Income

Table 20-5:
Real and Nominal Returns to Short-Term Investments
DMS Data: 1900-2010

	Nominal Total Returns			Inflation	Real Total Returns		
	Geom. Mean	Arith. Mean	Std. Dev.	Geom. Mean	Geom. Mean	Arith. Mean	Std. Dev.
Australia	4.57%	4.64%	3.94%	3.86%	0.68%	0.83%	5.40%
Belgium	4.98%	5.02%	2.93%	5.33%	-0.33%	0.01%	8.05%
Canada	4.68%	4.74%	3.59%	3.05%	1.58%	1.70%	4.88%
Denmark	6.23%	6.28%	3.35%	3.89%	2.25%	2.43%	6.04%
Finland	6.83%	6.87%	3.19%	7.32%	-0.46%	0.57%	11.89%
France	4.21%	4.23%	2.29%	7.21%	-2.80%	-2.28%	9.57%
Germany	2.25%	3.68%	9.62%	4.72%	-2.36%	-0.36%	13.23%
Ireland	5.00%	5.07%	4.03%	4.26%	0.71%	0.92%	6.67%
Italy	4.51%	5.07%	11.98%	8.45%	-3.63%	-2.54%	11.53%
Japan	4.96%	4.99%	2.39%	7.01%	-1.92%	-0.31%	13.94%
Netherlands	3.65%	3.67%	2.30%	2.92%	0.71%	0.83%	4.96%
New Zealand	5.46%	5.54%	4.24%	3.75%	1.65%	1.75%	4.68%
Norway	4.94%	5.00%	3.47%	3.74%	1.16%	1.41%	7.18%
South Africa	6.02%	6.17%	5.66%	4.92%	1.05%	1.24%	6.23%
Spain	6.19%	6.26%	4.01%	5.83%	0.34%	0.51%	5.87%
Sweden	5.53%	5.58%	3.11%	3.57%	1.90%	2.12%	6.81%
Switzerland	3.10%	3.12%	1.81%	2.30%	0.78%	0.90%	4.99%
United Kingdom	5.00%	5.06%	3.75%	3.95%	1.01%	1.20%	6.38%
United States	3.91%	3.95%	2.79%	2.96%	0.92%	1.03%	4.66%
Average	4.84%	5.00%	4.13%	4.69%	0.17%	0.63%	7.52%

instruments are blue diamonds. I also plotted the average of each group in pink, with the appropriate shape for each group.[8]

The overall trend is that higher historical risks have been associated with higher historical returns. As well, generally equities have the higher return and risk, long bonds have intermediate return and risk, and short-term instruments have the lowest return and risk. Returns to short-term instruments generally outpaced inflation, with an arithmetic average real return of 0.63% (average annualized cumulative real return of just 0.17%) against a standard deviation of annual returns of 7.5%. Real bond returns averaged 1.9% (average annualized cumulative return of 0.97%) with an average standard

---

[8] Bond and short-term data are from Tables 20-4 and 20-5, while equity data are from Table 5-1.

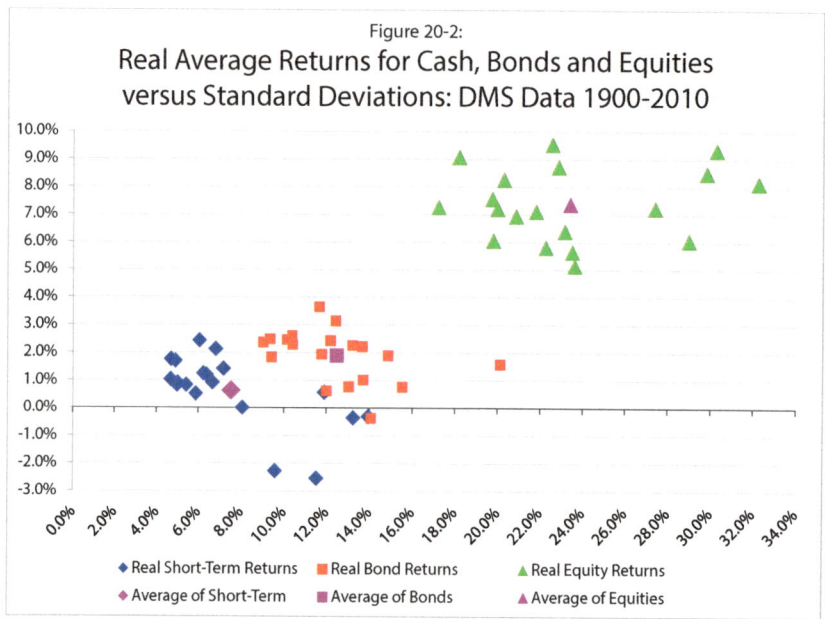

deviation of annual returns of 12.46%. Real equity returns averaged 7.37% (average annualized cumulative return of 4.74%) against an average annual standard deviation of return of 23.4%. Although Figure 20-2 cannot show the correlations between individual assets, you can see part of the point about risk and return made at the end of the previous chapter. Given the very high levels of risk associated with the higher real returns of equities, fixed income assets, with both lower returns and risk, may find a place in a portfolio designed to carry lower risk.

The picture is slightly more positive when we look at returns from 1950 onward, a time in which inflation was generally positive but fairly stable, with no very significant deflationary periods and fairly contained periods of high inflation. Figure 20-3 shows that only one country, Italy, experienced negative real returns to short-term investments, and the average annual real return to short-term was 1.38% (average annualized real return of 1.32%) with a standard deviation of annual return at 3.53%. Bonds generated an average real return of 2.97% (average annualized real return of 2.44%) against an average standard deviation of annual return of 10.13%. Equities

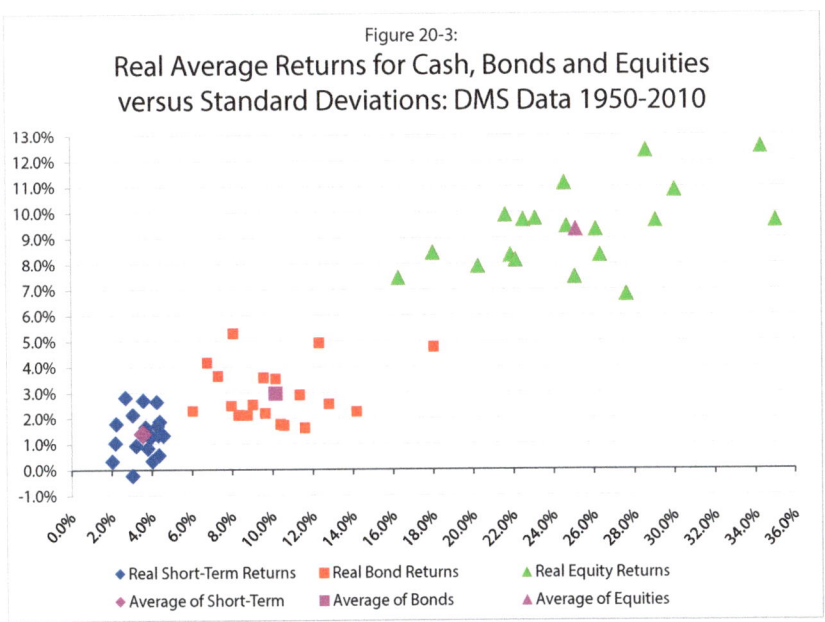

Figure 20-3: Real Average Returns for Cash, Bonds and Equities versus Standard Deviations: DMS Data 1950-2010

produced an average real return of 9.34% (average annualized real return of 6.46%) with an average standard deviation of 25.1%.

It is worth noting that over the past 60 years, and to a lesser extent over the whole 111-year period, returns to short-term investments have generally outpaced inflation. This has given an enhanced sense of safety to such investments, particularly to those issued by sovereign governments. But in the years since 2008, returns to short-term have trailed inflation, sometimes by substantial amounts. At the time of writing there is no sign that this situation will change in the near future, as nominal short-term rates in many developed markets continue to be close to 0%. Thus short-term instruments are now of very little use for the long-term investor, unless they are held for a very short time indeed.

It is also worth remarking that while returns to bonds and equities have also been very robust in the past 60 years, differences between country experiences are striking. As I show you a little about the mechanics of how bond returns are generated, you will see that much as with equities, you should not be lulled into complacency by strong average historical performance. As always, your starting point matters.

Chapter 21:

Yields, Changes in Yield, and Returns

The bonds referred to in the previous chapter might be called *nominal* bonds. Generally a borrower structures the instrument to pay back the face value (or value borrowed) at maturity, which might range from 1 year to 30 years or more. He pays interest in the form of ongoing fixed payments, historically called coupons. The most common structure has two payments per year, with each payment being half the designated annual rate.[1] Thus a 4% nominal bond is a series of fixed cash flows of 2% semi-annual interest payments that are paid at the end of each interest period, with the final interest payment accompanied by the repayment of the original amount borrowed.

The term "nominal" refers to the fact that all the payments are fixed and known in advance. This means that

> **OVERVIEW**
>
> Returns to nominal bonds are shown to be a function of the starting yield to maturity and the return due to any change in yield.
>
> Key concepts:
>
> - an attribution model of return is developed similar to the model for equities;
> - comparing the bond and equity models shows the structural differences between the two asset classes;
> - the impact of inflation on bond returns is added to the attribution model, and explains how bond returns interact with inflation.

---

1 There are many possible bond structures, including different structurings of coupons, and features such as a call by the borrower (allowing him to retire the bonds at one or more specified early dates), and so on. These will not be discussed here.

nominal returns to lenders and nominal costs for the borrower are also known in advance if the bond is held to maturity, regardless of what happens with future inflation.

A bond's *yield to maturity* is the single interest rate for which, when used to discount each of the cash flows to a present value, the sum of those present values is equal to the current price. That is, price determines a yield to maturity, and conversely. For those who are unfamiliar with discounting a future value to a present value, just think of it as the reverse of investing. You understand that $100 invested at any of 10%, 5% and 0% for one year results in a future value of $110, $105 and $100 respectively. Conversely, the present value of $110 a year from now at a 10% discount rate, $105 a year from now at a 5% discount rate, and $100 a year from now at a 0% discount rate for the year is $100 in each case. Alternatively, if you consider a single future value such as $100 one year from now, then the present values discounted at 10%, 5% and 0% are respectively $90.91, $95.24 and $100. This latter way of looking at the relationship clearly shows that high or rising yields imply lower or falling prices and lower or falling yields imply higher or rising prices.

Since a bond's price determines its yield, and conversely, either prices or yields can be used to fully capture the value of, or the return to, a bond or bond portfolio. But we often talk about bond prices as being driven by interest rates and their changes rather than the reverse. For example, you may read that a central bank is raising or lowering rates or yields, or that yields are rising or falling due to expectations of rising or falling inflation. On the other hand, when we hear that investors are running to the safety of US Treasuries, it might be more natural to think of the demand to buy Treasuries causing investors to bid up prices rather than to bid down yields. Which way we choose to talk is really a matter of perspective and context.[2]

---

[2] Fixed income analysis usually treats the Canadian or US government bond market as having a term structure of interest rates, in which each future time is associated with a unique interest rate or yield to that maturity. Thus the price of

Just as the total return for holding an equity is the change in price plus any dividends and the return from their reinvestment, the total return for holding a bond is its change in price, plus its interest payments and any return from their reinvestment. That is how you account for portfolio cash flows and calculate returns for both stocks and bonds.

But for the purpose of historical analysis, and later for the purpose of forecasting, I articulated an attribution model for equity returns as a function of dividend yield, dividend growth, and the return generated by the change in dividend yield. Here I want to develop a similar attribution model of bond returns.

For example, if you buy a bond with a price equivalent to a 4% yield to maturity, and then both reinvest any payments you received at 4% and sell it for a price equivalent to a 4% yield to maturity at the end of your holding period, you will receive a 4% return. That is, under those two special conditions the starting yield to maturity equals the total return. In fact such a scenario is unlikely, as yields (and therefore prices) are constantly in flux: the available reinvestment opportunities for your cash flows will probably not remain at 4%, and it is unlikely that you will be able to sell the bond at 4%. But despite this, the starting yield to maturity of a bond, or better, of a portfolio of bonds, is a reasonable first-level approximation of returns over a longer-term time frame.

Figure 21-1 illustrates this. The blue line shows US bond yields at the end of each year, from 1871 to 2010, while the red line shows ten-year returns, moved so that the return above or below each blue point is the subsequent ten-year return. When you take a moment to think through the graph, you can see that at points on the blue line after which yields are rising, the related ten-year return is below the blue dot, because subsequent rising yields have caused prices to fall. Conversely at points after which yields are falling, the related subsequent return is generally above the blue dot,

---

a bond is actually the function of a series of individual rates associated with each cash flow. From this analytical point of view, interest rates are indeed primary.

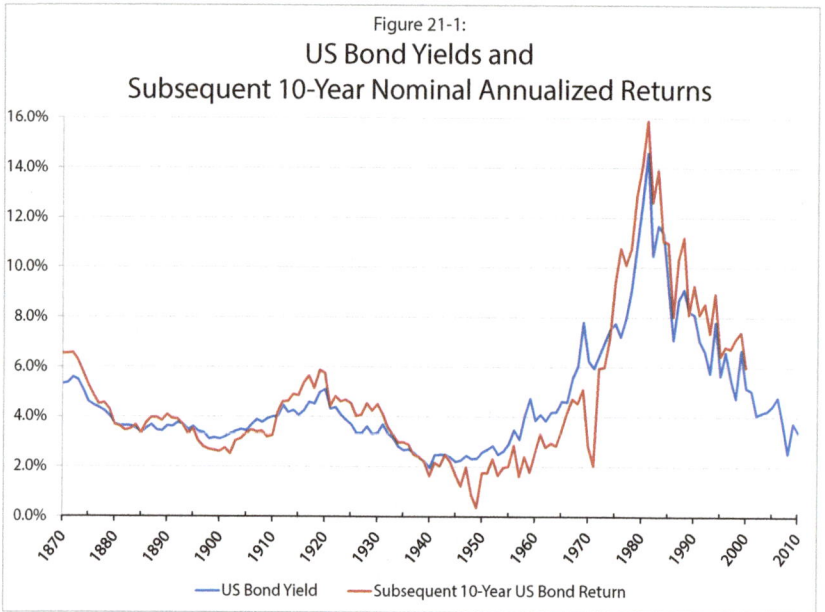

since falling subsequent yields have caused prices to rise. To give an extreme example, the yield at the end of 1971 was 5.95%, while the subsequent ten-year return was just 2.03%. During this decade, yields rose in all but one year, ending at 14.59%, which of course caused bond prices to fall. However, on average the current yield to maturity appears to be a good estimate of subsequent ten-year returns.

Indeed I can measure the strength of this relationship. Since the ten-year returns overlap, I cannot reliably apply statistics directly to the data in Figure 21-1. But just as with equity returns, I can look at non-overlapping ten-year periods,[3] of which there are 14. The linear regression to explain subsequent ten-year returns as a function of current yield is extremely strong, with an adjusted r-squared of 85.2% and a t-statistic of 8.71.[4] This suggests that current yield is a very good estimate of future returns over ten years.

---

3 As before, to obtain the maximum number of data points the return periods span decades ending 1880, 1890, and so on to 2010.

4 The t-statistic implies that the probability that the coefficient is really zero is 0.0002%.

By contrast, when I look ahead just one year, the returns appear to be much more volatile. Figure 21-2 plots US bond yields (the same blue line as in Figure 21-1), but this time the red line is for subsequent one-year returns. The volatile red line reflects the annual standard deviation of 7.6% mentioned in Table 20-1.

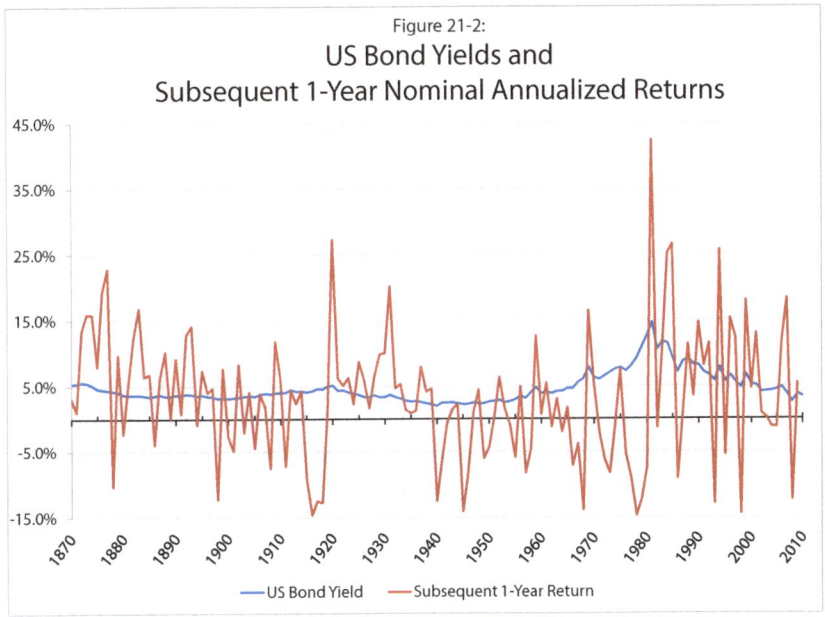

In fact the current yield is also important in explaining future one-year returns, although it is hard to see this in Figure 21-2. The linear regression that describes future one-year returns as a function of current yields has a very significant relation to next year's return, but it explains a smaller, though important, part of the variability of return with an adjusted r-squared of 23.8%.[5]

The explanation of how bond returns are calculated can be used to explain the volatility in Figure 21-2. Remember that if the bond's yield to maturity was not to change over the holding period of one

---

[5] The t-statistic of the coefficient of yields as explaining one-year future returns is 6.67, significant at better than the 0.0001% level.

year, you would receive a return equal to that yield to maturity,[6] with no return due to a change in price. So the volatility shown by the red line in Figure 21-2 *must come from changing yields,* which are equivalent to changes in price. In other words the return of a bond (or a portfolio of bonds, for that matter), is essentially a function of the starting yield to maturity plus the return due to changes in the yield to maturity during the holding period. This sounds a little bit like the equity attribution model, and can be symbolized as:

(21.1) $nbTR_t \approx Y_{t-1} + r\Delta Y_t$

where $nbTR_t$[7] is the nominal bond total return over period t
Y_{t-1} is the yield to maturity at the end of t-1 (that is, the starting yield for period t), and
$r\Delta Y_t$ is the return due to the change in yield to maturity over period t

I will demonstrate approximation (21.1) empirically rather than mathematically. Case 1 in Table 21-1 shows the historical regression mentioned in association with Figure 21-2: future one-year returns are explained as a function of starting yield to maturity. The coefficient associated with the starting yield is highly significant, and the adjusted r-squared of 23.81% means that 23.81% of the variability of one-year returns is explained by the starting yield to maturity. But in Case 2, I add the simple change in yield over the coming year as a second explanatory factor. The t-statistics and significance of both yield to maturity and the new yield-change variable skyrocket, and fully 98.46% of the variability of the one-year returns is explained. As you should expect, the coefficient of the yield change is negative, since an increase in yield implies a reduction of return, and conversely.[8]

---

6 Including a small return due to any reinvestment of the interest received.

7 Although the context normally makes the term "TR" (total return) unambiguous, from now on I will add "nb" or "eq" to "TR" to differentiate between total nominal return to equities as eqTR and total nominal return to nominal bonds as nbTR. Similarly real total returns will be symbolized as eqRTR and nbRTR.

8 The mathematics of fixed income is much more complex than that of equities. Despite this, while I think people intuitively "get" the impact of ongoing interest income, in the case of equities and dividend income this seems to be a blind spot. The importance of equity income is so much at odds with the current equity

Table 21-1:
Relating Factors to Subsequent 1-Year Returns to US Bonds

Case 1: Using starting Yield to Maturity only			
Variable	Constant	Starting YtM	
Coefficient	-2.678	1.665	
t-Statistic	-2.071	6.666	
Probability Coefficient is 0	4.018%	0.00000%	
Adjusted R-squared	23.81%		
# of observations:	140		
Case 2: Starting YtM + actual change in YtM			
Variable	Constant	Starting YtM	Actual Change in YtM over period
Coefficient	-0.471	1.167	-8.591
t-Statistic	-2.540	32.414	-81.890
Probability Coefficient is 0	1.219%	0.00000%	0.00000%
Adjusted R-squared	98.46%		
# of observations:	140		
Case 3: Starting YtM + Duration x actual change in YtM			
Variable	Constant	Starting YtM	Starting Duration x Actual Change in YtM over period
Coefficient	-0.768	1.253	-0.988
t-Statistic	-5.747	48.466	-114.015
Probability Coefficient is 0	0.000%	0.00000%	0.00000%
Adjusted R-squared	99.20%		
# of observations:	140		

I will come back to Case 3 in a moment, but Table 21-2 presents similar information for future ten-year returns (a subset of non-overlapping samples from the data underlying Figure 21-1). Case 1 shows the results as already reported, that starting yields have a very strong relationship with future ten-year returns, explaining 85.2% of their variability. When I add the future ten-year yield change in Case 2, the significance of the coefficients is very high, and the adjusted r-squared jumps to 99.53%.

In both tables I have given a Case 3, in which the interest rate change variable has been multiplied by a factor called *duration*. Duration is a measure of a bond's price sensitivity with respect to

---

culture that focuses on the possibility of short-term capital appreciation, that I felt the need to lay out the algebra of equity returns in detail.

Table 21-2:
Relating Factors to Subsequent 10-Year Returns to US Bonds

Case 1: Using starting Yield to Maturity only			
Variable	Constant	Starting YtM	
Coefficient	-0.780	1.156	
t-Statistic	-1.057	8.707	
Probability Coefficient is 0	31.129%	0.00016%	
Adjusted R-squared	85.20%		
# of observations:	14		
Case 2: Starting YtM with Actual Future Change in YtM			
Variable	Constant	Starting YtM	Actual Change in YtM over period
Coefficient	0.337	0.913	-0.533
t-Statistic	2.341	33.991	-19.139
Probability Coefficient is 0	3.914%	0.00000%	0.00000%
Adjusted R-squared	99.53%		
# of observations:	14		
Case 3: Starting YtM + Duration x actual change in YtM			
Variable	Constant	Starting YtM	Starting Duration x Actual Change in YtM over period
Coefficient	0.170	0.963	-0.055
t-Statistic	1.568	48.535	-24.959
Probability Coefficient is 0	14.512%	0.00000%	0.00000%
Adjusted R-squared	99.72%		
# of observations:	14		

changes in yield: specifically, it is the percentage price change given a 1% change in yield.[9] In Case 3, the yield change over any given future period is multiplied by the duration at the beginning of

---

[9] This concept of duration, sometimes called modified duration, is closely related to the concept of Macaulay Duration, which is a function of discounted cash flows: the time in years it takes for the bond's cash flows and their reinvestment at the current yield to maturity to earn back the initial price of the bond. Macaulay Duration, which is the calculation normally found in bond fund and ETF information, is stated in years, and for our purposes can be used as a proxy for modified duration. So for example, a duration of 6.75 years can be viewed as a sensitivity of 6.75% for a 1% change in yield.

The actual relation is: Modified Dur = MacaulayDur/(1+y/n) where y is the yield to maturity and n is the number of payments per year. Thus for a semi-annual pay bond, with a yield to maturity of 4%, and Macaulay duration at 6.75 years as above, the ModDur is 6.62%, close to the Macaulay duration number.

the period. You can see that in both tables, Case 3 has a slightly higher adjusted r-squared than Case 2, and that the t-statistics of the second and third coefficients of Case 3 are also higher. So adjusting the future yield change by the duration factor improves the already strong relationship.

This relationship from case 3 is captured by approximation (21.2), and provides an excellent attribution of bond returns over a holding period t: the total return of a bond or a portfolio of bonds for a period t is approximately the sum of the starting yield to maturity less[10] the starting duration multiplied by the yield change over the period. In symbols this is:

(21.2) $\text{nbTR}_t \approx Y_{t-1} - \text{Dur}_{t-1} * (Y_t - Y_{t-1})$

where nbTR_t is a bond's nominal total return for period t
Y_t and Y_{t-1} are the bond's yield to maturity at times t and t-1 respectively, and
Dur_{t-1} is the bond's modified duration at time t-1

You can think of the term $-\text{Dur}_{t-1} * (Y_t - Y_{t-1})$ as interpreting or estimating the term $r\Delta Y_t$ in (21.1), the return due to a change in yield to maturity.

Of course you can precisely calculate the actual returns to a bond or portfolio of bonds over history without using this approximation, although it is a handy way to quickly estimate the returns to a bond portfolio if you know the starting yield to maturity and duration, and the ending yield to maturity.[11]

Comparing the form of (21.1) with approximation (7.7), the analogous approximation for local market equities, provides a succinct way of comparing bonds and equities.

(7.7) $\text{eqTR}_g \approx DY_g + DG_g + r\Delta DY_g$

---

10 "Less" rather than "plus", because the duration is given as a positive percentage number, and the relation between interest rate changes and price changes is negative.

11 The approximation is more accurate, the shorter the period over which it is calculated. In the next chapter when I apply the attribution to longer periods, I calculated it over shorter periods such as months and years as I did for equities, and then accumulated the results over the longer term.

(21.1) $\text{nbTR}_t \approx Y_{t-1} + r\Delta Y_t$

Apart from the fact that I am not implicitly generalizing (21.1) across multiple periods, the key difference is that there is no yield growth component for bonds analogous to DG for equities. Cash flows are fixed by the definition of the bond, and (short of default) do not vary over the life of the instrument. We saw that dividend growth was linked with economic growth, and it is this growth factor that allows equities to keep pace with, and in many "normal" cases actually outpace, inflation. The fact that a nominal bond does not have a growth factor that adjusts to inflation helps to explain why bonds performed so much worse than equities in the higher inflation regimes (see Tables 20-2 and 20-3).

To make this point explicitly, remember that real returns are nominal returns net of inflation effects,

$\text{RTR}_t \approx \text{TR}_t - I_t$

So subtracting inflation from both sides of (21.1) yields approximation (21.3):

(21.3) $\text{nbRTR}_t \approx Y_{t-1} + r\Delta Y_t - I_t$

Approximation (21.3) makes it very clear that inflation is subtracted "off the top", directly eroding the starting yield to maturity. That is, if the yield to maturity at the start of a period is 3%, and inflation over the holding period is 2.5%, then the real return is 0.5% adjusted for any return due to yield changes.

This contrasts with the equities. Subtracting inflation from both sides of (7.7), to define equity real total return, yields what I will call (7.8*):

(7.8*) $\text{eqRTR}_g \approx DY_g + DG_g + r\Delta DY_g - I_g$,

But since $DG_g - I_g$, is just real dividend growth or RDG_g, this becomes approximation (7.8):

(7.8) $\text{eqRTR}_g \approx DY_g + RDG_g + r\Delta DY_g$

The fact that dividends have tended to grow with the economy[12] provides at least a partial hedge to inflation, while nominal bonds do not provide such a hedge, and the contrast between (21.3) and (7.8) and (7.8*) shows exactly why this is so.

But it's actually worse than this, because there is good reason to believe that the last two terms of (21.3) interact with each other: higher inflation is usually accompanied by, and possibly causes, higher yields. This point is really about *inflation expectations* rather than actual inflation. Since investors understand (21.3) (or something very like it), if current yields are 3% but then general expectations about inflation over the next period rise to 3% or higher, why would prospective purchasers buy bonds to yield 3% to lock in a 0 or negative real return? If this indeed becomes the accepted view of inflation, then in order to attract purchasers, sellers will have to offer lower prices, which equates to selling at higher yield levels. Conversely if expected inflation falls, potentially increasing real returns, purchasers will have to bid higher prices (or lower yields) to entice sellers to sell.

There is certainly empirical evidence that this relationship holds, at least in terms of actual inflation and actual yields. For example, Figure 21-3 shows US bond yields and one-year inflation for each year-end from 1950 onwards. The statistical relationship is very strong, with yields (blue line) generally rising as inflation (red line) rises, and conversely.[13] You can also see that at almost all year-end points (55 of 61 cases), current yields had a positive spread over 12-month CPI change, no matter what the inflation rate. The implication here is that if inflation is generally positive, and were it to rise over a holding period, an investor would not only be hurt by the fact that inflation is rising, which reduces real return, but by the fact that yields might be rising as well, causing a negative return due to the change in yield component $r\Delta Y_t$.

---

12 At least when inflation remains relataively low. We saw that as inflation rose to double digits, evidence grew that dividends might fall behind nominal growth.

13 The t-statistic of the coefficient in the regression of yield as a function of trailing one-year CPI is 6.52, which means that the probability that the relationship is not positive over this period is substantially below 0.001%.

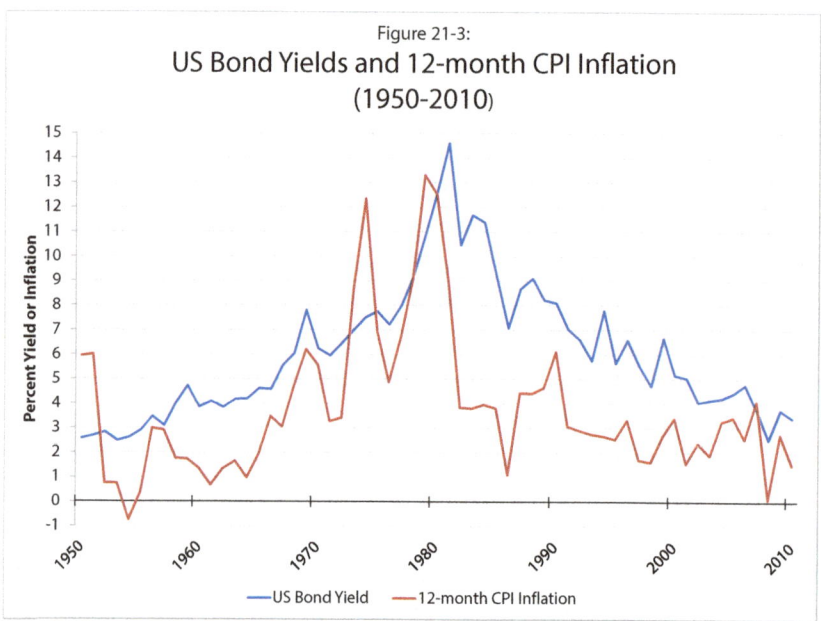

Figure 21-3:
US Bond Yields and 12-month CPI Inflation (1950-2010)

To put numbers to this, suppose that an investor is holding a long bond portfolio with a duration of ten years and a starting yield of 3.5%. If he expects inflation of 2.5% over the next year, his expected real return is 1%. But what if inflation actually rises from the 2.5% expected at the beginning of the period to 3.5% at the end of the year, while the yield to maturity of the portfolio rises in tandem to end the year at 4.5%, maintaining the differential of 1%. Rather than the expected real return of 1%, the rise in inflation wiped that out: 3.5% yield − 3.5% inflation = 0% real return. But worse, the rise in bond yields of 1% means that the portfolio lost 10% (1% x duration of 10). To summarize:

$$nbRTR_t \approx Y_{t-1} + r\Delta Y_t - I_t$$
$$\approx 3.5\% - 10\% - 3.5\%$$
$$\approx -10\%$$

where -10% is the estimate of $r\Delta Y_t$ developed in approximation (21.2): a duration of 10 multiplied by a yield change of 1%.

The important lesson is that there is a strong positive relationship between nominal bond yields and inflation. Theoretical work puts this in terms of inflation expectations and yields, but there is some

Yields, Changes in Yield, and Returns 247

evidence of a relationship between yields and actual current inflation. I will revisit the importance of inflation expectations in the next chapters, as I discuss the forecasting of bond returns.

A final point is that just as with equities, you may choose to invest in foreign fixed income securities denominated in foreign currencies. As you would expect, foreign currencies will work just the same with bonds as with equities, and so I will not work through the details that were presented in Chapters 8 and 9. I will simply assume that foreign currency elements can be added if and as needed. Obviously, your treatment of currencies for equities, such as adopting the view that long-term real or nominal returns to FX are 0, has to be mirrored by your treatment of currencies for bonds and any other assets not denominated in your home currency.

Chapter 22:

Forecasting Returns to Nominal Bonds

Given my approach to forecasting returns to equities, and given the discussion of bond returns and attribution to this point, you will likely have a very good idea of what will come next. But before I explicitly lay out an approach for forecasting returns to nominal bonds, I want to examine the components of bond return and risk in more detail.

The top section of Table 22-1 shows the annualized returns for the components of attributed returns to US bonds from 1871 to 2010, along with their standard deviations. This is based on approximation (21.2) which was applied year by year to annual data, with each component being

> **OVERVIEW**
> First, the bond attribution model is applied to historical bond returns.
> - 96% of long-term nominal US bond returns are due to annual starting yield, but most of their volatility is due to changing yields;
> - high inflation is negatively correlated with returns due to changing yield.
>
> Second, the bond attribution model is turned into a model of expected nominal and real returns.

accumulated over time. The bottom portion of the table gives the return attribution for each of the six inflation regimes that were isolated in the work on equities, sorted from low to high CPI in column 5. Here approximation (21.2) was used on monthly data, and the components of return were accumulated for each sub-period.

The first column gives the cumulative return based on the starting yield to maturity for each period (year or month) assuming

Table 22-1:
Attributed Returns to US Bonds
Based on Annual Data (1871-2010)

	(1) Return Due to Starting YTM	(2) Return Due to ΔYTM	(3) Total Attributed Return	(4) Total Actual Return	(5) CPI CPI
Overall: 1871/01-2010/12					
Annualized Return	4.64%	0.07%	4.71%	4.84%	2.07%
Annualized Standard Dev.	2.25%	6.63%	7.41%	7.60%	5.86%
By Inflation regime ranked from lowest to highest CPI					
Period 3 (1920/07-1933/05)	3.86%	1.47%	5.39%	5.35%	-3.84%
Period 1 (1871/01-1897/07)	4.09%	0.77%	4.88%	4.85%	-2.55%
Period 6 (1991/01-2010/12)	5.42%	1.73%	7.24%	7.61%	2.50%
Period 4 (1933/06-1967/12)	3.09%	-0.76%	2.32%	2.35%	2.90%
Period 2 (1897/08-1920/06)	3.89%	-0.76%	3.10%	3.07%	5.39%
Period 5 (1968/01-1990/12)	9.13%	-1.73%	7.26%	7.76%	6.15%
Correlation with CPI		-0.75			
Probability correlation is 0		8.72%			

that the yield remains constant over the period. The second column is the cumulative return due to the change in yield to maturity. The third column gives the total attributed return, the period-by-period accumulation of the first two components. The fourth column allows you to compare the actual nominal return with the attributed return in column three, while column five gives accumulated CPI. Columns four and five are duplicated from Table 20-1.

Focusing on the top part of the table, the most obvious point is that over the very long term, the return due to starting yield to maturity contributes 96% of total return (4.64% versus the total of 4.84%). Return due to the change in yield, as estimated by approximation (21-2), contributed just 1.5% of total return, as gains and losses due to this factor roughly balanced out over history. A small portion of total return remains unexplained. By contrast, while the volatility of the starting yield component was very low at only 2.25%,[1] which is 30% of the magnitude of the total volatility of

---

[1] A good question is: why is there any volatility at all to this component? The answer is that in this study, the attribution is performed on an annual basis, and

bond returns of 7.6%, the volatility of the yield change component was 6.63%, which is 87% of the magnitude of the total volatility of bond returns. So most of the volatility of bond returns was due to the change of yield component of return.

The bottom part of Table 22-1, which presents the attribution for each inflation regime, shows that while the returns due to starting yields still dominate, the returns due to change in yield have now become a larger component of return. The individual regimes are sorted by lowest average inflation to highest average inflation, and several important relationships can be seen. On the one hand, while there is a positive correlation of 0.49 between the return due to starting YTM and CPI, it is not significant,[2] and so is not reported in the table. On the other hand the second column, return due to the change in bond yield, has a negative correlation with CPI of -0.75, and the relationship is marginally significant.[3] This means that higher inflation regimes have been accompanied by rising yields and negative returns to this factor, while lower or negative inflation regimes have been accompanied by falling yields and positive returns to this factor. Thus the discussions from the previous chapters about the relationship between inflation and yields dovetails perfectly into the attributed structure of bond returns. Real bond returns are negatively correlated with CPI (Table 20-2), and bonds do not provide an inflation hedge (Table 20-3), because of the return due to the change in bond yields that accompanies changes in inflation.

With these insights in hand, I will turn approximation (21.1) into a model for formulating *expected returns* for bonds or bond portfolios. That is, expected nominal bond return over the coming period is my current bond yield plus the expected return due to any change in yield:

(22.1) $E(nbTR_t) \approx Y_{current} + E(r\Delta Y_{future})$

---

is then linked together over time. Since starting yields change from period to period, there is some volatility associated to the starting yield to maturity over time.

2 The t-statistic is 1.153, and the probability that the correlation is 0 is fairly high at 31.3%.

3 The probability that the correlation is 0 is 8.72%.

If I have no forecast of future yields, then (22.1) suggests that my expected return should be the current yield to maturity. Figure 21-1 and the regression in Case 1 of Table 21-2 supports that this is a very reasonable expectation.

On the other hand if I expect that yields will change over the forecast horizon, then I can estimate the implications of this change by using the interpretation of the return due to the change in yield to maturity as a function of duration times yield change, analogous to approximation (21.2).

$$(22.2)\ E(nbTR_{future}) \approx Y_{current} - Dur_{current}*(E(Y_{future}) - Y_{current})$$

Approximation (22.2) makes it clear that the only unknown or forecast element in the expression is future or ending yield to maturity, since duration and current yields are known.[4]

To give a quick example, in early 2012 the weighted yield to maturity of the iShares Dex Canadian Universe Bond ETF was 2.5% with an average duration of 6.62 years. Suppose you believe that Canadian rates will move up to at least 4.0% at the end of your ten-year forecast horizon, then the impact of rising rates would be -6.62%*(4.0%-2.5%) or -9.93% unannualized for ten years, which is approximately -1% per year. In that case you would expect your starting yield of 2.5% to be reduced by 1% due to rising yields, for an all-in forecast of 1.5% annualized return over ten years. If you are not willing to take a view about future yields, then you should use the current yield to maturity of 2.5% as your estimate of future nominal bond returns.

In order to make a forecast of real returns for nominal fixed income, you need to adjust for inflation expectations, by subtracting expected inflation from both sides. Using the more detailed (22.2), this becomes:

$$(22.3)\ E(nbRTR_{future}) \approx Y_{current} - Dur_{current}*(E(Y_{future}) - Y_{current}) - E(I_{future})$$

---

[4] I am not showing you how to calculate yield to maturity and duration, but if you are an investor in a fund or ETF, you should be able to check on the yield to maturity and duration of your fund. For example, ETF suppliers provide this information on a daily basis.

On the one hand, if you do not want to forecast a change in future yields, you also might not choose to forecast a change in future inflation, so your expected inflation would be current inflation. In this case your real return expectation is current yield to maturity less current inflation, with an expected return due to a change in yield of 0%. On the other hand, because we have seen that inflation expectations interact with yield expectations, a forecast of a change in inflation naturally suggests an accompanying change in yield, and conversely, although nothing in (22.3) says that this *must* be true. Inflation can rise or fall and, at least in theory, nominal rates could remain the same, with the result that real yields would change. For example, in Figure 21-3 real yields, defined as nominal yields less trailing one-year inflation (the gap between the blue and red lines) varied from point to point over the 60 years covered by the graph, and in a small set of cases was negative. While there is a link between inflation and nominal yield, they are distinct and require separate forecasts.

As I have talked about current inflation, I have been implicitly referring to recent actual or realized inflation. For example, in Figure 21-3 bond yields from each year-end were paired with 12-month inflation over that year. You can think of this as using recent past inflation as an estimate of current inflation expectations. In the next chapter as I introduce real return bonds, you will see a simple and more compelling way of determining the market's current inflation expectations. But for now I will continue to use the simple assumption that "current" inflation is estimated by recently realized actual inflation.

So let's take stock of the situation as of the spring of 2012. As with equities, I will look at assets from a Canadian point of view. But the approach can be used by any investor, just by substituting information about your home market. Table 22-2 presents five bond funds that a Canadian investor might be interested in. The two Canadian funds cover the overall universe and the long end of the market respectively, and include all investment grade credits (government of Canada, provincial government, and investment grade corporate bonds). The two US funds focus on special

Table 22-2:
Forecasting Local or Foreign Returns to Bond Fund Holdings
(No currency forecasts) March 31, 2012

		CN Universe Bond Index (ETF)	CN Long Bond Index (ETF)	US Corp. Bond Index (ETF)	US High Yield Bond Index (ETF)	EM Bond Index (ETF)
1	Current Yield	2.49%	3.53%	3.65%	6.90%	5.11%
2	Forecast Return to ΔYTM	0	0	0	0	0
3	Forecast Nominal Return (local or foreign market) (1+2)	2.49%	3.53%	3.65%	6.90%	5.11%
4	Forecast Inflation	2.50%	2.50%	2.50%	2.50%	4.50%
5	Forecast Real (local/ or foreign) Return (3-4)	-0.01%	1.03%	1.15%	4.40%	0.61%
Sensitivity Analysis: suppose interest rates rise by 1% over 10 years						
6	Forecast ΔYTM	1.00%	1.00%	1.00%	1.00%	1.00%
7	Current Duration	6.62	13.5	7.44	4.22	7.34
8	Return to ΔYTM (unannualized)	-6.62%	-13.50%	-7.44%	-4.22%	-7.34%
9	Return to ΔYTM (annualized)	-0.68%	-1.44%	-0.77%	-0.43%	-0.76%
10	Forecast nominal return including 1% rise in yields (3+9)	1.79%	2.04%	2.85%	6.44%	4.31%

opportunities not readily available to the Canadian home market, a diversified US corporate investment grade bond portfolio and a US high yield (low credit rating) corporate bond portfolio. The fifth fund is an emerging markets bond fund, reflecting government debt of emerging markets.

Row 1 shows the current yield, and row 2 assumes that no change of yield is forecast. This results in the nominal return forecast in local terms for each market in row 3. Local inflation forecasts are taken from Table 18-2, and so row 5 shows real return forecasts from the local market perspective. Please note that currencies have not been added to the equation here.[5]

---

[5] This is a good time to review the impact of currencies, but so as not to bog down the basic theme here, I leave this to you, with this guide. Remember that two basic views were, first, the assumption that real returns to FX would be 0%, or alternatively, that nominal returns to FX would be 0%. Of course you can have non-zero forecasts as well, if you believe you have reason to make them. I suggested that the assumption that real returns to FX are 0% is motivated by

Forecasting Returns to Nominal Bonds

The bottom half of Table 22-2 shows the implications of forecasting a 1% rise in yields over a ten-year horizon — think of this as a kind of sensitivity analysis. The impact on return (rows 8 and 9) is a direct function of the average duration[6] of each portfolio, with longer durations implying a more negative impact.

While I discussed the fact that many people would see the equity forecasts in Table 18-2 as very low relative to their informal expectations, Table 22-2 presents even lower forecasts for bonds. It is only by taking on significant term or duration risk, with Canadian long bonds, or significant credit risk, with US corporate or high yield bonds, that local market real return forecasts are 1% or higher. And any concern that yields may rise would further dampen the prospects for positive real returns. To be sure, at this point I am not taking into account the risk dimension, which I will bring into play as we build portfolios in Part 4, and you must remember that equities are substantially more risky than bonds. Nevertheless, at this point in time realistic real return expectations for bonds are low.

The fact that I am making such low forecasts now prompts me to restate an important theme: your starting point matters. Since we are now in a period of very low yields, I hope that you understand how difficult it will be for bonds to generate robust long-term returns. Since the current (March 2012) Canadian universe yield is 2.5%, the only way you can receive more than 2.5% for such an investment over a period of, say, ten years is if yields were to fall further.

---

long-term data analysis, and is the assumption I prefer as my neutral stance. In that case real local/foreign forecasts in row 5 will have the same numerical value as real return forecasts from the point of view of my home market. Nominal returns to FX are thus expected to reflect the inflation differentials, and in my forecasts the only differential forecast is with emerging markets. Table 18-2 showed that the implication of this differential is that nominal FX is expected to have a negative impact on emerging market investments. If you prefer to assume that nominal returns to FX are 0, or any other assumption, then you must work out the implications for nominal and real home market forecasts given your assumptions.

6 Durations, along with the yields, were taken from the i-Shares website for ETFs reported in Table 22-2.

By way of contrast, think of how different my forecasts would have been at the end of 1999. At year-end, US government bond yields were about 6.6%, which on my approach would have suggested ten-year forecast returns of 6.6%, with expected real returns in the range of 3.5% to 4%. As it turned out, actual nominal returns over the eleven years from 2000-2010 were 7.15%, reflecting additional gains due to falling yields, while real returns were 4.6% as inflation stayed moderate at 2.43%.

This is much higher than my forecast would have been at the end of March 2012, the date at which Table 22-2 was compiled. At that point nominal US government bond yields had fallen to 2.17%, and so forecasts based on US government bonds alone would be commensurately lower. In my view you must evaluate the current situation, using the information that the markets give you, in order to place your bets appropriately.

Chapter 23:

Inflation and Real Return Bonds

In Chapter 20, I gave a historical overview of nominal and real returns to fixed income assets, where we found that for 6 of 19 countries, cumulative annualized nominal returns to bonds failed to outstrip inflation over the 111-year history. In Chapter 21, I identified bonds as described so far as *nominal* bonds: they do not provide an inflation hedge because cash flows (interest payments) are fixed in nominal terms. Since nominal bonds have no growth component, investors will tend to respond to rising inflation by requiring higher nominal yields which means driving down their prices. Of course this causes negative returns for existing bond holders, although it makes the bonds more attractive for prospective buyers.

> **OVERVIEW**
>
> Real return or inflation-protected bonds are described, and both real and nominal returns to real return bonds are approximated using the attribution framework.
>
> Key points:
> - the framework is used to compare returns to nominal and real return bonds;
> - it is also shown how forecasts for real returns and inflation have different implications for the expected returns for nominal and real return bonds.

To deal with exactly this point, *real return* or i*nflation index-linked* bonds[1] were developed. They are designed to compensate

---

1 These are usually issued by governments, which have the "revenue growth" (taxation power) to cover rising interest payments due to inflation. The earliest issuer was Israel in 1955, with programs in the UK and Australia beginning in the 1980s, and Sweden, Canada, New Zealand and the US in the 1990s.

for changes in inflation by building inflation growth into interest payments. If you start with a fixed coupon rate as a percentage of the principal borrowed, just as with a nominal bond, but adjust the principal amount to be repaid for changes in an inflation index such as a country's official CPI index, then coupon interest payments along with the value of the principal repayment amount will rise in lockstep with inflation, and the initial coupon rate provides a real (after inflation) return.[2]

Were you to buy a real return bond at a particular real yield to maturity, reinvest interest payments at that real yield to maturity, and then either hold it to maturity or sell it at the same real yield to maturity, your total real return would equal the starting real yield to maturity. This is perfectly analogous to nominal bonds, except that now I am referring to real rather than nominal yield to maturity. However, just as I observed with nominal bonds, neither the reinvestment opportunities nor the real yield at which you sell the bond are likely to be the same as your starting real yield, meaning that the total real return over your holding period will differ from your starting real yield to maturity due to the change in yield.

The relationship is captured by approximation (23.1):

(23.1) $rrbRTR_t \approx RY_{t-1} + r\Delta RY_t$

where $rrbRTR_t$ is the real return bond total real return over t,
RY_{t-1} is the real yield to maturity at the end of t-1 (that is, the starting yield for period t), and
$r\Delta RY_t$ is the return due to the change in real yield to maturity over period t

Again, in parallel with nominal bonds, the return due to the change in real yield is a function of the change in real yields over period t times the modified duration of the real return bond, so (23.1) can be expanded to

(23.2) $rrbRTR_t \approx RY_{t-1} - Dur_{t-1}*(RY_t - RY_{t-1})$

---

[2] In the case of Canadian real return bonds, inflation is adjusted using Canadian CPI with a three-month lag. Thus an interest payment will approximately adjust for average inflation over the previous six-month coupon period.

Inflation and Real Return Bonds

Finally, nominal returns to a real return bond held over a period are its real return plus the inflation component built into the inflation-adjusted principal of the bond:

(23.3) $\text{rrbTR}_t \approx \text{RY}_{t-1} + r\Delta\text{RY}_t + I_t$

When you compare the nominal returns to real return bonds in (23.3) with nominal returns to nominal bonds in (21.1),

(21.1) $\text{nbTR}_t \approx Y_{t-1} + r\Delta Y_t$

you see immediately that the real return bond is *hedged* to inflation: its nominal return grows as inflation grows, while the nominal return of the nominal bond is determined without reference to inflation. Of course this doesn't mean that the investor who holds real return bonds is guaranteed to receive a nominal return equal to his starting real yield plus inflation, unless he holds the bonds to maturity. This is because the term $r\Delta\text{RY}_t$ can generate negative returns if real yields rise.

I've noticed several investment guides for retail investors suggesting that real return bonds are less risky than nominal bonds. This is actually a problematic claim, and sorting it out will shed a little light on the workings of real return bonds. In the first place, Table 20-1 showed that the annual volatility of real returns to nominal bonds was actually higher than the volatility of nominal returns to nominal bonds over the US history examined. To be sure the real returns to nominal bonds as calculated there are not the same as real returns to real return bonds, the concern here, but I think of this as some evidence that there is nothing intrinsically "less risky" about the concept of real bond returns.

That point aside, in order to fairly compare the riskiness of these two asset types in an absolute sense, you would have to compare them on an "apples to apples" basis: for example, compare nominal returns to nominal bonds with nominal returns to real return bonds. In the end this is an empirical question, and a major barrier to answering it is that the history of real return bonds is relatively short.[3] But our

---

3 Not only are real return bonds a relatively recent phenomenon, the data are particularly difficult to find without access to professional data services. The

analytical framework at least gives a hint as to what is going on. For example approximations (21.1) and (23.3) show how nominal returns are generated for both nominal and real return bonds:

(21.1) $nbTR_t \approx Y_{t-1} + r\Delta Y_t$

and

(23.3) $rrbTR_t \approx RY_{t-1} + r\Delta RY_t + I_t$

We have seen that most of the volatility of nominal returns to nominal bonds in (21.1) comes from the change of yield component $r\Delta Y_t$ over time. Similarly most of the volatility of nominal returns to real return bonds in (23.3) will come from the sum of the change in real yield component $r\Delta RY_t$ plus inflation as real yields and inflation evolve over time. While we can't know in advance what the impact of inflation will be on the volatility of nominal returns to real return bonds, we can assume that it will have a positive impact: any volatility in inflation will very likely increase the volatility of nominal returns to real return bonds. So nominal returns to real return bonds can only be less risky or volatile than nominal returns to nominal bonds if $r\Delta RY_t$ is less volatile than $r\Delta Y_t$. When you compare two bonds or bond portfolios of the same duration, this implies that nominal returns to real return bonds will only be less volatile than nominal returns to nominal bonds if changes in real yields are systematically lower than changes in nominal yields.

I am not aware of any theoretical strictures that would suggest that this is true. I already pointed out that a non-market-based interpretation of real returns to nominal bonds showed that real returns to nominal bonds were at least as risky as nominal returns to nominal bonds (Table 20-1). In addition, the limited historical data for real yields to real return bonds supports the idea that real yield changes are as volatile as nominal yield changes. For example, Figure

---

US Department of the Treasury provides more easily accessible data than most governments, and Figure 23-1 below shows long-term real returns from January 2000. While the Canadian government gathers lots of data at taxpayers' expense, it limits access to the data, and charges high fees for data that are accessible. Some data are available from the Bank of Canada, but for some reason it limits access to just ten years of yields (and of course no prices).

23-1 compares 12 years of yields of nominal long US Treasury bonds with the real yields of long US TIPS, the US Treasury Inflation Protected Securities. You can see that real yields (the red line) have fallen by 4.11%, from a high of 4.4% in January 2000 to a low of 0.29% in February of 2012. Over the same time span, nominal treasury yields fell 4.28%, from a high of 6.87% to a low of 2.59%. One major anomaly is highlighted by the magenta circle that covers October through December of 2008, where real yields spiked while nominal yields fell. But this short-term behaviour likely affected the volatility of both nominal and real returns in a similar fashion.

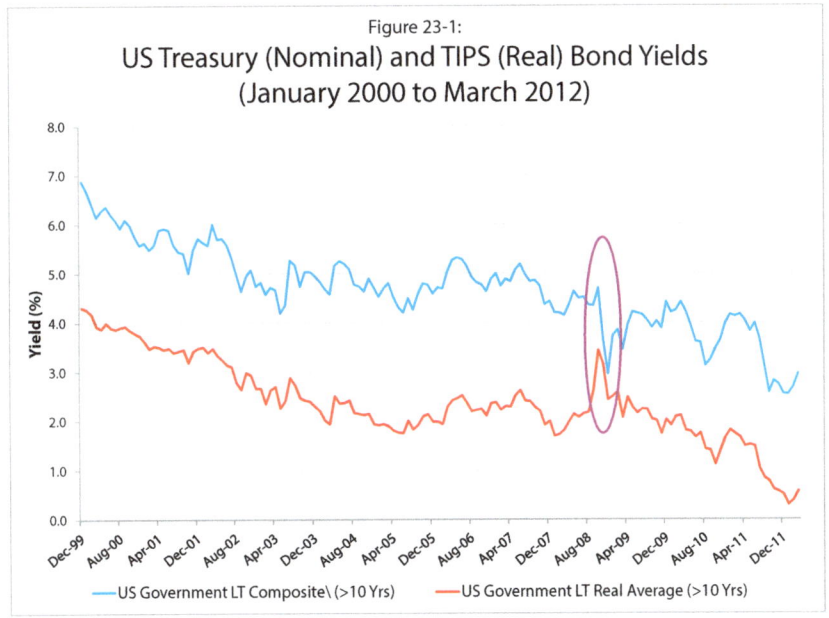

Similarly the Canada Real Return Long Term bond series fell 3.31% from a high of 3.67% in April 2002 to a low of 0.36% in January 2012, while over the same time span the Canada Long Term nominal bond series fell 3.33% from a high of 5.84% to 2.51%.[4]

In sum, while nominal and real return bonds may have similar absolute risk levels over some time frame, their returns are driven

---

4 Long nominal and real bond yield series are provided by the Bank of Canada on its website. The website does not provide details of the composition of the series, or other relevant information such as duration.

by different, though to some extent related, factors which the analytical framework helps us identify. For example, in a period as just described, with low and relatively stable inflation, and with both real and nominal moving together in the same direction, the analytical framework shows why the returns and risks experienced by long nominal bonds and long real return bonds can be expected to be similar, assuming similar durations. However, during a time of stable real yields with rising inflation, the framework suggests that there could be a significant divergence of nominal return, and possibly a divergence of risk as well.

Just as with nominal bonds, the attribution framework can be turned into a forecasting framework: the expected real return to a real return bond or portfolio is the current real yield plus any expected return due to a change in real yields. Using the more detailed formulation we have:

(23.4) $E(rrbRTR_{future}) \approx RY_{current} - Dur_{current} * (E(RY_{future}) - RY_{current})$

All the terms in (23.4) are known today except future real yield to maturity, in parallel with the forecast of nominal returns to nominal bonds. If you choose not to forecast changes in real yields, then today's real yield is a reasonable forecast of expected real return.

In order to forecast nominal returns to real return bonds you need to add a forecast of future inflation, which is a second unknown:

(23.5) $E(rrbTR_{future}) \approx RY_{current} - Dur_{current} * (E(RY_{future}) - Y_{current}) + E(I_{future})$

But an interesting point here is that you can choose to use the market's forecast of inflation, which is the difference in yield between the nominal yield to maturity of a nominal bond of the same term as the real yield of a real return bond. For example, the April 30, 2012 yield of Government of Canada long-term bonds (Bank of Canada series) was 2.61%,[5] while the Real Return Long-Term bond series was 0.57%. The geometric difference, 2.028%, encapsulates the market's

---

5 If you compare these yields to those of the Canadian ETFs I used in Table 21-2, remember that they both include provincial government and corporate credits. So the Canadian Long Bond Index ETF has a current yield to maturity that is approximately 1% higher than long-term Canada bonds mentioned here.

then-current consensus position on future inflation over the term of these two bonds, since it is the expectation of inflation that causes a difference between the nominal and real yield. This market-derived estimate of expected inflation can be used in equation (23.5), or in any other context where you need to forecast inflation over the relatively long term.

Just as you have to make sure that your real and nominal FX forecasts are consistent with your inflation forecasts (Chapter 17), you have to make sure that your forecasts for real return bonds, nominal bonds, and inflation are consistent. For example, the April 2012 market-based forecast of inflation, at just over 2%, is lower than the forecast of 2.5% for Canada that I used in earlier chapters, which was based on historical inflation over the past 20 years. Since I choose to keep the forecast of 2.5%, you can see that I may want to adjust my long-term expectations for real long-term yields or nominal long-term yields (or both), to accommodate the fact that my long-term inflation forecast is higher. That is, if I assume that long-term real rates remain at the current level of 0.57%, then my forecast of the long-term nominal yield will have to rise from the current level of 2.61% to approximately 3.2% in order to reflect my inflation forecast.

If I assume that real yields will remain constant over my investment horizon, then this is the only adjustment I need to make. But suppose I am concerned that real yields of about 0.5% are unsustainable, and that real yields should rise back to higher levels. For example, the actual average real return to nominal US bonds over the very long term from 1871 to 2010 has averaged 2.71% (Table 20-1), while over the 111-year DMS history (Table 20-4) real bond returns have averaged 0.97% across all 19 countries. More recently, real yields for real return bonds have averaged 1.96% in Canada over the past ten years, and 2.39% in the US over the past 12 years. If the current real yield of roughly 0.5% is an unsustainable anomaly, then real yields could rise over the next ten years, perhaps back to the 2% level. But for the purposes of my forecast right now, I will assume that real yields will rise by 0.5% to about 1%. With this forecast change to real yields, the impact on my nominal bond forecast is an increase of 1%, consisting of 0.5% due to a forecast of inflation that is higher than the market-implied rate, and a 0.5% rise due to my forecast of rising real yields.

Table 23-1 summarizes all of this information and shows the effect of these inflation and real yield forecasts on the nominal expected returns of both nominal and real return Government of Canada long bonds. The top section of Table 23-1 summarizes current market data: the nominal yield of the long-term nominal bond series at April 2012 was 2.61% (row 1), the current real yield of the long-term real return bond series was 0.57% (row 2), so the market-implied inflation rate was 2.03% (row 3). The middle section summarizes my forecast changes. Rows 4 and 5 reflect my forecast increase of 0.5% to real yields and 0.5% to inflation over ten years, for an assumed total impact of a 1% increase to nominal yields (row 6).

Table 23-1:
Creating Consistent Forecasts
for Real and Nominal Government Bonds

		Government of Canada long-term nominal bond series	Inflation	Government of Canada long-term real return bond series
	Current Market April 2012			
1	Current Real Yield	2.61%		
2	Current Nominal Yield			0.57%
3	Market-Implied Inflation Rate		2.03%	
	Forecast Changes			
4	Forecast Increase in inflation		0.50%	
5	Forecast Increase in real yield			0.50%
6	Forecast Increase in nominal yield (=4+5)	1.00%		
	10-Year Forecast of Annualized Nominal Return			
7	Due to starting yield	2.61%		0.57%
8	Due to forecast change in yield	-1.50%		-0.83%
9	Due to forecast inflation			2.50%
10	Total Forecast Return	1.11%		2.24%

Inflation and Real Return Bonds

The bottom section shows how the forecast changes affect my expected returns. First, approximation (22.2) says that the expected return of a nominal bond is the sum of the current yield of 2.61% (row 7) plus the return due to the expected change in nominal yield. Since the expected increase in nominal yield is 1%, and I estimate that the modified duration of the Government of Canada nominal long bond series is 14 years, the return due to the change in expected yield is -14% over ten years, or -1.5% per year (row 8), for a total return of 1.11% annualized (row 10).

But second, the effect of this forecast on a real return bond portfolio is somewhat different, because the forecast of a 1% increase in nominal yields came in two parts: a 0.5% increase in real yields plus a 0.5% increase in inflation relative to the current market-implied rate. Only the increase in real yields hurts the expected nominal return of real return bonds: with a duration of 16 years, the increase in yield of 0.5% implies a loss of 8% over ten years, or -0.83% per year (row 8). However, all inflationary changes are passed on as increases in principal and coupon payments. So approximation (23.5) says that forecast nominal return to a real return bond or portfolio is the sum of starting real yield of 0.57% (row 7), the return due to the forecast change in real yield of -0.83% (row 8), and the forecast inflation of 2.5% (row 9), for a total of 2.24%.

Of course neither the forecast return of 2.24% to a Government of Canada real return long bond portfolio, nor the forecast return of 1.11% for the nominal Government of Canada long bond portfolio, matches expected inflation of 2.5%. But you can see that any further increases in inflation would cause an additional divergence of return. For additional rises in inflation would be passed on to the real return bond investor as gains in nominal return, while the nominal bond investor would suffer further losses to the extent that nominal yields rose to reflect those increases in inflation.

In Table 22-2, I showed the impact of an increase of 1% to nominal yields of a number of Canadian and non-Canadian bond portfolios of different durations. The forecasts in Table 23-1 are for long bond portfolios that only contain Government of Canada credits, while the Universe and Long Bond portfolios in Table 22-2 contain provincial and corporate credits as well. As a consequence, their starting yields, and hence forecast returns, are slightly higher.

Chapter 24:

Correlations and Other Asset Classes

In the opening chapter of Section 3, I added the concept of imperfect correlation as an additional criterion in a search for useful investment opportunities. My overview of fixed income as a useful investment alternative to equities is completed by observing that fixed income investments generally have a low positive correlation with equities in one's home equity market, and so provide a useful and diversifying asset class.

Table 24-1 illustrates this by adding historical correlations for three Canadian nominal bond indexes to the four Canadian dollar-based equity investments examined in Chapter 19, all of which can be easily invested in by retail and small institutional investors. These are the DEX Canadian Universe bond index that essentially encompasses the complete Canadian bond market of "investment grade" bonds, the DEX Short-Term bond index that encompasses the subset of maturities of less than five years, and the DEX

> **OVERVIEW**
> The usefully low correlation between fixed income returns and equity returns is demonstrated. Three criteria are suggested for choosing additional asset classes to further broaden your investment opportunities:
> 1. additional investment vehicles must be accessible to your scale of investing and have a reasonable cost;
> 2. you should have a conceptual or theoretical basis for believing that the sources of return for alternative assets differ from current opportunities;
> 3. usefully low historical correlations with existing alternatives should confirm this difference.

Long-Term bond index that encompasses the subset of maturities of greater than ten years. Table 24-1 shows correlations over the 1988–2010 period, the longest term over which I have data for the Emerging Markets component.

Table 24-1:
23-Year Correlations — Assets in Canadian Dollars
(Monthly Returns 1988/01-2010/12)

	CN Equity	US Equity (CAD)	EAFE Equity (CAD)	EM Equity (CAD)	CN Short Bonds	CN Univ. Bonds	CN Long Bonds
CN Equity	1						
US Equity (CAD)	0.63	1					
EAFE Equity (CAD)	0.55	0.63	1				
EM Equity (CAD)	0.60	0.54	0.58	1			
CN Short Bonds	0.13	0.11	0.07	0.08	1		
CN Univ. Bonds	0.22	0.19	0.14	0.12	0.93	1	
CN Long Bonds	0.26	0.22	0.18	0.13	0.80	0.96	1

As you might expect, correlations among the bond indexes themselves are very high, and so you might only choose one of these as an investment vehicle at any time depending on the duration you wanted. But in all cases the correlations with equities denominated in Canadian dollars are quite low. Table 24-2 shows the same relations, with the addition of Canadian real return bonds, but the correlations are calculated on the monthly data over five years starting in 2006. As I showed in Chapter 19, correlations over the 2006–2010 period

Table 24-2:
5-Year Correlations — Assets in Canadian Dollars
(Monthly Returns 2006/01-2010/12)

	CN Equity	US Equity (CAD)	EAFE Equity (CAD)	EM Equity (CAD)	CN Short Bonds	CN Univ. Bonds	CN Long Bonds	CN RRB
CN Equity	1							
US Equity (CAD)	0.54	1						
EAFE Equity (CAD)	0.66	0.82	1					
EM Equity (CAD)	0.80	0.60	0.83	1				
CN Short Bonds	-0.27	-0.04	0.05	-0.05	1			
CN Univ. Bonds	-0.02	0.13	0.23	0.16	0.84	1		
CN Long Bonds	0.13	0.22	0.31	0.26	0.60	0.94	1	
CN RRB	0.39	0.36	0.44	0.49	0.29	0.57	0.67	1

were considerably higher among the equity assets, but the correlations between bonds and equities remain very low, and in some cases are actually negative.

Investors whose home market is not Canada can perform the same exercise, although you would substitute home market bond products if your home market is of reasonable size and complexity. Large investors may hold a significant portfolio of international bonds, although currencies then come into play. My own approach, especially for smaller portfolios, is to pick and choose specialty portfolios from outside Canada to supplement broad Canadian market indexes, since the Canadian bond market is large and robust on its own. Canadians can find ETFs (see Part 4), that invest in such areas as high-yield US corporate bonds, and Emerging Market country debt. In some cases these are even available with hedged currency. Investors from small countries, with less diversified and possibly riskier debt markets, may want to have a global or regional bond portfolio as their default portfolio.

As a long-term investor I would like to find additional investment opportunities — that is, additional sources of return and risk. But to have a real impact on my investment portfolio, they have to differ significantly from the returns and risks from global equities and bonds that are already under consideration. While I am not going to analyze additional asset classes in great detail, I will outline an approach that you can use to examine possible additional investments.

First, as a retail or smaller institutional investor your investment opportunities will be more limited than those of a very large fund or institution, so there is no point in spending time thinking about investments that are not readily accessible to you. Consequently, in many cases you will want to begin by determining that there are potential investment vehicles that have an acceptable cost structure. I will cover the topic of costs in detail in Part 4, but for now I just want to put the idea on the table as an obvious starting point.

Second, I would like to place any additional investment opportunities within a conceptual framework that shows me *how and why the new opportunity should differ* from existing investments. The simple analytical framework that has been developed gives some hints as to how to begin the process. The framework has suggested three generic sources of return so far: yields from cash flows, real and/or nominal growth of cash flows, and returns due to changes in yield. Equity returns are derived from all three sources: cash flows from dividends, real and nominal dividend growth that was arguably related to productivity or economic growth, and returns from changes in dividend yields. Nominal bond returns are driven by cash flows from interest payments based on a nominal yield, no growth component, and returns from changes in nominal yield that are driven by the changing structure of interest rates. Real return bonds have returns generated by cash flows based on a real interest rate, growth in interest payments from an inflation-matching mechanism, and returns from changes in real yields. In all three cases the return-generating mechanism is quite different from the others. In order to identify usefully different assets or asset classes, you need to look for ways in which their components of return differ from those outlined above.

Third, if I can identify additional assets that I believe have usefully different return-generating properties from a theoretical or conceptual analysis, I hope to be able to find empirical evidence that supports this. Here the most important justification would be imperfect historical correlations with existing investments.

I will briefly outline two examples, focusing on the second and third points. In both cases I know that the first point is covered, that there are relatively inexpensive and easily-traded investment vehicles that are appropriate for retail and smaller institutional investors.

My first example is real estate. While larger institutions such as pension funds favour direct investment in real estate,[1] for smaller investors this almost certainly means investing in REITS, real estate

---

1 They can control costs and leverage, and since their holdings are periodically valued through an appraisal process, they can portray their assets as having less volatility than market-traded vehicles.

investment trusts,[2] which would likely be held in a fund or ETF. In general, real estate investments generate income from property rents and related management fees, and in some cases from mortgages, and property values may also increase in value over time. Rents and fees may be affected by changing demand, and ideally will be managed so that they can grow in line with reasonable rises in inflation. However, rents and other fees are likely not subject to "productivity growth". So REITs generate yields from real estate cash flows, and the cash flows may grow with inflation. But since REITs are traded investment entities, they are also subject to price or yield changes as market valuations change over time.

Given this introductory analysis, you can start to make the case that returns from REITs are potentially quite different from returns from equity and bond investments. First, REIT yields are based on cash flows from a different source. Second, while cash flows may have a growth component related to inflation, growth is by no means guaranteed to rise with inflation as it is with real return bonds, and there is little reason to believe that it will outpace inflation over time as equity dividend growth may. Third, price changes due to changing yields may or may not be related to equity returns, but this is partly an empirical question. I will come back to correlations in a moment.

A second example is investment in commodities through publicly traded investment vehicles. I am thinking of commodities as a broad exposure to the inputs of food production and manufacturing: agricultural products, natural resources including metals and the inputs to energy production such as coal, oil and gas and their derivatives.[3] One potential attraction of commodities in general is that they may be a partial hedge to inflation, certainly to the extent that inflation is caused by the increased prices of the inputs of production. Whether or not commodities can provide a long-term growth component in excess of inflation is an interesting

---

2 REITS are set up as trusts and are required to distribute virtually all of their income to unit holders, thereby avoiding corporate taxes.

3 I would suggest that specific bets on particular commodities, such as gold or oil, are far beyond what most investors should be involved in, but other opinions will differ.

question, and the answer will depend in part on the particular broad commodities benchmark you are considering.

Since commodities do not have an income component (and hence no yield), all of the return is due to changes in commodity prices. Without a yield, commodity returns are quite different from other assets we have discussed, and so within my simple framework I think of commodity returns as due to growth (in price). So it's pretty clear that from a conceptual point of view, commodity returns are different from bond and stock returns.

But for both REITs and commodities, the answer as to whether they are likely to provide usefully different potential sources of risk and return needs to be confirmed by an empirical study. For illustrative purposes Table 24-3 adds in the correlations of a Canadian REIT index and the Canadian dollar translation of the Goldman Sachs Commodities Index (GSCI). While I have long histories for various commodity returns, my REIT data only begin at the end of 1999, so this determines the time span of the data presented in the table.

Table 24-3:
11-Year Correlations — Assets in Canadian Dollars
(Monthly Returns 2000/01-2010/12)

	CN Equity	US Equity (CAD)	EAFE Equity (CAD)	EM Equity (CAD)	CN Short Bonds	CN Univ. Bonds	CN Long Bonds	CN RRB	CN REITS	GSCI (CAD)
CN Equity	1									
US Equity (CAD)	0.62	1								
EAFE Equity (CAD)	0.66	0.80	1							
EM Equity (CAD)	0.75	0.65	0.80	1						
CN Short Bonds	-0.19	-0.13	-0.01	-0.09	1					
CN Univ. Bonds	-0.01	-0.06	0.11	0.04	0.87	1				
CN Long Bonds	0.10	0.01	0.18	0.13	0.67	0.94	1			
CN RRB	0.24	0.12	0.24	0.24	0.24	0.45	0.54	1		
CN REITS	0.57	0.40	0.50	0.52	-0.03	0.15	0.22	0.27	1	
GSCI (CAD)	0.32	0.01	0.16	0.17	-0.11	0.02	0.08	0.25	0.18	1

Over this 11-year period REITs are less correlated with equities than equity markets are correlated among themselves, averaging about 0.50. As you might expect, the highest correlation is between Canadian REITs and the Canadian equity market at 0.574, but this is still a low and useful correlation. Correlations between REITs and fixed income are much lower.

GSCI commodities in Canadian dollars have even lower correlations with both equities and fixed income. Given the resource-based nature of the Canadian market, it is not surprising that the highest correlation is with Canadian equities, at 0.318. Correlations with fixed income are virtually 0. While I do not show this in a table, over the 23 years from 1988 to 2010 presented in Table 24-1, correlations between the GSCI commodities index and other assets are even lower, averaging 0.018, with the highest correlation of 0.17 holding between commodities and Canadian equities.

Table 24-4 presents similar data for the five years from 2006 to 2010. Just as correlations between equities are higher, correlations between REITs and equities and between commodities and equities are higher over this period, although correlations with fixed income are not.

Table 24-4:
5-Year Correlations — Assets in Canadian Dollars
(Monthly Returns 2006/01-2010/12)

	CN Equity	US Equity (CAD)	EAFE Equity (CAD)	EM Equity (CAD)	CN Short Bonds	CN Univ. Bonds	CN Long Bonds	CN RRB	CN REITS	GSCI (CAD)
CN Equity	1									
US Equity (CAD)	0.54	1								
EAFE Equity (CAD)	0.66	0.82	1							
EM Equity (CAD)	0.80	0.60	0.83	1						
CN Short Bonds	-0.27	-0.04	0.05	-0.05	1					
CN Univ. Bonds	-0.02	0.13	0.23	0.16	0.84	1				
CN Long Bonds	0.13	0.22	0.31	0.26	0.60	0.94	1			
CN RRB	0.39	0.36	0.44	0.49	0.29	0.57	0.67	1		
CN REITS	0.68	0.51	0.61	0.58	-0.16	0.13	0.26	0.32	1	
GSCI (CAD)	0.55	0.21	0.35	0.42	-0.23	-0.09	0.00	0.35	0.31	1

So both REITS and commodities meet my criteria of providing returns and risks that are conceptually different from the equity and bond assets we have considered in detail, and have usefully different historical correlations. These are good candidates for providing additional investment opportunities. In order to use these assets in an investment program, you would need to take the final steps of forecasting returns, but I will not take that project on here.

In Parts 2 and 3 I have developed an approach for generating expected returns for equities, nominal bonds and real return bonds that go beyond mirroring past returns over some historical period. But so far I haven't said anything about forecasting expected risks and correlations. In fact it is very difficult to do more than use historical risks and correlations for your forecasts, and that is what I will be doing in Part 4.

From my perspective, the important point is to make sure that you use a long enough history that a very wide range of market environments is covered. My rule of thumb is to measure risks and correlations using the longest data series that I have, unless I have developed other measurement tools. For example, I would never use risks and correlations based on a short five-year time frame as in Table 24-4, and even the correlations based on 11-year monthly returns in Table 24-3 are too short for my comfort. With short time spans investors can get lulled into complacency when volatility is lower than it has been over the longer term.

You can argue that such complacency had set in for investors in the 1990s. At the beginning of 1998 the ten-year (120-month annualized) standard deviation of US equities had fallen to 12% while five-year standard deviations had fallen below 11%, both measures extremely low compared to the longer-term average of more than 18%. Such low levels of volatility may have contributed to the overconfidence of managers and pension funds as equities rose to unsustainable levels in 1999: many investors over-committed to equities on the assumption that equity risks had systematically fallen and would remain lower in future. This happened to a lesser extent in 2008, as just before the crash five-year standard deviations returned to a low of 12%.

There are very sophisticated quantitative analyses that can be used to measure, and possibly to forecast, risks and correlations. But for most of us, acknowledging the risks of longer-term history is the more prudent course.

Part 4:

The Realities of Investing: Costs, Investment Vehicles and Portfolio Construction

Chapter 25:

The Challenges of Active Management within Asset Classes

In all of the discussions and analysis to this point I have talked about investing and forecasting in terms of broad markets: Canadian stocks or bonds, US or other country equity markets, or diversified foreign composites such as EAFE or the Emerging Markets (EM) indexes. I have purposely avoided the topic of *active management within asset classes*, picking stocks or bonds to build portfolios that one hopes will outperform a particular market or benchmark index. Yet this is the focus of almost all that we read about investing in books, magazines, newspapers and brokerage reports.

I want to begin by reminding you that I am and have been an active manager, and that I believe that under the right circumstances active management can play an important role in portfolio strategy. However, it is very difficult for the average active manager, even the average *professional* active manager, to add value. Even worse, it is also very difficult for potential investors in an active manager's strategy to determine with any confidence whether the strategy will add value in the future, even if it has in the past. All active managers who truly understand the nature of markets and their work within them, will

> **OVERVIEW**
>
> Active managers are unlikely to outperform broad market benchmarks after costs, and both simple arithmetic and empirical evidence strongly support this point.
>
> Most investors will find it difficult to identify managers who will justify their fees going forward. So investing in the lowest-cost investment vehicles that generate broad market returns may be the best strategy for most investors.

understand the points I make in this chapter. Investors who consider purchasing active management services should understand them too.

In a deservedly famous short article "The Arithmetic of Active Management" (Sharpe 1991), William Sharpe makes the following points.

If "active" and "passive" management styles are defined in sensible ways, it must be the case that:

(1) Before costs, the return on the average actively managed dollar will equal the return on the average passively managed dollar, and;

(2) After costs, the return on the average actively managed dollar will be less than the return on the average passively managed dollar. (Sharpe 1991, p.7)

Pick any set of securities you like, for example the S&P/TSX Composite Index of larger Canadian stocks. Sharpe's argument is essentially this: if you define a passive investor as one who holds all securities in proportion to their market capitalization, then over any performance period all passive investors must receive the return of the market, before costs. But this means that the average return of all other investors in the market — the non-passive or "active" investors — must also equal the market return before costs. Thus the first point is made: before costs the return of the average passively managed dollar must equal the return of the average actively managed dollar.

The second point follows directly, since the costs of passive management are known to be much lower, on average, than the costs of active management.

Rather than dismissing the argument with a shrug, as too many people are inclined to do, it is instructive to think about it and its implications. Sharpe discusses several reasons why sometimes active managers may incorrectly appear to beat passive managers on average, and I encourage you to read his paper. But I want to focus on a line of reasoning about active management that is consistent with Sharpe's arithmetic. For it is quite possible that the portfolios of "professional" active investment managers, as opposed to the portfolios of the whole universe of active (non-passive) managers, could outperform market averages in some or all individual markets. This would be explained if the "non-professional" managers — all other active portfolios — underperformed on average. The idea would be that professional expertise and training raises them above the level of the average active investor.

While this idea, if true, would indeed be compatible with Sharpe's arithmetic, you might be surprised to find that the "pros are better" idea does not hold up to empirical inspection. This has been shown time and again by both straightforward studies such as Standard & Poor's ongoing "Indices versus Active" reports[1], as well as more complex and nuanced academic studies. One of the most comprehensive recent studies is by Fama and French (F&F 2010). Using a large sample of US equity mutual funds from 1984 to 2006, and using a number of techniques including some that adjust for the fact that individual funds have differing exposures to risk factors, they find that before expenses the aggregate of all active equity mutual funds generated market portfolio returns, while after expenses the net return underperformed by roughly the cost of management fees.[2]

Rather than delving into their study in detail, let me just show you some simple results found by examining several samples of Canadian mutual funds. There is no sophisticated analysis here. For example, there is no adjustment for individual fund risk and the sample is not adjusted for the size of the assets under management — funds are weighted equally. But this analysis shows what a consumer will face when he goes to a mutual fund database and looks for possible investment vehicles.

Table 25-1 is based on the Globe and Mail Canadian equity mutual fund database, with several adjustments.[3] It shows the

---

1 Published on their website at:
   http://www.standardandpoors.com/indices/spiva/en/us
2 F&F 2010, p. 1921.
3 First I required a minimum of three years of returns. Then funds identified in their name as pooled funds were removed, since generally their fee structures and clientele are different from mutual funds. Funds identified as ETFs were removed, as were funds clearly identified as index funds. The idea was to look only at actively managed (and in this case Canadian equity) mutual funds. I would

Table 25-1:
Canadian Mutual Funds, Globe & Mail Data
Canadian Equity Mandates
Returns Data ending Dec. 2010

	1-Year	3-Year	5-Year	10-Year
Highest Manager	38.10%	18.08%	9.99%	10.99%
Median Manager	13.50%	-0.62%	3.82%	5.11%
Average Manager	14.03%	-0.41%	3.95%	5.06%
Standard Deviation	3.94%	2.88%	1.84%	2.28%
Lowest Manager	-1.20%	-9.63%	-1.58%	-3.47%
S&P/TSX Total Return	17.61%	1.45%	6.70%	6.67%
Average Manager less Benchmark	-3.58%	-1.86%	-2.75%	-1.61%
Current MER	2.53%			
# in Sample	378	378	294	142
# > benchmark	56	87	24	26
% > benchmark	14.81%	23.02%	8.16%	18.31%

distribution of returns for one-year, three-year, five-year and ten-year periods all ending at December 2010, and compares them to the benchmark returns which are assumed to be the S&P/TSX Total Return Index. The blue highlighted row shows the value added or lost of the average fund return relative to the benchmark, here in all cases negative. The current (2010) management expense ratio or MER is 2.53%, and is the average of the individual fund MERs. Since management expenses are included in fund returns, the returns in the first four rows are after the expense of the MER. The bottom of the table shows the size of the sample, and the number and percentage of funds that outperformed the benchmark after fees.

Several points are worth highlighting. Over all four periods the average fund substantially underperformed the benchmark after fees, and in the one- and five-year periods the underperformance was by more than the current MER of 2.53%. The percentage of funds that outperformed the benchmark ranged from a high of just 23% over three years, to a low of 8.16% over five years. That is,

---

guess that some pooled funds and index funds that were not identified as such remain in the sample.

over five years an investor had less than a 10% chance of having a fund that outperformed the benchmark, and over ten years, less than a 20% chance. Neither number takes into account that some underperforming funds went out of business, either returning capital to investors or more likely being purchased and merged with other more successful funds.[4]

I also looked back over this sample on a year-by-year basis, and found that the average fund underperformed the benchmark in nine of ten years, outperforming only in 2001, although that year the outperformance was substantial at 6.8%. Despite that first great year, the cumulative underperformance over the ten years was -1.61% annualized.

The same simple information as that displayed in Table 25-1 can be easily calculated for other mutual fund samples. For example Table 25-2 shows the results for Canadian international equity mutual funds invested with an EAFE benchmark (in CAD), while Table 25-3 shows the same information for Canadian bonds with a DEX Canadian Bond Universe index benchmark.

The international data sample in Table 25-2 again shows that the average fund underperformed the benchmark in all four periods. However the underperformance was by less than the MER of 2.65%, so before costs it is possible that the average manager may be showing a small amount of skill, although without significant testing you cannot tell whether it is skill or luck.[5] For example, over ten years the average manager underperformed the benchmark by -2.04%, which is 0.61% less than the current MER.

---

4 This is called "survivorship bias": the funds no longer in the sample almost certainly had lower-than-average returns, so the true average return is likely lower over history. Without belabouring the point, you can imagine that if a fund company buys the funds of another fund company, any consolidation or merging of similar funds will reflect the track record of the more successful fund. It is also unlikely that funds with better-than-average records would simply go out of business.

5 In addition to the question of skill versus luck, there is also a potentially serious survivorship bias, as previously mentioned.

Table 25-2:
Canadian Mutual Funds, Globe & Mail Data
International (EAFE) Equity Mandates
Returns Data ending Dec. 2010

	1-Year	3-Year	5-Year	10-Year
Highest Manager	19.00%	4.02%	4.67%	4.73%
Median Manager	2.50%	-8.38%	-2.73%	-2.37%
Average Manager	2.20%	-8.00%	-2.42%	-2.28%
Standard Deviation	4.77%	3.12%	2.42%	2.59%
Lowest Manager	-12.40%	-15.99%	-10.10%	-9.73%
EAFE (CAD) Total Return	2.40%	-6.67%	-0.21%	-0.24%
Average Manager less Benchmark	-0.20%	-1.33%	-2.20%	-2.04%
Current MER	2.65%			
# in Sample	215	215	144	72
# > benchmark	110	62	26	14
% > benchmark	51.16%	28.84%	18.06%	19.44%

Again going back over ten years of year-by-year data, the average fund only outperformed the benchmark in 2001, and that was by just 0.044%. For the one-year period ending 2010, 51% of managers outperformed the benchmark, despite the slight underperformance of the average relative to the benchmark. But over five and ten years an investor had less than a 20% chance of choosing a fund that outperformed the benchmark after costs.

Finally the bond sample in Table 25-3 also shows underperformance in all four periods. While the underperformance is slightly less than the current MER of 1.77%, the underperformance of 1.65% over ten years is close to the MER. However, the number of managers outperforming the benchmark appears to be somewhat lower than for the equity samples, ranging from 6.85% to 15.14%. As well, over the past ten years managers underperformed in nine of ten years, only outperforming in 2009 by 0.74%.

To summarize, a possible response to Sharpe's arithmetic of active management argument was that professional active managers as a group might outperform market returns, implying that non-professional active managers would underperform. There is little

Table 25-3:
Canadian Mutual Funds, Globe & Mail Data
DEX Canadian Universe Bond Mandates
Returns Data ending Dec. 2010

	1-Year	3-Year	5-Year	10-Year
Highest Manager	12.90%	8.99%	6.38%	7.88%
Median Manager	5.30%	4.60%	3.51%	4.40%
Average Manager	5.44%	4.84%	3.74%	4.68%
Standard Deviation	1.63%	1.22%	0.89%	0.97%
Lowest Manager	-4.20%	-1.69%	1.99%	1.98%
Canadian Bond Universe Total Return	6.74%	6.19%	5.25%	6.33%
Average Manager less Benchmark	-1.30%	-1.35%	-1.51%	-1.65%
Current MER	1.77%			
# in Sample	317	317	240	146
# > benchmark	40	48	21	10
% > benchmark	12.62%	15.14%	8.75%	6.85%

evidence of this before costs, and definite evidence that after costs they underperform on average. The hope and belief of every professional active manager is that there is a subset of active managers who really have skill and can indeed add value over time, and of course that he is a part of that subset.

My point here is not to denigrate active management or managers, but rather to highlight the difficulty that smaller investors face when they try to hire active management services. The problem with mutual funds is their cost structure: with fees of 2.5% and higher for equities, and 1.77% for bonds, the probability is low that actively managed funds you choose will outperform the market.

You should understand that large institutional investors face different conditions. In the first place, the fees that they pay for external active managers are roughly an order of magnitude lower than those of mutual funds. In the second place, they employ significant resources to help them identify managers with skill — that is, managers that they have reason to believe will outperform their market benchmarks. Related to this is the fact that large investors generally have much greater access to information about managers and their strategies, information not available to retail and smaller institutional investors. They also have sophisticated performance measurement systems to evaluate whether or not their hiring decisions turn out to be validated. In some cases they also develop their own team of internal managers, to potentially lower their costs further. But even pension funds and foundations find the task difficult, and broad studies across pension funds show that many fail in the endeavour to add value relative to broad market indexes.

In my view the rational response for smaller investors, including many professionals who want the best possible expected return for a diversified set of assets, is to invest in the broad market at the lowest possible cost. In the next chapter I focus on the benefits of cost reduction versus the "hope" of value added within asset classes.

Chapter 26:

Certain Cost Reduction versus Uncertain Value-Added (and the case for ETFs and other index funds)

Whether or not the average manager can outperform their broad market benchmarks before costs, when you add in mutual fund costs of more than 2.5% for equities and almost 1.8% for bonds, there is almost no chance that the average manager can outperform his benchmarks.

To emphasize the magnitude of those costs, remember that the DMS data in Chapter 6 pegged long-term nominal returns to the US market at 9.4% and real returns at 6.25%, while the World Ex US was 8.16% or 5.04% real. Assuming MERs of 2.5%, these out-of-pocket costs are 26.6% of US historical nominal returns, 40% of US historical real returns, 30.6% of World Ex US (roughly EAFE) historical nominal returns, and 49.6% of World Ex US real returns. Then remember that from our current standpoint we are starting with low dividend yields and little prospect of additional returns

> **OVERVIEW**
>
> Average costs of index-tracking ETFs are an order of magnitude lower than the average costs of actively managed mutual funds.
>
> The investment impact of costs is treated as the trade-off between a small certain underperformance of a portfolio of ETFs versus the small probability (or hope) for the outperformance of a portfolio of actively managed funds.
>
> Key result:
>
> - the almost certain reduction in costs of a portfolio of passive ETFs has a high probability of outperforming a more costly portfolio of active funds.

due to falling dividend yields. With my Canadian equity forecast of 5.64% nominal return and 3.06% real return in Table 17-4, the MER of 2.5% is 44.3% of my nominal expected return and fully 81.7% of my real expected return.

Although MERs for bonds are lower, the lower historical and forecast returns make the situation even worse. To focus only on Canada, the historical geometric returns from the DMS data were 5.21% nominal and 2.1% real (Table 20-4), so assuming an average MER of 1.8%, costs would have eaten up 34% of nominal returns and 84.3% of real returns. Going forward, with very low starting yields and the potential for rising yields harming bond returns if inflation rises, an optimistic real return of 0.5% before the MER implies a negative real return, less than -1.2%.

Institutional investors face much lower costs for active management, and their costs for using passive or index-tracking management is probably 0.05% and in some cases much lower. So institutions who choose to forgo active management can virtually guarantee themselves benchmark returns for portfolio exposure to broad market indexes. But even smaller retail investors have an alternative to expensive mutual funds: these are *exchange traded funds* or ETFs. The goal of the original developers and providers of ETFs was to create very low-cost funds that are designed to mimic the performance of benchmarks.[1] Unlike mutual funds, in which daily purchases and sales of units at the end of each day usually require a net purchase or sale of assets within the fund, ETFs trade like stocks — investors buy and sell existing units at any point during the day. However, the supply of outstanding units can increase or fall as units are created or redeemed by *designated brokers*. These brokers can

---

[1] Some of the early providers, such as Barclay's Global Investments and Vanguard, were at least in part motivated by the principles behind indexing strategies captured by Sharpe's Arithmetic of Active Management argument. Now that ETFs have become a major success, the financial services industry is trying to turn them into higher fee-generating vehicles, by introducing sometimes questionable complexity, and in some cases "active" management. The drive to increase fees is the natural course of things with the financial industry, and investors should be aware of this tendency. Fortunately many fine examples of ETFs remain that continue the tradition of very low-cost broad investment vehicles.

create blocks of units by delivering a precisely defined set of assets that mirrors the existing assets in the fund, and receiving a block of units in return. Blocks of units can also be redeemed by reversing the process and receiving securities that can then be sold. This means that after the initial fund setup, all of the transactions required to increase or decrease the number of fund units happen outside the fund, without any performance impact on the fund, and without any immediate tax consequences to the fund either.

The key for small investors is that you can find ETFs that track the broad indexes I have been discussing, but that have MERs of an order of magnitude less than mutual fund fees. Table 26-1 gives

Table 26-1:
A Sample of the Lowest-Cost Broad Market ETFs
Easily Accessible to Canadian Investors (August 2012)

Canadian Equities	Currency	Ticker	Exchange	Manager	MER	Sample Portfolio Allocation	Contrib. to MER
S&P/TSX Comp. Index Fund	CAD	XIC	TSX	iShares	0.25%		
S&P/TSX 60 Index Fund	CAD	XIU	TSX	iShares	0.17%		
MSCI Canada Index	CAD	VCE	TSX	Vanguard	0.09%	20%	0.02%
US Equities							
S&P 500 Index Fund	USD	VOO	NYSE	Vanguard	0.05%		
MSCI US Market Hedged to CAD	CAD-hedged	VUS	TSX	Vanguard	0.15%	5%	0.01%
EAFE Equities							
MSCI EAFE Hedged to CAD Index	CAD-hedged	VEF	TSX	Vanguard	0.37%	10%	0.04%
MSCI EAFE Index	USD	VEA	NYSE	Vanguard	0.12%	5%	0.01%
Emerging Markets Equities							
MSCI Emerging Markets Index Fund	USD	VWO	NYSE	Vanguard	0.20%	10%	0.02%
Canadian Bonds							
DEX Universe Bond Index Fund	CAD	XBB	TSX	iShares	0.30%		
Barclays Cdn Aggregate Bond Index	CAD	VAB	TSX	Vanguard	0.20%	50%	0.10%
Portfolio Totals:						100%	0.19%

an example of a set of funds appropriate for a Canadian investor, and I have generally chosen the fund with the lowest MER where duplicates are available.[2] You can see that Canadian, US, EAFE and Emerging Markets equities are all represented, and both US and EAFE equities are available with currency hedged to Canadian dollars. Note that the unhedged EAFE and EM ETFs trade in US dollars on US exchanges, and currencies are unhedged to the USD, and so of course are unhedged to CAD when held by a Canadian-based investor. Since the ETFs I am showing you are designed to mimic or track their benchmarks, before fees they track the benchmarks very closely, while after fees they generally underperform by the amount of their MERs.

To the right is a sample portfolio consisting of 50% bonds and 50% equities, some of which are currency-hedged. The overall MER is calculated in the right-hand column, and comes out to just 0.19%. Given the average MERs of more than 2.5% for equities, and 1.77% for bonds, a 50-50 stock bond portfolio allocated in a similar fashion using Canadian mutual funds might be expected to have an average MER of close to 2.2% — 11 times as large.

Think about this: assuming you would make the same long-term allocations whether you invested in mutual funds or ETFs, you can save a guaranteed 2% per year for the life of your investment. That 2% gain relative to the average mutual fund cost is virtually certain. What would be the benefit of investing in mutual funds instead? Presumably you hope to beat the odds of underperforming the market, or at least the related ETFs, and believe that your funds will add value. That is, you want to trade a certain gain of 2% (relative to the average fee of mutual funds) for the uncertain hope of a potential gain of more than 2% above the average fund. What are the chances of this happening, for example over a ten-year period?

To create a simple example, suppose that you want to hold a portfolio of four mutual funds to cover a basic spectrum of opportunities: Canadian, US and EAFE equities along with Canadian

---

2 In addition to low MERs, trading liquidity is a consideration, and I am not taking that into account here.

bonds. In the previous chapter I showed you distributions of mutual fund returns over several periods, including the ten years ending in 2010 for Canadian and EAFE equity funds and Canadian bonds. For illustrative purposes I assume that a Canadian-based sample of US-focused mutual funds would approximate the Canadian equity sample. Using the characteristics of each sample I "simulated" the results of picking a portfolio of four funds with a ten-year investment period, and tested to see what the probability was that such a portfolio would outperform the aggregate benchmark.

For each of the four fund choices I drew 10,000 cases from a random normally distributed sample that had the same mean and standard deviation as the appropriate manager sample, so I had four sets of 10,000 "fund returns". I assumed a 50-50 bond-stock portfolio, with the three equity funds equally weighted within the 50% equity portion, and so generated 10,000 possible portfolio returns using that portfolio allocation. Only 2.1% of the 10,000 sample portfolios outperformed the ten-year composite benchmark with the same allocation and just 3.2% outperformed the equivalent ETF portfolio, assuming a 0.2% cost.

For comparison purposes I created a second test that equally weighted the four sample funds, and the results were slightly better with 5.1% of the 10,000 portfolios outperforming the equally weighted benchmark, and 7.1% outperforming an equivalent ETF portfolio after costs. In either case these are slim odds that you could select a portfolio of mutual funds that would outperform an ETF-based portfolio after costs. Thus the bet of forgoing the certain cost reduction of 2% by using ETFs on the hope of outperforming those ETFs in aggregate has very low odds of winning.

While it is crucial to understand that lower cost, and potentially higher return, alternatives to mutual funds are available to smaller investors, ETFs are in themselves no panacea. I cannot deal in depth with some of the issues that need to be considered when comparing the pros and cons of ETFs relative to mutual funds, without departing significantly from my main line of reasoning. Moreover, since these issues are highly dependent on each investor's actual circumstance, it is difficult to give a simple overview. Nevertheless, I would like to point out a number of the more critical issues that should be examined by an investor.

In the first place mutual fund providers will counter that they are conferring many benefits other than performance, such as portfolio strategy advice, fund selection, planning and reporting, which are not available for those "do it yourself" investors who use ETFs. While there is some truth to this, consumers will have to decide whether the 2% or more cost differential to ETFs is justified by those additional benefits.[3] Alternatively, can you provide the planning, asset allocation and reporting yourself or through the services of your (discount) broker, or can you obtain some subset of these services from an independent adviser at reasonable cost?

Second, an ETF portfolio will also bear trading costs, and these have to be factored in when comparing total returns to mutual funds. Not surprisingly, the mutual fund industry will suggest that trading costs are very high, and will erase a large part of that 2% cost gap, while proponents of ETFs will deny this. I will briefly mention some of the things to consider in the Appendix to this chapter, but again the costs you will face depend on the amount of trading you do, and includes both explicit and implicit costs. The kinds of strategies I endorse would involve very low trading volumes or turnover, and as I expect that a large portion of your portfolio would be held for very long periods, ongoing trading costs would be very low.

Third, while many individuals, and small institutions such as small pension funds and foundations, will be investing in a non-taxable environment, those fortunate enough to hold investment assets outside of their tax-sheltered Canadian RRSPs and US IRAs have to consider the tax implications of investing. Again your actual situation has to be taken into account, and so it is difficult to generalize. But there are several potential tax efficiencies that can accrue to ETFs relative to actively managed mutual funds.

---

3 You also need to evaluate whether a salesman is truly independent, and gives you purchase and sale advice that is completely in your personal interest. Does a salesman have incentives to sell his clients funds from certain "fund families", perhaps those sponsored by the organization he works for?

The first applies specifically to ETFs that track broad capitalization-based equity indexes versus actively managed equity mutual funds that are benchmarked against those same indexes. Capitalization-based indexes have very low turnover relative to actively managed portfolios, and it is turnover or trading that produces realized taxable capital gains. Individuals can compare the historical tax consequences of broad ETFs they might be interested in with the tax consequences of funds they hold.[4] Of course dividend and interest income is likely similar in both cases. Some mutual fund companies offer "tax efficient" structures, but you have to pay significant extra fees for these, and you would need to do an objective analysis (not one done by a mutual fund provider) to evaluate the efficacy of these relative to ETFs.

The structure of ETFs and the way they are traded also has an impact on their tax efficiency. Since mutual funds potentially receive a net purchase or sale every day, this requires the purchase or sale of securities within the fund on an ongoing basis. That is, taxable transactions occur continually even if strategic trades are not made. By contrast, while the purchase or sale of existing ETF units creates a taxable event for the investor, it does not create a taxable event within the ETF trust, since nothing has happened inside the trust itself. Moreover when new units are created, or existing units are redeemed, the creation or redemption occurs outside of the trust, again without immediate tax consequences to the trust itself.

All of these additional issues need to be evaluated by a careful investor, and perhaps the issue of "advice" is the most important one. It is the difficulty of finding good and reasonably-priced independent advice, as well as the difficulty most people find in actually tracking

---

4 Generally speaking you can expect that higher turnover will tend to generate higher realized capital gains. I don't have access to a broad sample of mutual fund turnover or tax information, so it is difficult to generalize. But by way of example, I compared capital gains data over a seven-year period for a broad Canadian equity ETF versus a bank-managed mainstream equity mutual fund that I believed to have modest turnover. The capital gains averaged 1.36% per year for the ETF versus 5.37% per year for the mutual fund, and in addition the ETF happened to outperform the mutual fund before taxes.

and rebalancing their portfolios, that makes a packaged mutual fund solution so attractive from an operational point of view. But industry fees are so high that they are value-destroying, and there is little evidence that the advice provided through the fund distribution mechanism makes up for the cost of those fees.

The fact that most small investors need packaged solutions has generated a great deal of support from independent pension fund consultants for the idea of a very low cost optional and supplemental government-sponsored investment plan for Canadian investors. But for investors who want to take on the challenges of managing their own portfolios, I believe that a disciplined strategy implemented with broad market ETFs is very likely to outperform a comparable portfolio of mutual funds after costs. The certainty of reducing costs by using ETFs is a decided advantage.

Appendix: more on the trading costs of ETFs

Careless and badly executed trading could certainly raise ETF trading costs to uneconomic levels, but I will lay out the parameters here that would allow small investors to experience small and reasonable trading costs. My assumptions include the following:

- a small number of relatively liquid ETFs that track broad market indexes will be used for most of the portfolio;
- turnover will generally be low, and I'll assume 10% turnover annually, which implies total purchases and sales of 20% of the portfolio's value;
- a discount broker is used. With a portfolio size of $50,000 or more, trade execution costs should be $10 or less in Canada, and probably less for US-based investors. For accounts of this size and larger, there are generally no additional administration fees.

Here's how I estimate trading costs for this kind of portfolio. First a $10 cost per trade implies $0.10 per share for a 100 share trade, $0.02 per share for a 500-share trade, and $0.01 per share for a 1000-share trade. The fact that only a few securities are held at any time, and that trade volume should be very low, implies that larger trades should be the norm. For the sake of the example I will assume that trades average at least 500 shares, but as a portfolio grows larger so should the trade size. Direct commission costs are the main *overt* or easily identifiable cost of trading.

But other and larger costs of trading are hidden. The most obvious hidden cost is the bid-ask spread. If you assume that the current "fair" value is the middle of that spread, and that for most retail-sized orders for liquid ETFs you will be able to buy on the ask and sell on the bid, then your spread cost is half of that spread. The Vanguard Group website[1] presents a study of average bid-ask spreads for their ETFs trading on US exchanges over a 30-day period, in both a dollar amount and as a percent of market price. In dollars the spreads of their S&P500, EAFE and EM ETFs are respectively $0.01, $0.02 and $0.01, while the spread for their intermediate-term bond fund is $0.03. Of course the spreads of more focused and less liquid ETFs can be substantially higher. My observation is that the spreads of liquid Canadian ETFs are probably double those in the US, in the range of $0.02 to $0.04. But for the sake of this analysis, I will make the very conservative assumption that bid-ask spreads are as high as $0.06, which makes half the bid-ask spread $0.03.

In addition, at any point in time the fair value of any index-tracking ETF is its net asset value or NAV, the weighted sum of the values of securities held, including dividends receivable. To the extent that the NAV strays below the current pricing of the ETF, this is an additional cost for a buyer, and to the extent that the NAV strays above the current price this is a cost for the seller. If ETFs are being constantly arbitraged, you would expect that NAVs would range within the bid-ask spread of its weighted holdings plus the cost of arbitrage. I can only measure this with end-of-day prices versus end-of-day NAVs, which may not reflect fluctuations within the trading day, but the tentative results are more or less in line with this idea. There is also no reason to think that fluctuations from fair value should be systematically against you or any other particular investor, since you will be both buying and selling, and the strategies I will discuss have little relation to current market momentum. So for the sake of argument let me posit another $0.03 cost to reflect divergence from fair value, although I believe that on average this number will be close to 0.

Adding up these three factors, a 500-share trade might cost as much as $0.08 per share, although I actually believe it will be much less than this, since my assumptions are very conservative. This cost

---

1   At https://advisors.vanguard.com/VGApp/iip/site/advisor/investments/bidaskspread

Appendix: more on the trading costs of ETFs

of $0.08 per share should be evaluated relative to the market price of the unit. For example, for a $20.00 unit price, this amounts to 0.4%. But remember that I am assuming a turnover of 10%, which means that sales plus purchases total 20% of the market value of the portfolio. Thus 0.4% on the 20% of the portfolio traded comes to 0.08% of the total portfolio, and again I believe that this is a very high estimate. So on this assumption, the 0.19% MER from Table 26-1 becomes an ongoing 0.27% cost after trading. Even if you double those trading costs again (for example you double the turnover, or your ETF strays far from its NAV than I am supposing), the total is still at 0.35%, a substantial saving relative to mutual fund implementation.

Chapter 27:

The Key Component of a Comprehensive Investment Strategy: Asset Mix

I examined historical nominal and real returns and risks for equities, and developed a return attribution approach that I have used to create forecasts of expected returns for equities. In a similar fashion I examined historical returns and risks of fixed income assets, and established a parallel system for generating expected returns. Finally, as part of my introduction of fixed income investments I introduced the idea of diversification due to imperfect correlations.

> **OVERVIEW**
>
> On average, over 90% of the variability of a portfolio is due to its evolving asset mix. In addition, on average 100% of a portfolio's return is due to its evolving asset mix. The second result is consistent with the earlier observation that it is difficult for active managers to add value within asset classes.

One of the implicit consequences of the discussion of diversification is that it is unlikely to be sensible to simply invest in the asset with the highest expected return. Risk matters, and investors should be looking for a combination of expected return and risk that meets our investment needs (as yet undefined). But I haven't said anything about how we can go about doing this.

My starting point is to demonstrate that the dominant driver of any portfolio's investment returns is its *asset allocation*, the exposure to each of the broad equity, fixed income and any other assets (or asset classes) that it holds. To let the cat out of the bag, I'm actually going to suggest that asset allocation is the *only* thing that should matter for most investors, apart from reducing both explicit and implicit costs, but I'll get to that conclusion in due course. After establishing this general result here, in Chapter 28 I will show the impact of specific historical asset allocations using historical returns, illustrating how risk and correlation have interacted with returns over time. Historical asset allocation results serve as forecasts for future investments only to the extent that you believe that historical returns, risks and correlations will continue into the future. In Chapter 29 I will show the impact of applying my specific forecasts that reflect the facts related to evolving market conditions, building portfolios that may evolve over time.

You can begin to see why asset allocation is crucial in a very direct way, without any statistical analysis, by examining Figure 27-1. To keep the graph simple, I have plotted year-by-year returns of just two assets, Canadian equities and bonds, using the DMS data from 1960 to 2010. The central red line gives year-by-year equity return, while the two outer red lines give the index return plus and minus 4%, which is approximately the standard deviation of one-year

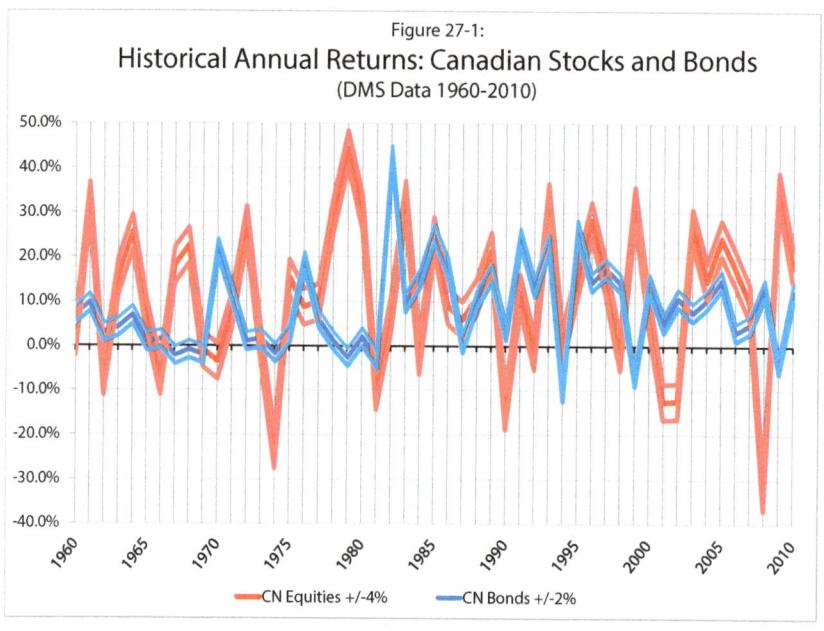

The Key Component of a Comprehensive Investment Strategy: Asset Mix 299

manager returns around the average for mutual funds as we saw in Chapter 25.[1] The central blue line gives the year-by-year bond returns, and the outer lines give the index return plus and minus 2%. Again, 2% approximates the standard deviation of bond manager returns around the index.

At each point the red lines indicate a span of 8% (index +/-4%). But in most years the volatility of the lines implies that most of your return is dependent on whether or not you actually invested in equities, rather than where you are within the distribution of +/-4% around the index return. Similarly the blue lines indicate a span of 4%, and again most of your return is determined by whether or not you invested in bonds rather than where you are within the distribution of bond returns. Were you to limit your portfolio to the two asset classes in Figure 27-1, then I think it is also intuitive that for any mix of the two assets, the same point would also hold. That is, in any one year most of your return would be due to the average returns of stocks and bonds along with the proportions in which you held them, rather than on whether your stocks and bonds outperformed or underperformed the general markets.

To be sure, if you could outperform the equity or bond index by 4% or 2% respectively on a consistent basis year after year, that outperformance would make a huge difference after a few years. While such systematic outperformance is indeed possible, the mutual fund examples showed that there is a very low probability of achieving that over multiple years. But without making any assumption about investors' abilities to link together outperformance year after year, there are many empirical studies that demonstrate the dominance of the asset allocation decision on portfolio returns.

These studies are discussed and replicated in a clear and insightful article by Roger Ibbotson and Paul Kaplan: "Does Asset Allocation Policy Explain 40, 90, or 100 Percent of Performance?" (see I&K 2000). Imagine that you have a large sample of portfolios,

---

1 Remember that the standard deviation of fund returns was not actually centred around the index as my example suggests here, but I simply want to indicate the variability of active management relative to an index.

say pension funds or multi-asset "balanced" mutual funds, with monthly or quarterly returns over a lengthy period such as ten years or more. Assume as well that at the beginning of each monthly or quarterly period you have the starting asset mix, the percentage allocated to each asset class, as well as benchmark returns for each asset class. For each period you can calculate the *return to the asset mix* for each portfolio, by using its asset mix weighting and attributing the subsequent benchmark return to each component.

Here's a first thing you might do. For each portfolio calculate a linear regression that explains the period-by-period portfolio returns as a function of period-by-period returns to its asset mix. The r-squared of that regression tells you how much of the actual returns are explained by the policy mix. For example, an adjusted r-squared of 85% means that *85% of the variation in return of the portfolio was due to its ongoing and changing asset mix*. Do this for all the portfolios in the sample and pool all of the results. The mean of the sample results is the average adjusted r-squared, which tells you the average percentage of variability explained by asset mix. The two original studies, which are often cited by investors as "the Brinson studies",[2] found the average r-squared to be 93.6% and 91.5% respectively for a sample of pension funds. Ibbotson and Kaplan find slightly lower results for their samples of mutual funds and pension funds,[3] but conclude that on average approximately 90% of the *variability* of individual fund returns is explained by policy asset mix.

Figure 27-2 gives an example of a regression for an individual portfolio, just as it would be calculated in this first test. The portfolio is composed of just those two assets, a simulated Canadian equity

---

2 The two studies are:

Brinson, Gary P., L Randolph Hood and Gilbert L. Beeobower, "Determinants of Portfolio Performance", *Financial Analysts Journal*, July/August 1986, pp. 39-48; and

Brinson, Gary P., Brian D. Singer and Gilbert L. Beeobower, "Determinants of Portfolio Performance II, An Update", *Financial Analysts Journal*, May/June 1991, pp. 40-48.

3 I&K 2000 give results for the two studies mentioned in the previous footnote, along with their own, in Table 2 p. 29.

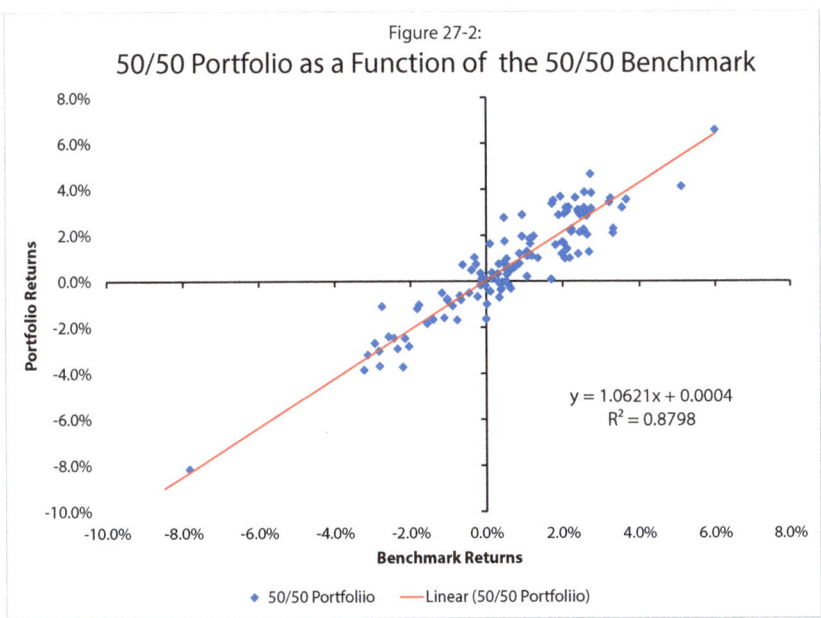

portfolio and a simulated Canadian bond portfolio.[4] You can see that the fit of the 50-50 portfolio was very close to the 50/50 benchmark, and the r-squared was just under 88%.

The background ideas that I was trying to convey with Figure 27-1 are related to this first finding. That is, most of the period-by-period performance in the portfolio of Canadian stocks and bonds in that graph — the "ups and downs" or variability of return — would be due to the proportions of each asset held, and very little would be explained by the value added or subtracted relative to each index.

Investors often incorrectly describe the Brinson studies as showing that on average 90% of a *portfolio's return* is due to its ongoing asset mix — they drop the crucial term "variability". To repeat, the Brinson methodology shows that on average roughly 90%

---

4 While I would have preferred to use actual portfolios such as mutual funds, for some reason it is quite difficult to find monthly or quarterly returns for long periods of history. My hypothetical Canadian equity portfolio had a standard deviation of 5.3% around its benchmark, while the bond portfolio simulation had a standard deviation of 2.2% around its benchmark. Each "return" is drawn from a normally distributed random sample.

of the *variability of a portfolio's return* is due to its ongoing asset mix. However, there is a second test[5] that can be done with these data, that speaks directly to the question of fund returns.

Suppose you take the data and calculate the total return for each portfolio for a period of five or ten years, along with the cumulative return to the ongoing asset mix over the same period. Divide the cumulative return to the asset mix for each portfolio by its actual cumulative return. If they are identical, the ratio would be 1.0, meaning that 100% of the fund's return was due to the asset mix. If the ratio is greater than 1.0, then the portfolio has underperformed its asset mix, and conversely if the ratio is less than 1.0 then the fund has outperformed its mix (added value through changing the asset mix within each period, or by having active management within asset classes that on average outperformed the asset class benchmarks). Ibbotson and Kaplan find that on average for their mutual fund sample, slightly more than 100% of return is due to asset mix, meaning that balanced mutual funds slightly underperformed their evolving asset mix. For pension funds the average was 99%. They point out that the pension fund sample was before expenses, so that after costs the number would climb close to 100% as well.

You might find this astounding, but I repeat: *on average, all of the return of a fund or portfolio is due to its asset mix.* This is not to say that there is not a significant range of performance. For example, in

---

5 In I&K 2000 this is actually the third of the three tests. I will not discuss the second test in detail here, which shows that roughly 40% of the *difference or variability* in cumulative performance across the sample of portfolios is due to their differing asset mix. The other 60% is due to such factors as value added or lost within the various asset classes, costs, and changing allocations within each performance period.

This is a totally intuitive result as well. For example, at one extreme if two portfolios happened to have the same asset allocation over time, then clearly all of the difference in their cumulative performance would be due to factors other than asset allocation. At the other extreme, if two portfolios held exactly the same index funds, but had different asset allocations, then 100% of their cumulative performance differential would be due to asset mix. But most portfolios differ both in asset mix and in the asset class portfolios that are used to implement it, and on average the asset mix difference explains 40% of the performance differential.

their pension fund study Ibbotson and Kaplan found that for 50% of the funds examined (25th to 75th percentile) the percentage of total return explained by the return to the asset mix ranged from 96% to 102%,[6] while the 25% below and above the middle 50% were much more widely skewed. You also have to understand that this result does not imply any evaluation of the particular asset mix decisions that have been made. What it says is that *given the particular set of asset mix decisions made by a fund over time,* even professional pension fund managers find it difficult to add value beyond their asset mix decisions. That should be a sobering thought, but it is consistent with the idea that within markets, the average manager has difficulty outperforming the market even before fees, and most underperform after fees.

Now that I have demonstrated the importance of asset mix, I will illustrate a process for building a multi-asset portfolio strategy.

---

[6] I&K 2000 Table 7 p.32.

Chapter 28:

Returns, Risks and Correlations in Portfolio Construction

As I begin discussing investment portfolios and building an ongoing investment strategy, I will follow my usual game plan and begin by looking at history. What would have happened in the past had you combined multiple assets in portfolios over time? I will start with a "constant mix" approach that illustrates the interaction of return, risk and correlations between asset classes. Combined with the idea that historical returns and risks can be used as proxies for future expected returns and risks, investors often use the historical results as a basis for choosing an ongoing portfolio asset mix. I will discuss some issues with this approach, and in the following chapter I will show how using my dynamic forecasts rather than historical averages can potentially improve our asset allocation.

Long-term historical returns and risks across asset classes have often been appropriately ordered, with higher historical returns being accompanied by higher historical risks or volatility. To

> **OVERVIEW**
>
> A historical perspective on portfolio construction is developed using historical returns, risks and correlations from 1900 to 2000. Maximum return portfolios for each level of risk are calculated.
>
> **Key findings:**
>
> - at lower levels of risk the benefits of imperfect correlation yield much higher returns than those of individual assets at the same level of risk;
> - on the assumption that historical returns, risks and correlations are your best estimate of future returns, an approach to choosing an asset mix is outlined;
> - some implications of holding a constant mix portfolio are illustrated.

give an example, let me take the perspective of a Canadian investor at the end of 2000 who is looking at long-run history for four main asset classes: Canadian bonds, Canadian equities, US equities (in Canadian dollars), and the rest of the developed equity market outside of North America which is approximately EAFE (also in CAD). The data are from the DMS dataset, and I'm going to ignore the fact that the data probably weren't available in this form for several more years.[1] Table 28-1 shows what the investor would have seen.

Table 28-1
Geometric and Average Returns, Risks and Correlations
CAD perspective, DMS Data 1900-2000

	CN Bonds	CN Equities	US Equities	World Ex US
Annualized Return (CAD)	4.97%	9.33%	10.55%	8.89%
Arithmetic Average Return	5.35%	10.64%	12.37%	10.40%
Standard Deviation	9.04%	16.82%	19.57%	18.46%
CN Inflation	3.15%			
Annualized Real Return	1.76%	5.98%	7.17%	5.56%

Correlations	CN Bonds	CN Equities	US Equities	World Ex US
CN Bonds	1			
CN Equities	0.088	1		
US Equities	0.190	0.787	1	
World Ex US	0.099	0.478	0.393	1

Despite the fact that equity markets outside of Canada had begun to turn down in 2000, as technology and telecom stocks began to recede from stratospheric levels, the long-term historical returns to stocks around the world were strong. Over the 101 years ending in 2000, Canadian bonds returned 4.97% in nominal terms, for a real return of 1.76%. Canadian equities returned 9.33%, for a real return of 5.98%, and non-Canadian equities performed strongly as well in Canadian dollars. At a standard deviation of 9.04%, Canadian bonds exhibited slightly more than half the risk of Canadian equities at 16.82%, and less than half the risk of non-Canadian equities.

---

1 Their *Triumph of the Optimists: 101 Years of Global Investment Returns*, in which these data were first made widely available, was not published until 2002.

Correlations were also usefully low, with only Canadian-US equity correlations substantially over 0.5.

Figure 28-1 presents the arithmetic average returns and standard deviations of the four asset classes placed on a return-risk graph. Equities are clustered higher and to the right-hand side of the graph, while Canadian bonds (the red square) are far to the left and lower. The blue line and blue dots represent *maximum return* portfolios for each level of risk, based on the historical correlations, risks and returns in Table 28-1,[2] and assuming that a constant mix of assets is held over history. Since the data underlying the graph are annual returns data from the DMS dataset, this is just like assuming that the portfolios are rebalanced to the same proportions at the beginning of each year, whatever those proportions happen to be.

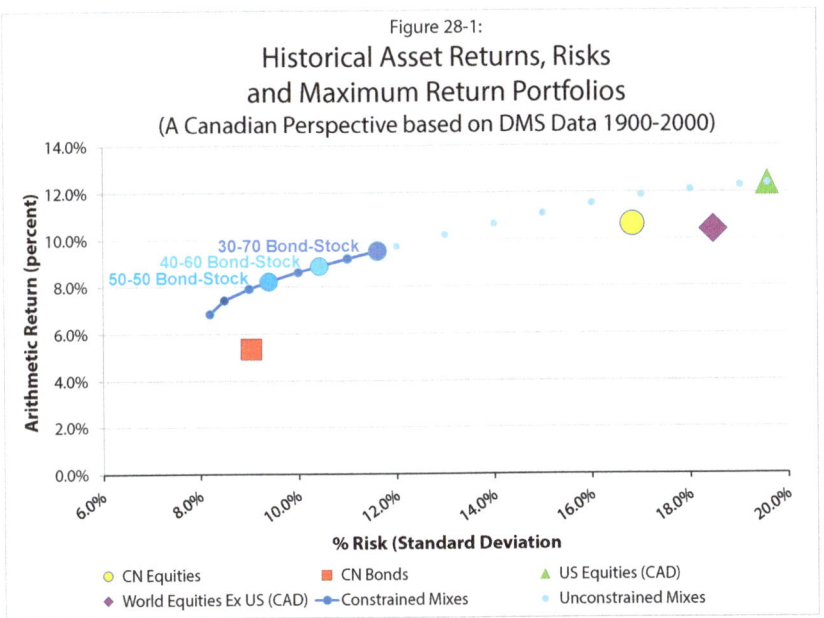

---

2 These maximum return portfolios are calculated using a mean-variance optimizer, specifically the Solver application in Excel. I am not going to give details here as to how this is set up, but it is easy to find references about using Solver if you are interested. The data in Table 25-1 are all that is needed for this simple problem. In a real working situation, where optimization assumes a normal distribution of returns, the averages and standard deviations would be of logarithmic returns.

The three large blue circles represent three maximum return portfolios that have specific asset mixes that are often mentioned as long-term asset mix allocations. The first on the left has 50% bonds (hence 50% equities divided among the three equity indexes used), the second has 40% bonds and 60% equities, while the third on the right has 30% bonds and 70% equities.[3] The return, risk and specific allocations for each are shown in Table 28-2 below.

Table 28-2:
Historical Arithmetic Returns, Risks and Allocations
For the Three Constant Mix Portfolios in Figure 28-1

Bond - Equity Mix	Arithmetic Average Return (CAD)	Risk (Standard Deviation)	CN Bonds	CN Equities	US Equities (CAD)	World Ex US (CAD)
			\multicolumn{4}{c}{Percentage Allocation}			
50-50	8.20%	9.39%	50.0%	17.2%	14.4%	18.4%
40-60	8.86%	10.43%	40.0%	15.6%	22.6%	21.8%
30-70	9.53%	11.65%	30.0%	13.9%	30.9%	25.3%

I also want to note that the heavy blue line represents maximum return portfolios based on *constrained* weights for each asset, with bounds that might have been in place for an institutional investor.[4] The lighter blue dots continue with unconstrained portfolios, ending with an allocation of 100% in US Equities. The portfolios beyond the dark blue line are too heavily weighted in equities to be considered as feasible institutional portfolios.

The maximum return portfolios give dramatic illustrations of the point made in Part 3 of this book, that combining assets with imperfect correlations can generate portfolios with more attractive return-risk characteristics than the individual assets have on their own. For example, the 50-50 bond-stock portfolio has a historical risk of 9.39%, only marginally higher than the 9.04% of bonds on

---

3 The actual mix of equities in the equity portion is just the result of the optimization: the maximum return portfolio that happened to have the percentage exposure to bonds that I wanted to highlight.

4 Canadian equities were constrained to between 10% and 35%, and the remaining two equity classes were constrained between 5% and 30%.

their own. But its arithmetic average return of 8.2% was an attractive 2.85% higher than the 5.35% arithmetic average return of bonds on their own. This large boost in potential return with almost no realized incremental risk is the result of the imperfect correlations between the equities themselves and with bonds. As you move up the line of dots to the right, the incremental return relative to the underlying assets diminishes, until the final "mix" is just 100% of the highest return asset, US Equities in CAD. You can also verify that the historical return-risk calculations "work" by calculating period-by-period returns for any particular asset allocation.[5]

Figure 28-1 shows *historical* returns and risks for the individual asset classes, and shows what maximum returns could have been obtained historically for each level of risk using a constant asset allocation weighting. But graphs like this have also sometimes been used to help determine the *future* asset mix for an investor such as a pension fund that has been established to fund future pension liabilities, or an individual who has to fund his expenditures after retirement.

To dramatically simplify, the process might be something like this. Given your knowledge of the liabilities or future payouts that you face, along with the value of your current investments and a schedule of future funding contributions that you expect will be made to bolster the assets of the fund, you can calculate a required return on your investments that will fully fund those liabilities.[6] Then if you were to accept the view that historical averages and risks

---

[5] To give one example, since the DMS data are annual, I calculated year-by-year returns for the 50% bond example, based on the asset mix weights. This is to say that the portfolio was "rebalanced" at the beginning of each year to that asset mix. The arithmetic return and risk numbers were 8.2% and 9.39%, exactly as estimated from the historical correlations and standard deviations.

[6] Of course this is not a "back of the envelope" endeavour for a pension fund — actuaries and other pension plan consultants focus on understanding the liabilities, potential funding, and required returns, and these assumptions and calculations have to be approved by a regulatory regime. An individual can perform an exercise of a similar kind on a smaller scale, using a spreadsheet to plot the potential growth of current investments and future contributions, against the value of the outlays he expects to make after retirement, accounting for inflation.

are the best estimate for future average returns and risks, at least over the long term, you can choose a portfolio mix from Figure 28-1 as your investment mix going forward. You will pick a portfolio mix with an expected return that matches or betters your required return, although you also have to be willing to bear the accompanying expected risk of not matching that expected return.

For example, suppose that in 2000 you calculated that your required real return was 4% (after inflation), and you estimated long-term inflation to be 3%. Then your nominal required return is roughly 7% (properly 7.12% with compounding). Now, you need to be a little careful here, because the long-run required return of 7.12% is a *geometric average return*, the rate you require assuming that you received it year after year, without volatility. In order to compare it with the arithmetic average returns displayed in Figure 28-1, you have to convert it into an arithmetic average return, matching the volatility of the comparison point. For example, using a standard conversion formula[7] the required geometric return of 7.12% is equivalent to an arithmetic average return of 7.52% at a volatility of 9.39% as shown by the 50-50 bond stock mix. So if you accept historical average returns as your expected future long-term returns, the expected return of 8.2% from this 50-50 bond-stock mix provides a small cushion of 0.68% over the required return of 7.52%, while you have to bear a risk of 9.39%.

Of course you can choose a more aggressive mix with a higher expected return if you are willing to accept the higher risk that accompanies it. Imagine that you move up and to the right along the line of maximum return portfolios taking on tiny increments of additional risk. For each additional unit of risk you receive a little more return, but given the shape of the line the additional return diminishes with each step. At some point you will judge that the additional return does not justify the next increment of risk. That is, your *aversion to risk* will make the incremental return unattractive, and you will have reached the point at which you have maximized the benefits or

---

7 I gave a simple approximation for this conversion in the Appendix of Chapter 3, and if you use that formula you get a required arithmetic return of 7.56%, slightly higher than I get using a more complex formula.

utility of return given the risks. This is your *optimal* portfolio, which provides you the maximum expected benefit consistent with your forecasts of return and risk, along with your risk aversion.

I am not going to present these ideas of *risk aversion, utility* and *optimal portfolios* in a formal way here, but I think that the basic ideas given in the previous paragraph are fairly intuitive, and that the step-by-step approach to determining your portfolio choice is a sensible idealization of what you might actually do. There are four key assumptions that underly the selection process as described:

- First, your forecasts determine the expected return and risk opportunities that are available to you.
- Second, you benefit from higher expected returns, which add to your utility, and you dislike or are harmed by risk, which lowers your utility. In this context only the benefits or utility from higher returns and the harm or negative utility from higher risk are viewed as determining the net benefit or net utility you receive from investing in a portfolio.
- Third, your personal or institutional risk aversion can be understood as the lowest change in return that you will accept as a consequence of accepting an incremental unit of risk — it is the rate at which falling utility due to increased risk *is exactly balanced* by the increase of utility due to increased return.
- And of course the fourth unstated assumption is that you want to maximize your benefits or utility.

From these assumptions we know in advance that you must choose one of the maximum return portfolios, since for any risk level (negative utility) they provide the best return (positive utility). The particular maximum return portfolio you choose is determined by your risk aversion.

In the Appendix to this chapter I will add just enough additional structure to enable me to draw a picture that captures these ideas, for those who find that kind of thing useful. But the basic concepts that I have outlined help to conceptualize what you are doing when you choose a portfolio. Moreover once you identify a particular portfolio, such as the 50-50 bond-stock mix in Figure 28-1 as your portfolio choice, you can use its expected returns and risks to infer your risk aversion. You can then use your implied risk aversion to choose portfolios consistent with your first choice as circumstances change. I will show you how that works in the next chapter.

To come back to the year 2000, suppose that you had chosen your long-term investment mix on the basis of the long-term historical returns in Table 28-1 and the consequent maximum return portfolio opportunities shown in Figure 28-1. While you would have realized that over the next 12 years returns might be quite different from history, you would have assumed that the more aggressive equity-mix portfolios would perform better. Table 28-3 shows the actual results, with returns and risks of the mix portfolios measured assuming annual rebalancing back to the long-term "policy" mix. Note as well that the table provides returns for indexes that are investable using index funds or ETFs, rather than the historical DMS data, and all the subsequent analysis will use those indexes.

Table 28-3:
Subsequent Annualized Returns and Risks
CAD Perspective, S&P and MSCI Data 2001-2012

	CN Universe Bonds	CN S&P/TSX Equities	US S&P500 Equities (CAD)	EAFE Equities (CAD)	50-50 Bond-Stock Mix	40-60 Bond-Stock Mix	30-70 Bond-Stock Mix
Annualized Return (CAD)	6.37%	5.25%	-0.84%	0.12%	4.43%	3.62%	2.79%
Arithmetic Average Return (CAD)	6.39%	7.13%	-0.06%	1.43%	4.67%	3.96%	3.25%
Standard Deviation	1.94%	19.91%	12.58%	16.54%	7.38%	8.62%	9.90%

Bonds had the highest annualized return at 6.37%, while exhibiting extremely low volatility over the period. All three equity classes significantly underperformed bonds, with much higher volatility that was close to their historical levels. Since bonds were the best performing asset class, the cumulative annualized returns of the various asset mixes were dominated by the size of their bond exposure. Thus the 50-50 bond-stock mix returned 4.43%, the 40-60 mix returned 3.62%, while the 30-70 mix returned 2.79%. While the realized returns of the three asset mixes are in the reverse order relative to the longer-term history shown in Table 28-2, the realized risks are in the expected rank order, although at slightly lower levels.

Although these returns are not devastatingly bad, they are certainly low relative to long-term history. If you deduct the 1.9% for Canadian inflation over this period you see that real returns for the static mix portfolios were quite thin, ranging from approximately 2.5% to 0.9%. This also assumes that your investment was costless, but if you add in the average level of costs that small Canadian investors face with mutual funds, you would have had difficulty obtaining positive real returns.

Still, such an asset allocation strategy would have achieved more than word of mouth suggests many smaller investors actually obtained, and is not far from what a pension fund might have expected to receive.[8] For interest, Table 28-4 shows the year-by-year nominal returns for the four assets, along with the returns for each of the three mixes. At the beginning of every year the asset mix portfolios have been rebalanced back to their chosen allocation. You can see that investors who followed this simple diversified investment approach fared relatively well. Even in a difficult year like 2008, returns were -10.8% for the 50-50 portfolio — a disappointing but not frightening result.

---

8 For reference, I calculated benchmark returns for three major Canadian public pension plans who provide annual reports on their websites: the Ontario Teachers' Pension Plan Board (OTPPB), the Ontario Municipal Employees Retirement System plan (OMERS), and the Healthcare of Ontario Pension Plan (HOOPP). Over the 12-year span considered here, their benchmark returns were respectively 5.4%, 5.35% and 6.42%.

In my examples the asset mix is very simple, using only Canadian Universe bonds and the three equity asset classes. Simply adding a 10% allocation to Emerging Markets equities, and reducing exposures to the other equity classes, generated a benchmark return of 5.39% for the 50-50 bond-equity mix, right in line with both the OTPPB and OMERS benchmarks. In addition to emerging market equities, the three pension fund benchmarks also benefited from a broader selection of assets, including inflation-protected fixed income, commodities, alternative assets such as hedge funds, and direct holdings in real estate, infrastructure and other non-traded direct investments. In some cases the benchmarks also evolved considerably over this period.

Table 28-4:
Year-by-Year Returns to Asset Classes and Constant Mix Portolios
CAD Perspective, DMS Data 2001-2012

	CN Universe Bonds	CN S&P/TSX Equities	US S&P500 Equities (CAD)	EAFE Equities (CAD)	50-50 Bond-Stock mix	40-60 Bond-Stock Mix	30-70 Bond-Stock Mix
2001	8.1%	-12.6%	-6.4%	-16.3%	-2.0%	-3.7%	-5.4%
2002	8.7%	-12.4%	-22.9%	-16.5%	-4.1%	-7.2%	-10.4%
2003	6.7%	26.7%	5.3%	13.8%	11.2%	11.0%	10.8%
2004	7.1%	14.5%	2.8%	11.9%	8.7%	8.3%	8.0%
2005	6.5%	24.1%	2.3%	11.2%	9.8%	9.3%	8.8%
2006	4.1%	17.3%	15.4%	26.4%	12.1%	13.5%	15.0%
2007	3.7%	9.8%	-10.5%	-5.3%	1.0%	-0.5%	-2.1%
2008	6.4%	-33.0%	-21.2%	-28.8%	-10.8%	-13.7%	-16.5%
2009	5.4%	35.1%	7.4%	12.5%	12.1%	12.0%	11.9%
2010	6.7%	17.6%	9.1%	2.6%	8.2%	8.0%	7.9%
2011	9.7%	-8.7%	4.6%	-9.5%	2.2%	1.5%	0.7%
2012	3.6%	7.2%	13.4%	15.3%	7.8%	8.9%	10.1%
Annualized Return Dec. 2000 to Dec 2010 (Table 28-3)							
	6.4%	5.3%	-0.8%	0.1%	4.4%	3.6%	2.8%

Now I want to step back for a moment and think about how you would justify the idea of investing in a constant-mix portfolio, an approach that is often preached if not quite strictly practiced. One implication of using long-term history as your forecast of future returns is that your forecasts are essentially unchanged from year to year. To be sure, cumulative returns evolve slowly over time, as we saw for US equities in Figure 12-1, but this evolution is slow, and hardly noticeable from one year to the next. Given that historical risks and correlations likely evolve even more slowly than returns, then with the further assumption that your risk aversion hasn't changed, your portfolio allocations will remain very stable. So the idea that your portfolio strategy can maintain a constant mix over time is a pretty clear consequence of (1) unchanging forecasts of return and risk based on historical values, and (2) the assumption of no change in your risk aversion. Were your aversion to risk to change, without a material change to your forecasts, you would essentially select alternative portfolios from Figure 28-1. But as long as both (1) and (2) hold, the same portfolio continues to be optimal for you.

I have portrayed this strategy as including an annual rebalancing, largely because the DMS data are annual. But what exactly should drive you to rebalance at all? Given the assumption that your forecasts for individual asset returns and risks remain the same (or very similar) over time, if your various assets rise or fall at roughly the same rate, they will remain at roughly the same relative allocations, and your expected portfolio returns and risks will remain the same. But suppose one or more of the assets noticeably outperforms the others and you let your allocations "drift" as the outperforming asset takes a heavier weight in your portfolio.

First, if I assume that equities as a group strongly outperform bonds, then over time your allocation to equities will increase. This means that your portfolio is becoming riskier, and assuming that your long-term forecasts haven't changed, your portfolio has moved up and to the right on the curve in Figure 28-1. If your risk aversion has not changed, you shouldn't want this increased risk. That is, given your risk aversion, the increased expected return due to the higher equity allocation is less than what you require to compensate you for the increased risk you are now bearing. As a consequence you should "rebalance" back to your starting point. Conversely, suppose bonds strongly outperform, as they did in the 12 years from 2001 to 2012 shown in Table 28-4. Bonds will become a higher weighting in your portfolio, which means its total expected risk is falling as it begins to move down and leftward on the curve of Figure 28-1. Once again, if your risk aversion has not changed, you should want to increase your risk in order to obtain more expected return, by rebalancing your portfolio back to its starting weights.

When you maintain this strategy on an ongoing basis, the yearly (or more frequent if desired) rebalancing essentially forces you to sell "winning" or outperforming assets and buy "losing" or underperforming assets. Given that your forecasts of risk and return have not changed significantly, this also means that you are maintaining a constant level of expected risk and return. Thus the idea of portfolio rebalancing to a constant asset mix is a natural consequence of essentially unchanging forecasts of return and risk along with an unchanged risk aversion. In practice you might use cash flows from contributions, withdrawals and income to rebalance on an ongoing basis, with annual or semi-annual reviews of your weightings to make additional adjustments as required.

I want to suggest that investors can potentially do better than following a constant mix strategy based on these assumptions. But I hope you see that maintaining a portfolio strategy on the basis of these assumptions has actually given investors who controlled costs a reasonable outcome over a very difficult decade. Diversification across asset classes has indeed worked.

Appendix: more on risk aversion, utility, and optimal portfolios, part 1

I mentioned in the text of this chapter that I would give you a picture of how these concepts interact, but to do so I would need to add a little more structure to them. The assumption that allows me to draw this picture is the idea that a person's risk aversion is constant with respect to different levels of risk, at least in the range in which he is choosing between diversified portfolios.

I characterized risk aversion as the lowest additional incremental return that an investor will accept to take on another unit of risk. To say in addition that his risk aversion is *constant* is to say that the level of incremental (change in) return required to take on an incremental (change in) risk does not change for different levels of return or risk. This means that on a graph that plots return versus risk, risk aversion is the slope of a straight line $y = mx + b$. The slope m is the ratio of (change in y)/(change in x), and b is the y-intercept, the value of the line where x is 0. I also need to mention that in this context, risk is taken to be variance rather than standard deviation.

Appendix Figure 1 shows three such lines labelled L1, L2 and L3, along with the historical data from 1900 to 2000 from Figure 28-1. But the difference here is that the horizontal axis is variance rather than its square root, standard deviation, as originally presented. Thus a line like L1 shows a linear relation between expected return and expected variance of the form: expected return is a function of risk aversion times expected variance plus the constant, or

$$E(r) = RA*E(Variance) + C$$

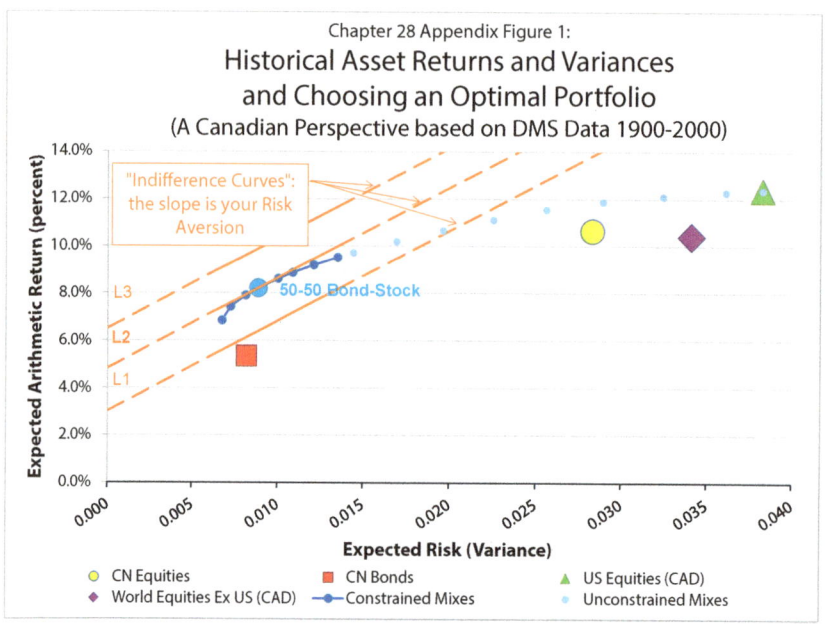

For the three lines that are shown, the constant C intercepts the vertical y axis at 3%, 4.819%, and 6.5% respectively where expected risk or variance is 0. I am *indifferent* between any two points on a line such as L1 because as I move up the line from the intercept, I am adding return as I add risk at the lowest rate I find acceptable — each additional incremental risk is exactly compensated by the incremental return. Because of this, these lines are often called *indifference curves*. Given my indifference between points on the line, I can say that the intercept for L1 at 3% captures the *certainty equivalent utility* of all the points on the line. That is, I am indifferent between (or find equal value or utility in) *any* of the risky points on the line and the intercept at 3% expected return with 0 expected variance.

Finally, the graph shows what it means to maximize utility when I choose an optimal portfolio. Since I want to maximize my utility or benefit, I want to choose a portfolio that sits on the highest possible indifference curve, which is equivalent to saying that I want the highest possible value of the constant C. Given the curve of the line of maximum return portfolios, there will only be one such portfolio. In this case L2 intersects with the maximum return set at the 50-50

Appendix: more on risk aversion, utility, and optimal portfolios, part 1

bond-stock mix which has an expected return of 8.199%, and a variance of .008825 (equal to a standard deviation of 9.39%). The intercept of 4.819% is the certainty equivalent value or utility of the portfolio. Clearly any indifference curve with a higher intercept than L2 (and so a higher utility) will not hit a maximum return portfolio, so L2 maximizes the intercept or utility, and the 50-50 bond-stock portfolio is optimal for me. To put this another way, any movement along the line of maximum return portfolios to the right or to the left of the optimal portfolio will put me on a lower indifference curve: a move to the right gives me less return than is required to justify the increased risk, and a move to the left reduces my return by more than the reduction in risk requires, and so neither generates maximum benefit to me.

Of course you understand that I created this example by working backwards: I decided that the 50-50 bond-stock portfolio is optimal, and I used it to calculate my risk aversion. That was used as the slope of the various "L" lines. The point now is that if I accept that the slope of those lines captures my risk aversion, I can now apply that to new situations and new forecast sets, assuming that my risk aversion has not changed. I show this idea informally in the next chapter, and extend the graphical approach in its appendix.

Chapter 29:

Applying Dynamic Forecasts to Portfolio Construction

In Chapter 12, I suggested that using long-term returns as forecasts for future returns is problematic. In that context I was focusing on equities, but the points I made hold for any asset with volatile returns. First I expressed discomfort with an attempt to find a theoretical link between past average returns and future expected returns that assumes that surprises or unexpected returns net out to zero over time. I also suggested that past average returns appeared to be ineffective as forecasts. But in the end a key point for me is that using your longest history as your forecast of future expected returns implies that information about the current market environment has no bearing on future returns. If that is indeed your belief, then historical averages are your best (perhaps only) guide.

> **OVERVIEW**
>
> As a contrast to using historical averages as forecasts, dynamic forecasts for year-end 2000 are developed, and maximum return portfolios are calculated. Using the portfolio construction approach from the previous chapter, an optimal portfolio is derived.
>
> The consequences of using dynamic forecasts over the 2001-2010 period are examined. There is some evidence that taking into account ongoing market information would have enhanced portfolio returns and lowered portfolio risks relative to static mix strategies.

However, I suggest that the analysis in Parts 2 and 3 supports the idea that information about current markets should inform your forecasts about future returns, and I have discussed many aspects of this point of view. But a simple example in Table 29-1 gives a dramatic illustration. It compares the returns and risks from the first 81 years of the DMS data set with those from the last 30 years.

Table 29-1:
Returns and Risks in CAD
DMS Data: History to 1980 and Subsequent Returns

	CN Bonds	CN Equities	US Equities (CAD)	World Ex US (CAD)
Historical Returns: 1900 to 1980				
Annualized Return (CAD)	3.15%	9.09%	9.23%	7.96%
Arithmetic Average Return	3.37%	10.51%	11.22%	9.39%
Standard Deviation	6.69%	17.49%	20.47%	17.81%
Subsequent Returns: 30 Years 1981 to 2010				
Annualized Return (CAD)	10.95%	9.03%	9.84%	8.67%
Arithmetic Average Return	11.47%	10.34%	11.08%	10.48%
Standard Deviation	10.98%	16.54%	16.52%	20.45%

Equity returns and risks were similar in both periods. However the annualized bond returns of 10.95% over the past 30 years were astonishingly 3.48 times higher than the returns of 3.15% annualized over their previous history, and outperformed all three equity classes. With a standard deviation of 10.98% bond risk was also 1.64 times higher relative to previous history, although it remained substantially lower than equity risk. Thirty years is a long time for the "natural" return-risk rankings to be out of kilter, with the lower-risk asset outperforming.

Of course what has happened here is not a mystery given our analytical framework. At the end of 1980, Canadian government bond yields were averaging close to 13.5%. While none of those bonds remain today, and cash flows have all been reinvested at much lower rates, investors benefited from the initial high yields, which have fallen steadily over the three decades. This explains the high bond returns of the 30 years to 2010.

But also think of the situation for the forecaster. Had you been able to access long-term historical data at the end of 1980, you would have seen that the arithmetic average nominal return to bonds was 3.37% (Table 29-1), in contrast to the current yields of

Applying Dynamic Forecasts to Portfolio Construction

13.5%. Which would have been a better indicator of the future? Over the next decade ending in 1990, the DMS data peg Canadian bond returns at 13.13%. All in all, your starting point is crucial, and it seems counter-intuitive not to take current market information into account when making investment forecasts and portfolio construction decisions.

I will try to make this point in more detail by looking at the situation over the decade following the year 2000. I will apply my forecast approach retrospectively, to think about what an investor could have surmised about the future. In Table 29-2, I begin by developing forecasts for four basic asset classes, using data as of December 2000, much as I did for equities from a Canadian perspective in Table 18-3, and for Canadian Universe bonds in Table 22-2. Nominal bond yields and dividend yields are taken from the

Table 29-2:
Forecasts as of December 2000 from a CAD Perspective

	At Dec. 2000	CN Universe Bonds	CN S&P/TSX Equities	US S&P500 Equities (CAD)	EAFE Equities (CAD)
1a	Current BY	5.75%			
1	Current DY		1.25%	1.23%	1.56%
2	Forecast RDG		1.15%	1.07%	1.11%
3	Forecast rΔDY		0.00%	0.00%	0.00%
4	Forecast real local/foreign return (1+2+3)		2.41%	2.31%	2.69%
5	Forecast real FX			0.00%	0.00%
6	Forecast Home (Canadian) real equity return (4+5)		2.41%	2.31%	2.69%
6a	Forecast Home real bond return (1a-Cdn inflation in 7)	3.17%			
7	Forecast Canadian inflation		2.50%		
8	Forecast Home (Canadian) nominal equity return (6 + 7)		4.97%	4.87%	5.25%
8a	Forecast Home (Canadian) nominal bond return (8a=6a+7)	5.75%			
9	Historical Standard Deviation	9.04%	16.82%	19.57%	18.46%
10	Forecasts converted to Arithmetic Average Returns	6.09%	6.15%	6.48%	6.66%

Note: all additions and subtractions are geometric

historical data sets, and for illustrative purposes, real dividend growth forecasts are a simple function of historical real GDPPC growth.[1]

Because bond yields were relatively high and dividend yields were relatively low, the bond forecast based on current yields is the highest forecast at 5.75% (row 8a), while the equity forecasts range from 4.83% to 5.25% (row 8). The historical standard deviations at 2000 year-end (row 9) are used to convert the annualized return forecasts to arithmetic average return forecasts in row 10. Because of the low standard deviation of bond returns, the bond forecast is no longer the highest forecast, but obviously has the most attractive return/risk ratio.

Figure 29-1 shows the implications of these forecasts, and compares them with the results already shown in Table 28-1 and Figure 28-1. This graph is full of interesting information, so let me go through it in some detail.

First, let's focus on the returns and risks of the individual assets from row 10 of Table 29-2. Since I am still using the same historical risks and correlations for each asset, only the expected return has changed.[2] The dynamic forecasts for the three equity assets are much

---

[1] While the US RDG had been positive over the 30 years from 1970-2000, and close to its long-term historical average of approximately 1%, Canadian and EAFE RDG had been much more variable over this period, with stretches of negative growth. Yet in all three cases real GDPPC had been positive, accumulating to roughly 2% annualized. So I decided to base my RDG growth forecasts on real GDPPC growth. To make this a purely mechanical exercise that could be applied to other years in the example later in this chapter without further explanation, my forecast for RDG at any year-end is half the cumulative real GDPPC growth over the data span from 1970 to that point. This puts RDG forecasts for all three equity classes in the range of 1% to 1.5% at each year-end over the next ten years. This is a good forecast (as it turns out) for the US and EAFE, but badly understates the actual results for Canada. Clearly an investor working in real time could have taken a more nuanced approach to forecasting dividend growth.

[2] While short-term strategies sometimes adjust risks to reflect expectations over a short time frame, I think that it is dangerous to stray far from longer-term historical standard deviations as your measure of risk when you intend your forecast to hold for a longer time frame. In that case I want my risk numbers to reflect the full range of what is possible. However, correlations may be another matter. For example, if you believe that conditions such as inflation affect how stocks and

Applying Dynamic Forecasts to Portfolio Construction 325

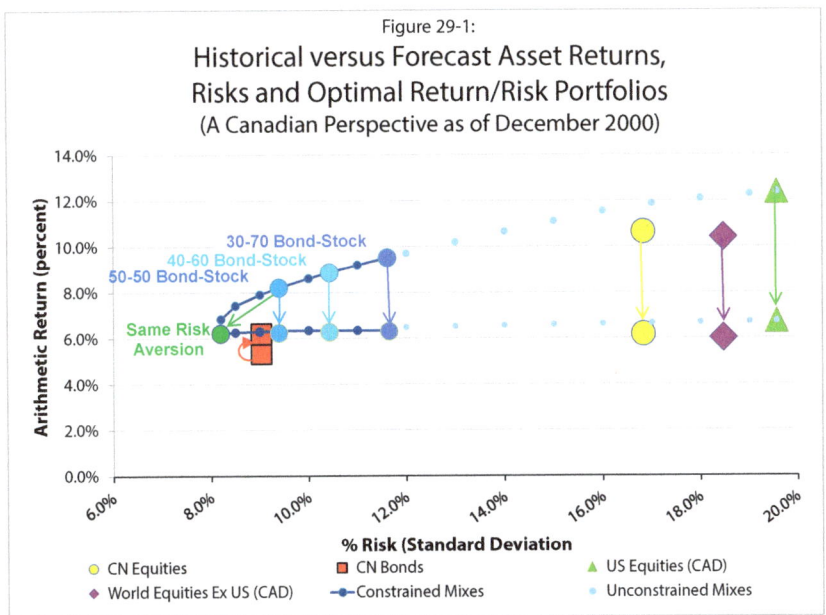

lower than their historical values, as shown by the yellow, purple and green arrows. However my bond forecast is slightly higher than the historical returns, and so the direction of the red arrow is upwards. Note that while the historical data from the previous chapter show equities with substantially higher returns that might justify their much higher risks, my new forecasts suggest that there is little or no incremental return to justify those much higher risks, since all forecasts are between 6% and 7%.

This last point is dramatized by comparing the two sets of blue lines and dots. These represent the maximum return portfolios at various levels of risk for the two sets of forecasts. Remember that the dots on the dark blue lines represent portfolios with assets constrained roughly as I expect institutional portfolios might be,[3]

---

bonds interact with each other, and you are willing to forecast inflation over your investment horizon, then you may want to adjust your expectations with respect to correlations as well. Some initial empirical findings on this topic will be posted on http://www.structuredcapital.com/ as supplementary material for this book.

3 As mentioned in the last chapter, Canadian equities were constrained to between 10% and 35%, and the remaining two equity classes were constrained to between 5% and 30%.

while the extended blue dots are unconstrained, and end with the highest return/risk equity asset in each case. The larger blue circles show the maximum return 50-50, 40-60 and 30-70 bond-equity asset mix portfolios as defined by the original historical data, which have the same risk but much lower expected return with the new forecasts. You cannot see this by inspecting the graph, but with the new dynamic forecasts, the three original constant mix portfolios are actually just below the maximum return line, although in all three cases they are very close to it. That is, with the new forecasts *they are no longer maximum return portfolios*, and for each of the three risk levels some other combination of the four assets provides a slightly higher expected return.

Perhaps the most obvious general observation is that all of the maximum return portfolios based on the new dynamic forecasts are lower than any of the maximum return portfolios based on the historical returns. But a second point is that the line or curve created by linking all of the newly calculated maximum return portfolios is much flatter than the original curve. This means that if you use the new forecasts you will likely pick a portfolio close to the left end of the line, since risk is much lower and you expect to receive almost no incremental return for taking on more risk. Indeed if I assume that a particular portfolio such as the 50-50 bond-equity portfolio correctly expressed your risk aversion with the original forecasts, *the same risk aversion would suggest that you select a much lower-risk portfolio with the new forecasts*, one which (as it turns out) has 74% in bonds. This change downward and to the left is shown by the green arrow and the portfolio is represented by the green circle.

There are a lot of moving parts in this last point, so let me go through it step by step. I'll begin with the historical data from the last chapter which are reproduced as the higher maximum portfolio line in Figure 29-1. First, assume that you identified a particular portfolio, such as the 50-50 bond-stock mix, as your asset mix. That means that you accept the risk aversion measure implied by that selection. You don't want to move upwards and to the right on the maximum return line because the additional return isn't compensated for by the additional risk you must take on. Nor do you want to move down and to the left, because the return you lose isn't compensated for by the risk reduction.

But with the new dynamic forecasts and the new lower set of maximum return portfolios, the portfolio that maximizes return given the same risk aversion ratio is now much further to the left, with substantially lower expected returns and expected risk. I will show this graphically in the appendix. The flatness of the new maximum return line, caused by the low forecasts of the higher-risk equities, means that taking on more expected risk is very unrewarding. In this extreme case you would have to have a very low risk aversion indeed in order to move further to the right.

I have been completely transparent as to how these new forecasts were created, and you can judge whether or not you think they would have been plausible forecasts at the end of 2000. You can check Table 28-3 from the previous chapter to see the subsequent ten-year returns for the four asset classes, and it's fairly clear they were better forecasts of the following decade than the original forecasts based on long-term history. But suppose that these dynamic forecasts had been updated continuously, or at least (given our data limitations) at the end of each year. Could they have been used to improve one's investment outcome over the decade of the 2000s? This is after all the crux of this approach to forecasting. While the forecasts are for an extended period such as ten years, conditions continually change which affect that long-term forecast, and so the optimal portfolio can be expected to change as the market conditions and forecasts change. The result should be an *evolving* rather than a static asset allocation.

Table 29-3 gives my year-by-year forecasts, created just as the 2000 year-end forecasts were created in Table 29-2. Two main points jump out here. First, the Canadian bond forecasts systematically fall throughout the decade, which directly reflects falling yields. Second, while equity forecasts were fairly consistent for the years 2001 to 2008, the 2009 forecast (at year-end 2008) jumped significantly as equity yields rose during the market downturn.

You have already seen the subsequent returns generated by rebalancing to one of the three constant mix portfolios in Tables

Table 29-3:
Year-End Expected Returns (Forecasts)

At Year-End	CN Universe Bonds	CN S&P/TSX Equities	S&P500 Equities (CAD)	EAFE Equities (CAD)
2000	6.09%	6.15%	6.48%	6.66%
2001	6.28%	6.47%	6.84%	6.37%
2002	5.72%	6.78%	7.28%	7.20%
2003	5.50%	6.06%	7.01%	6.84%
2004	5.14%	6.03%	7.05%	6.89%
2005	4.83%	6.01%	7.23%	6.80%
2006	4.93%	6.61%	7.20%	6.95%
2007	4.84%	6.82%	7.33%	7.30%
2008	3.54%	8.51%	8.58%	9.59%
2009	4.46%	7.09%	6.82%	7.43%
2010	3.96%	6.72%	6.61%	7.34%
2011	2.79%	7.09%	6.91%	8.35%
2012	2.65%	7.20%	7.00%	7.83%

28-3 and 28-4. I also suggested a justification for adhering to such a strategy, if your risk aversion is constant, and you accept essentially unchanging historical returns and risks as your best forecast of long-term future returns. The alternative approach now under consideration is to continue with the assumption that your risk aversion remains constant, but that portfolios are built using the new dynamic forecasts. I am going to assume that long-term history still gives a good estimate of future risks and correlations, so the only changes are due to the dynamic forecasts of return, that evolve as market conditions change. I call these the *dynamic forecast* strategies, and they result in evolving asset allocations.

Table 29-4 presents the results for the three dynamic forecast strategies, along with those of the three related constant mix portfolios. Columns 1, 4 and 7 summarize the returns of the three constant mix strategies presented in the previous chapter. Column 2 summarizes the results of the dynamic mix strategy which is rebalanced to the same risk aversion as the 50-50 bond-stock mix. Similarly, columns 5 and 8 summarize the results of the dynamic mix strategies which were rebalanced using the same risk aversion as the 40-60 and 30-70

Applying Dynamic Forecasts to Portfolio Construction   329

Table 29-4:
Comparing Constant Mix with Constant Risk Aversion Portfolios
Subsequent Returns in CAD, DMS Data 2001 to 2012

	1	2	3	4	5	6	7	8	9
	50-50 Bond-Stock Mix based on Hist. Returns to 2000	Constant Risk Aversion with Dynamic Forecasts	Cols 2-1	40-60 Bond-Stock Mix based on Hist. Returns to 2000	Constant Risk Aversion with Dynamic Forecasts	Cols 5-4	30-70 Bond-Stock Mix based on Hist. Returns to 2000	Constant Risk Aversion with Dynamic Forecasts	Cols 8-7
Annualized Return	4.43%	6.10%	1.60%	3.62%	5.95%	2.25%	2.79%	5.69%	2.83%
Arithmetic Average	4.67%	6.24%	1.57%	3.96%	6.13%	2.17%	3.25%	5.93%	2.68%
Standard Deviation	7.38%	5.68%	-1.70%	8.62%	6.40%	-2.22%	9.90%	7.20%	-2.70%

constant mix portfolios respectively. Columns 3, 6 and 9 show the differences.[4]

In each case the strategy using the same risk tolerance but dynamic forecasts outperformed its static mix counterpart, and perhaps even more importantly it demonstrated lower risks. To focus on just one example, the annualized returns to the dynamic forecast strategy in column 2 were 1.6% higher than the 50-50 constant mix strategy, while the standard deviation was considerably lower at 5.68% versus 7.96%.

Table 29-5 gives one example of the year-by-year returns, in this case for Columns 1 and 2, the 50-50 bond-stock portfolio and the related dynamic mix strategy, along with the allocations for the dynamic mix portfolio. Remember that the allocations for each year are actually from data at the previous year-end: for example, the allocation for 2001 was set at the end of 2000, and was not adjusted again until the end of 2001.

---

[4] Following my general practice, the differences between annualized returns are geometric, while the differences between arithmetic average returns and between standard deviations are arithmetic.

Table 29-5:
Comparing Returns and Allocations:
50-50 Bond-Stock Portfolio versus the Dynamic Forecast Strategy
(Allocations are from the previous year-end)

	Portfolio Returns to:			Allocations based on Dynamic Forecasts			
	50-50 Bond-Stock Mix based on Historical Returns to 2000	Dynamic Forecast Strategy with Constant Risk Aversion	Cols 2-1	CN Universe Bonds	CN S&P/TSX Equities	US S&P500 Equities (CAD)	EAFE Equities (CAD)
2001	-2.03%	2.86%	4.90%	74.1%	15.9%	5.0%	5.0%
2002	-4.12%	2.49%	6.62%	74.0%	16.0%	5.0%	5.0%
2003	11.25%	10.97%	-0.27%	70.0%	20.0%	5.0%	5.0%
2004	8.66%	8.40%	-0.26%	73.2%	16.8%	5.0%	5.0%
2005	9.76%	9.83%	0.07%	71.1%	18.9%	5.0%	5.0%
2006	12.06%	8.57%	-3.50%	68.2%	19.1%	7.7%	5.0%
2007	1.03%	4.00%	2.97%	65.9%	24.1%	5.0%	5.0%
2008	-10.83%	-7.14%	3.69%	63.6%	26.4%	5.0%	5.0%
2009	12.10%	15.30%	3.20%	48.4%	30.0%	10.4%	11.2%
2010	8.18%	9.40%	1.22%	64.6%	25.3%	5.0%	5.1%
2011	2.25%	3.51%	1.26%	63.1%	24.7%	5.0%	7.2%
2012	7.79%	6.69%	-1.09%	53.4%	27.9%	5.0%	13.7%
Annualized Return	4.43%	6.10%	1.67%				
Arithmetic Average	4.67%	6.24%	1.57%				
Standard Deviation	7.38%	5.93%	-1.44%				

If you focus on the bond allocation, you can see that the decade begins with a very high bond allocation of 74.1%, which falls over the years to 63.6% for the year 2008. While these allocations by no means predict the market turmoil of 2008,[5] the forecasts position

---

[5] Bond yields did not rise at the end of 2007, and both bond and equity markets remained quite complacent prior to the credit crisis. On average equity yields had risen very slightly, but this actually made them a little more attractive. The dynamic strategy did well despite this, mainly because the relationship between expected bond returns was still relatively high, while expected equity returns were still relatively low.

the bond-equity split much more conservatively than the 50-50 level of the constant mix, at 63.6% versus 36.4%. This means that the dynamic portfolio weathered the 2008 downturn better than the constant mix portfolio, returning -7.14% versus -10.85% for the static mix strategy. The rise in equity yields during the market downturn made stocks more attractive, so that at the end of 2008 bond allocations fell and equity allocations rose by a significant 15.2%, positioning the dynamic strategy to make additional gains in 2009 as equities rallied. It is interesting, however, that even during the equity downturn the subsequent allocation to equities only moved to a high of 51.6%, just slightly higher than the 50% level of equities in the original allocation at this risk aversion level.[6] Overall the dynamic mix outperformed the static mix portfolio in eight of twelve years, and, just as importantly, its risk has remained lower than that of the constant mix strategy.

Of course it is easy to "forecast retrospectively". While all of the elements in these forecasts were quite objective, and I tried not to "cheat" when making them, it's quite another thing to actually use such forecasts in real time when market sentiment may be very different than the consequences implied by the forecasts. This is one of several reasons why "historical simulations" should be treated with caution. It is always much easier to stick with principles and forecasts which you know won't have disastrous consequences than it is to implement those forecasts in real time, under conditions of full uncertainty.

I also want to be clear that these dynamic forecasts will not always work to either lower subsequent risk or add to subsequent return, relative to a constant mix strategy. In the first place, the very best forecasts work only a little more than half the time. In the second place, I have suggested that these forecasts are for the longer term, with a ten-year time frame in most of my examples. So while there is

---

6 Had this exercise been undertaken more frequently than once a year, for example at the equity market low at the end of February 2009, the equity allocation could have tilted a little higher. But that would have been a virtually perfect case of market timing, and it is not realistic to assume that you would have pulled that off.

nothing wrong with adjusting forecasts as conditions evolve — you are trying to get a better fix on the future — you should not expect that they will "come true" over (say) the next year due to short-term volatility, even if they turn out to be good forecasts over the longer term. In the third place, the main point of my rather crude simulation is to show *how* the dynamic forecasts can work, and how they can be used to generate evolving portfolio allocations. In particular, I am not advocating a mechanical annual forecast and rebalancing. It is just that the data here are annual, and to show you that the forecasts do indeed evolve and that there may be some information in them as they change, I am constrained to this simple approach.

In reality you would monitor the forecasts on an ongoing basis, and part of the judgment involved in managing a strategy is to determine under what circumstances you should implement your changing forecasts. This is not a mechanical process.

I also want to be clear that the alternative to any set of dynamic forecasts such as I have suggested is not a passive or "no forecast" alternative. I don't believe that any such alternative exists. Every investor must employ an asset allocation, and there is no alternative passive allocation that mirrors the passive alternative to active management within an asset class, such as Canadian equities or bonds. Any particular allocation choice must be justified by *something*, and that something has to be a set of asset class forecasts of one kind or another. In each case here my alternative or comparison strategy was based on a fixed allocation strategy with the same risk aversion parameter as the dynamic strategy. But this alternative was not in any sense passive: it was justified by using long-term historical average returns as forecasts.

Investors like to avoid taking responsibility for important forecasts, and perhaps using historical averages makes it seem like they are not going out on much of a limb when they do so. But really they are. The most important forecasts of all are those that determine your portfolio allocation. Remember that on average your asset allocation explains 100% of your return.

Appendix: more on risk aversion, utility, and optimal portfolios, part 2

This appendix picks up where the appendix from Chapter 28 left off. Since I am assuming that the 50-50 Bond-Stock portfolio was optimal using the original forecasts, the slope of indifference curve L2 expresses your risk aversion. Adding the new dynamic forecasts for year-end 2000, and the maximum return portfolios based on them, I want to find the new optimal portfolio. Figure 1 below reproduces Figure 1 from the previous appendix, along with the return-variance data for the dynamic forecasts and the maximum return portfolios based on them.

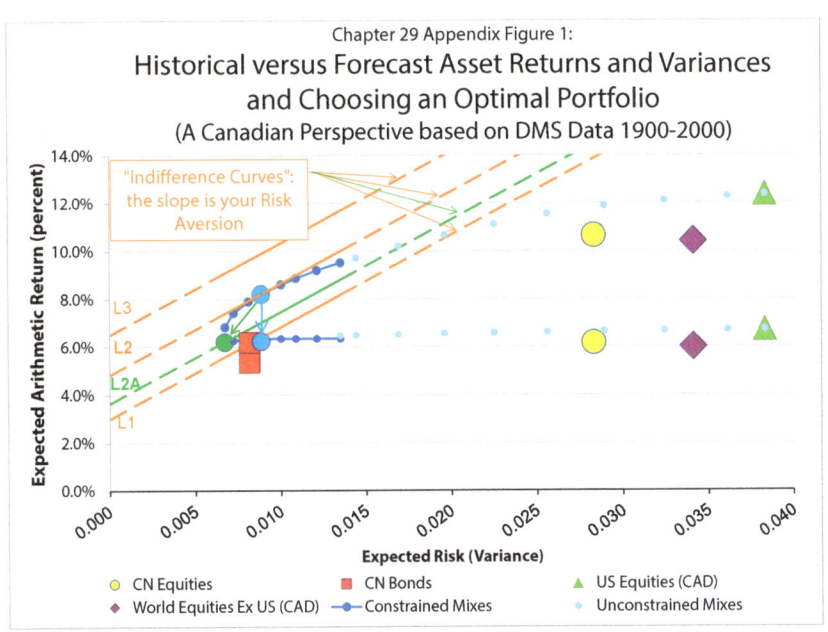

First, since your risk aversion is represented by the slope of your indifference curves, as long as your risk aversion does not change, all of your indifference curves are parallel to the original example lines L1, L2 and L3, no matter how the forecasts change. Second, in order to maximize utility you must find the maximum return portfolio that intersects the highest possible indifference curve. In this case that indifference curve is in green, and is labeled L2A, and it intersects the portfolio represented by the large green circle.

The green circle is almost, but not quite, at the far left of the line of maximum returns portfolios, a fact which cannot be seen on the graph given the scale. But the same conditions hold as they did for the optimal portfolio on the line of maximum return portfolios based on historical returns. Any movement along the line of maximum return portfolios to the right or to the left will put you on a lower indifference curve with a lower intercept. A move to the right gives you less return than required to justify the increased risk, and a move to the left reduces your return by more than the reduction in risk requires, and so neither generates your maximum benefit.

Chapter 30:

A Summary of Key Concepts

Investing is about forecasting, developing expectations of return and risk for an array of potential investment opportunities, and then building a portfolio based on those forecasts. But it's interesting the extent to which so many investors shy away from this "f-word". They "buy cheap", they "value" or evaluate, they base their portfolio allocation on history — in short, investors go out of their way to avoid saying that they are forecasting.

By examining history, we are able to observe a wide range of possible investment returns — possible because they actually happened. Of course some possible future outcomes may fall outside the range of history. But when we take into account 19 equity and bond markets, which contain episodes of huge annual losses (such as -88.4% in local terms for German equities and -93.7% for German bonds in 1948, and virtual bankruptcy with hyperinflation in 1922–23) and huge gains (such as +179.5% in 1979 for Norwegian equities), that historical experience is broad indeed. But most of history is less extreme, and we should expect that most future returns will fall within those extremes.

I used simple statistics to measure arithmetic and geometric average returns, to estimate historical risks as standard deviation of return, and to characterize relations between markets as correlations between returns. Just as important was the idea of using history to motivate, and then validate, the attribution analysis that characterized the generation of equity and bond returns. The equity version of the framework was modified to describe nominal bonds and real return bonds, and the differences in structure reflect the differing properties of these investment vehicles. Potentially the framework can also be modified to describe other investment vehicles such as REITS and commodities, although I only provided verbal descriptions of this.

As I developed the idea of forecasting returns, an underlying theme was the contrast between assuming that historical averages will reflect future average returns, and the idea that forecasts should be based on, or at least take into account, the current market environment. The attribution framework was turned into a forecasting framework, and I argued that at least some of the components of that framework may be forecast with some plausibility.

The concept of enhancing return-risk opportunities through the benefits of imperfect correlations among assets is fairly intuitive, and was illustrated with many different examples. The same principles apply whether you use forecasts based on historical averages, or forecasts based on some other approach, such as the dynamic forecasts I have suggested. I also gave evidence that for most investors, the most important, and perhaps the only important, investment decision is your asset mix: the allocation of your investments between broadly defined asset classes. On average, asset mix provides 100% of an investor's return.

Consistent with that result is the fact that costs are crucial. Even large institutional investors find it difficult to add value relative to broad market indexes across time, and the costs associated with retail investment products such as mutual funds can be devastatingly high. Achieving the goal of reducing costs, which can be accomplished with some certainty, is likely to be more profitable than trying to add value by choosing funds that you hope will outperform broad market averages.

While a set of forecasts for returns, risks and correlations determines an array of maximum return portfolios that you could hold, in order to choose one of the many possible portfolios you must determine which one best fits your investment needs: the combination of expected return and expected risk that maximizes your utility or satisfaction. The minimum amount of return you require to justify

A Summary of Key Concepts

taking on another unit of risk, which is a ratio of change in return to change of risk, measures your risk aversion. Assuming a constant risk aversion with stable forecasts of return and risk over time implies a constant asset mix in your portfolio with constant expected returns and risks. But a constant risk aversion with changing forecasts implies that your asset allocation, expected portfolio returns and expected portfolio risks will all evolve over time.

I have focused on the importance of asset allocation as the key to long-term investment success. But I have not dwelled on the obvious flip side, that systematically poor or haphazard asset allocation choices can completely undermine long-term success. There are no guarantees here, but a successful long-term investor will follow the key themes that I have just summarized. These include

- developing asset class forecasts that have more information than long-term historical averages;
- finding as many asset classes as possible to serve as potential investments, where each has a distinct source of return and, as a consequence, usefully imperfect correlations with existing investments;
- minimizing costs; and
- rebalancing when appropriate to reflect changing forecasts of returns, risks and correlations in light of your ongoing risk aversion.

The result is an asset allocation that evolves over time as forecasts change, rather than a static asset allocation that uses long-term historical returns as forecasts.

This framework encourages the development of consistent forecasts across asset classes, and for many investors that will be sufficient. For larger individual and institutional investors, who have access to more resources, these forecasts can be viewed as first-level approximations, a starting point for more detailed and comprehensive analysis.

I have kept the portfolio examples in Chapters 28 and 29 very simple, using only four asset classes: local Canadian bonds and equities, along with US and EAFE equities. I have mentioned that additional asset classes such as emerging market equities, REITS, real return bonds and commodities can also be analyzed within our forecasting framework, and would very likely enhance your potential return and lower or constrain your potential risk. Such investments are easily accessible to smaller investors through ETFs, and are staples of larger portfolios.

Beyond this, even smaller investors can extend their investment opportunities in fixed income investments by considering the properties of bond ETFs that cover shorter- or longer-term bonds, corporate and high yield bonds, and emerging market bonds. Equity coverage can be enhanced by considering alternative indexes that are not weighted by market capitalization, such as "fundamental" indexes that are weighted by balance sheet exposures, and low volatility indexes. But in all cases a similar approach can be taken, both for forming expected return forecasts, and for integrating these additional opportunities into a portfolio structure.

I have tried to make my discussions as accessible as I can to non-professional investors. Those who have an oversight role for a fund or foundation will often receive lots of information about history, expectations, risks and required returns. I hope this narrative will help you sort through the chaff and focus on the key investment issues your fund faces.

However, retail investors face a more difficult task. While I hope that the overall gist of the argument is helpful, the practical difficulties of putting all of this into effect are large. On the one hand, most investors will require some form of advice and management. But many of my contentions, including the crucial conclusion that reducing known costs offers more benefits than the small possibility of obtaining excess gains, are at odds with the interests of a large part of the retail-oriented financial services industry. At least this background may give you a little more information to help you evaluate what you are being offered.

On the other hand, for those who want to "do it yourself", the task of gathering data, making consistent forecasts, and building portfolios is daunting. One hope is that industry participants, such as ETF providers or discount brokers, will find a way to provide better data and portfolio construction tools for their clients. But regulators also play a role in making this difficult, because client use of investment data and tools, especially if instructions for their sensible use are provided, could be considered as giving investment advice, which is prohibited without a formal advisory relationship.

Given these realities, you can see why there is a move among Canadian pension experts who are not captive of the retail financial services industry, to explore and support the idea of a supplementary government-sponsored investment plan to help individuals to invest and save for retirement. A professionally run investment fund with long-term investment goals could provide an extremely low-cost investment alternative. Such a fund would not have to employ high-cost distribution systems, and would not have to return profits to its sponsor. It could also bypass the "know your client" and related advisory relationships mandated by provincial securities regulators, although it would not remove the need for personal financial planning and advice. Most importantly, it would challenge the financial services industry to provide better products, better service and better advice at lower cost, a goal which it seems unable to achieve on its own.

Bibliography

Arnott, Robert D. and Clifford S. Asness, "Surprise! Higher Dividends = Higher Earnings Growth", *Financial Analysts Journal*, January/February 2003, pp. 70-87. (A&C 2003)

Arnott, Robert D. and Peter L. Bernstein, "What Risk Premium is 'Normal'?", *Financial Analysts Journal*, March/April 2002, pp. 64-85. (A&B 2002)

Chang, Kelly H., "Currency Hedging: A Free Lunch?", MSCI Barra Research, April 2009. (Chang 2009)

Cutler, David M., James M. Poterba and Lawrence H. Summers, "Speculative Dynamics", *Review of Economic Studies*, (1991) 58, pp. 529-546. (CPS 1991)

Dimson, Elroy, Paul Marsh and Mike Staunton, *Credit Suisse Global Investment Returns Sourcebook 2011*, Credit Suisse AG, Zurich, Switzerland. (DMS 2011)

Dimson, Elroy, Paul Marsh and Mike Staunton, "Economic Growth", *Credit Suisse Global Investment Returns Yearbook 2010*, Credit Suisse AG, Zurich, Switzerland, pp. 13-19. (DMS 2010)

Dimson, Elroy, Paul Marsh and Mike Staunton, "The Worldwide Equity Premium: A Smaller Puzzle", a draft paper from April 2006 available at http://papers.ssrn.com/sol3/papers.cfm?abstract_id=891620 (DMS 2006)

Dimson, Elroy, Paul Marsh, Mike Staunton and Jonathan Wilmot, *Credit Suisse Global Investment Returns Yearbook 2010*, Credit Suisse AG, Zurich, Switzerland. (DMSW 2010).

Elton, E. J. and M. J. Gruber, "Risk Reduction and Portfolio Size: An Analytic Solution," *Journal of Business* 50 (October 1977), pp. 415-37. (E&G 1977)

Fama, Eugene F. and Kenneth R. French, "Luck versus Skill in the Cross Section of Mutual Fund Returns", *The Journal of Finance*, VOL. LXV, No. 5, October 2010, pp. 1915-1947. (F&F 2010).

Ibbotson, Roger G., and Paul D. Kaplan: "Does Asset Allocation Policy Explain 40, 90, or 100 Percent of Performance?", *Financial Analysts Journal*, January/February 2000, pp. 26-33. (I&K 2000)

Mauboussin, Michael J., "Share Repurchase from All Angles", Legg Mason Capital Management, June 11, 2012. (Mauboussin 2012)

Perold, André F. and Evan C. Schulman, "The Free Lunch in Currency Hedging: Implications for Investment Policy and performance Standards," *Financial Analysts Journal*, Vol. 44, No. 3, 1988, pp. 45-50. (P&S 1988)

Reuters Money, "How big is the public pension funding gap?", March 16, 2011 http://blogs.reuters.com/reuters-money/2011/03/16/how-big-is-the-public-pension-funding-gap/.

Sharpe, William F., "The Arithmetic of Active Management", *Financial Analysts Journal*, Vol. 47, No. 1, January/February 1991, pp. 7-9. (Sharpe 1991). This article is available on Sharpe's website at: http://www.stanford.edu/~wfsharpe/art/active/active.htm

Sharpe, William F., *Investments*, 3rd Edition, Prentice-Hall, Inc. Englewood Cliffs, New Jersey. (Sharpe 1978)

Shiller, Robert J., *Irrational Exuberance*, 2nd Edition, Currency Doubleday, New York, 2005. (Shiller 2005)

Smithers, Andrew, *Wall Street Revalued*, John Wiley & Sons Ltd., Chichester, United Kingdom, 2009. (Smithers 2009)

Whitehouse, Edward, *Pensions and the Crisis*, OECD media briefing, OECD 2009. (Whitehouse 2009)

Index

A

active management
   empirical evidence of added value, 279–283
   "The Arithmetic of Active Management", 278–279
   within asset classes, 277–284
Ambachtsheer, Keith
   expected returns, viii
   inflation regimes, 23
Arnott and Bernstein
   estimating future real dividend growth, 169–171
   relating real dividend growth to real GDPPC growth, 166–167
asset mix.
   See also portfolio construction
   choosing an ongoing mix, 309–311
   empirical studies demonstrating its importance, 299–304
   graphical illustration of importance, 298–299
   rebalancing to a constant mix, 312–316
   the dominant driver of portfolio return, 297–298
attribution model of equity returns
   and forecasting equity returns, 205–208
   applied to international markets, 73–74
   applied to the US market, 70–71
   derivation of, 79–85
   equations, 71
   examples, 75–78, 105–109, 203–204
   including currencies, 102–104
   introduced, 70–73
attribution model of returns to nominal bonds
   and forecasting bond returns, 251–256
   applied to the US bond market history, 249–251
   compared to the attribution of equity returns, 243–244
   developing a model for nominal returns, 236–243
   for real returns, 244–247
   volatility and changing yields, 239–240
attribution model of returns to real return bonds
   and forecasts for real return bonds, 262–265
   for nominal returns, 258–259
   for real returns, 258

B

baseball.
   and investing, 2–3
   learning the game, 1–2
Big Mac index
   illustrated, 95–96
bond returns.
   See returns to fixed income
bonds
   bond yields and inflation, 245–246
   comparing nominal and real return bonds, 259–261
   nominal bonds described, 235
   nominal vs real yields and market-implied inflation, 262–263
   real return or inflation indexed bonds described, 257–258
   volatility and changing yields, 239–240
   yield to maturity, 236

C

correlation
   between equities, bonds, and other asset classes, 272–273

between equity and bond indexes, 267–268
between equity indexes, 220–221
illustrated, 39
imperfect correlation and diversification, 218–223
imperfect correlation as a criterion for useful investment opportunities, 220–224, 267–274
costs.
See investment costs
currency hedging
described, 92–93
discussion of why and when you might hedge, 194
not a free lunch, 93
currency impact on returns
adds complexity to underlying returns (four cases), 91–93, 193
concept of hedging currency exposures, 92–93
currency illusion, 88, 89
examples, 88–91
terminology, 87

D

diversification
and imperfect correlation, 217–220
and imperfect correlation, examples, 221
and multiplying investment opportunities, 215–216
and reducing risk, 216–217
and reducing risk, examples, 222–223
and undiversifiable risk, 217, 219–220
not in itself an investment strategy, 220
dividend growth
nominal, 68–69
range of historical real growth, 163
real, 69
dividends
and their impact on total return, 66–67
dividend yield
for selected indexes and dates, 162
historical US, 67
dynamic forecasts
as of December 2000, 322–323
consequence compared with constant mix strategies 2000-2010, 326–332

implications for portfolio construction, 324–326

E

economic growth and equity market returns
and the components of return, 131–132
empirical evidence for lack of correlation, 117–123
in fact not correlated, 114
often believed to be positively correlated, 113–114
positive correlation between real GDPPC growth and real dividend growth, 132–133
equity indexes
price index, 15
total return index, 15
equity returns.
See also returns to equities
and volatility of the components of return, 149–151
ETFs
benefits of low cost, 287–289
described, 286–287
estimating implementation costs, 293–296
potential difficulties in using them, 289–292
expected dividend yield
and current dividend yield, 153
conceptual relationships, 157–161
dividend yield not used as a valuation measure, 161–162
historical relationships, 153–159
expected real dividend growth
and historical averages, 164–165
developing a simple forecasting framework, 165–171
examples of forecasts, 172–174
expected return due to the change in dividend yield
and the concept of valuation, 179–181
forecasting implies a change in valuation, 178–179
Shiller P/Es or CAPE, 181–186
the "no forecast" approach and some implications, 176–178

two approaches to forecasting, 175
expected returns to equities.
   See forecasting equity returns
expected returns to foreign exchange.
   See also currency hedging
   and consistency with other forecasts, 191–192
   and relative purchasing power parity, 189–191

F

fixed income returns.
   See returns to fixed income
forecasting equity returns.
   See also expected dividend yield; expected real dividend growth; expected return due to the change in dividend yield
   examples, 196–200
   models of expected return, 148
   using the components of return, 147–148
forecasting using historical averages.
   See also dynamic forecasts
   conceptual problems, 140–141
   empirical validity questioned, 141–146
   how this might be justified, 139–140
foreign exchange.
   See also currencies; currency impact on returns
   real returns defined, 100–101

G

gross domestic product (GDP)
   real versus nominal, 114–115
gross domestic product per capita (GDPPC)
   explained, 115–116
   growth in GDPPC a proxy for productivity growth, 115

H

history
   learning from, 8–9
   how do you get there from here?
   and expected returns to equities, 209–212

I

indifference curves
   illustrated, 317–318
   used in optimization, 318–320, 333–334
inflation
   and impact on international returns, 52, 55–57
   and impact on returns, 22, 24–25
   as forecasted by real and nominal market yields, 262–263
   US CPI 1871-2010, 17
   US CPI by sub-periods, 21–25
investing
   an approach to finding additional investment opportunities, 269–274
   and expectations, 5–6
   and forecasting, 6
   definition, 3
   examples of, 3–4
   reasoned or rational, 6
investment costs
   certain cost reduction versus possible value-added, 288–289
   of broad market ETFs, 287–288
   of mutual funds compared to average historical returns, 285–286

L

linear regression
   illustrated, 39–41
line of best fit.
   See linear regression

N

nominal returns
   defined, 17

O

optimal portfolio
   derived, 311, 317–320

P

portfolio construction
   based on a constant mix allocation, 305–308
   based on long-term historical returns, risks and correlations, 305–307
   using dynamic forecasts, 321–332

purchasing power parity (PPP)
and the Big Mac theory, 96
explained, 96

R

real returns
defined, 17
relative purchasing power parity (RPPP)
empirical evidence, 98–102
illustrated, 96
return due to the change in dividend yield
defined, 70
returns
annualized, defined, 35–36
arithmetic average, defined, 36
cumulative, defined, 35
international equity returns compared to US equity returns, 52–54
relating average and annualized returns through variability, 38
the effect of variability on, 36–37
returns to equities
due to changes in equity prices, 15
due to dividends, 15
international equity markets 1900-2010, 52
nominal versus real, 17
US equity market 1871-2010, 16
returns to fixed income
and international inflation, 229–230
and US inflation, 227–228
compared to equity returns, 230–233
international short-term instruments 1900-1020, 230–231*
US bond returns 1871-2010, 226–227
risk aversion
characterized, 311, 317

S

Sharpe, William F.
definition of investing, 3
Shiller, Robert J.
cyclically adjusted P/E ratios (CAPE), 181–186
historical returns to equities, 16
US data, 15
standard deviation
defined, 37
introduced, 32

properties of, 32
statistical significance
illustrated, 41–43
Summary
and outline of book, 9–11

V

variability.
See also standard deviation; variance
illustrated, 29–31
of equity returns, 29, 59–63
over the longer term, 46–50
variance
defined, 37

CPSIA information can be obtained at www.ICGtesting.com
Printed in the USA
LVOW01*2002130913

352385LV00001B/1/P